RELIGION AND HEALTH

RELIGION AND HEALTH

By

JAMES J. WALSH, M.D., Ph.D., Sc.D. ETC.

GYAN

Published by

GYAN

Gyan Publishing House
5, Ansari Road
Daryaganj, New Delhi-110002
Phone: 011-47034999, 9811692060
E-mail: books@gyanbooks.com

Distribution Network
gyanbooks.com
India, USA, Canada, UK, Australia, France

ISBN : 978-81-212-6488-4 (PB)
First Published, 1920

2nd Impression 2022

Printed at: Gyan Press, Delhi.

RELIGION AND HEALTH
Author: JAMES J. WALSH

RELIGION AND HEALTH

BY

JAMES J. WALSH, M.D., Ph.D., Sc.D. etc.

1920

To

HIS EMINENCE JAMES CARDINAL GIBBONS

AN EXEMPLAR OF RELIGION AND HEALTH
FOR OUR GENERATION

CONTENTS

RELIGION AND HEALTH

INTRODUCTION

Physicians are agreed that there is no entirely satisfactory definition for health. We all know quite well what we mean when we use the word, but it does not admit of such exact limitations as would make a scientific formulation of its meaning. Religion is another of the words which, in spite of its common use, is extremely difficult to define exactly, and it has often been said that we have no definition that will satisfy all those who profess religion and certainly not all those who have made a study of it from the standpoint of the science of theology. As is true of health, each of us knows pretty thoroughly what we mean when we use the word, though our definitely formulated signification for it might not meet with the approval of others, especially of those who are exacting in their requirements. With the two principal words in the title incapable of exact definition, it might seem that the subject matter of this book would be rather vague at best and unpromising in practical significance. But all this indefiniteness is in theory. There are no two words in the language that are more used than health and religion, none that are less vague in practice and no two subjects have a wider appeal or a more paramount interest. The linking them together for discussion in common because of their mutual influence will serve to throw light on both of them and undoubtedly help toward a better understanding of each.

Ordinarily the most satisfactory definition of a word can be obtained from its etymology. Unfortunately in the matter of religion there is a very old-time division of opinion as to the derivation of the word which makes etymology of less definite significance than usual. Cicero suggested that *religio* came from *relegere,* to go through or over again in reading, speech or thought, as prayers and religious observances generally are repeated. On the other hand St. Augustine and Lactantius insisted on deriving *religio* from the Latin verb *religare*, which means to bind again, to bind back, to bind fast. The word obligation has an analogous origin and illustrates the meaning of religion as if its form from etymology should have been religation.

It is this latter derivation that has been most commonly accepted in the modern time. A man may recognize the existence of God and yet not feel any particular obligations toward Him, but if he binds himself anew to the deity whom he recognizes, by trying to make his life accord with the divine will as he views it, then he practices religion. James Martineau said, "By religion I understand the belief and worship of Supreme Mind and Will, directing the universe and holding moral relations with human life."

What will occupy us in this book is the effect of this profound feeling and sense of obligation toward a higher power on health, that is, on that wholeness of body and mind which constitutes a normal condition for human beings.

There are many more relations between the two words than would at first be suspected or that most people might think possible. The old high German word *haelu* or *haelo*, from which our word health is derived, meant also salvation. The original root *hal* means haleness or wholeness and also refers to healing, and curiously enough the word holiness is derived from the same root. Holiness has now come to refer to perfection, or at least normality of soul, while health refers to normality of body. Our word health is related more directly to whole than it is to heal, in spite of the feeling there might be because of the spelling that the latter word must represent its immediate origin. Holiness of soul exactly corresponds in etymology with wholeness of body.

Cardinal Newman would, I suppose, be an authority on the subject of religion as satisfying for most people as could be found. In his "Grammar of Assent", which he wrote in order to define as exactly as might be possible just how men came to admit certain propositions with special reference to the acceptance of religion, he gave a definition of what he meant by the word in as simple words as it is possible to use, perhaps, to express so large a subject. He said: "By religion I mean the knowledge of God, of His Will, and of our duties toward Him." Matthew Arnold, who represents among English-speaking peoples almost the opposite pole of thought to Cardinal Newman, in what concerns religion, suggested in "Literature and Dogma" that "Religion, if we follow the intention of human thought and human language in the use of the word, is ethics heightened, enkindled, lit up by feeling; the passage from morality to religion is made when to morality is applied emotion." Both of these men, in spite of their distance apart, insist on duty as the essence of religion. Matthew Arnold calls it ethics and says nothing as to the foundation of it; the great English

Cardinal speaks very simply of our duties toward God. Newman says nothing of the emotions but appeals only to the reason, while, curiously enough, the rationalizer in religion emphasizes the emotions.

Between these two definitions there is a world of difference that we shall not attempt to bridge, for we want to treat of the relations and above all the interaction of religion and health in the widest sense of these terms. The "Century Dictionary" definition more nearly resembles that of Cardinal Newman than Matthew Arnold's formula, but it generalizes in a way that would describe the practice of religion for a greater number of people and especially for those who still believe that there are more gods than one. It runs: "Recognition of and allegiance in manner of life to a superhuman power or superhuman powers, to whom allegiance and service are regarded as justly due."

Even this definition is not too broad for the subject matter of this book, for I am one of those who believe that there is a blessing on every sincere effort of worship of the Higher Power, no matter how groping it may be. Above all, every regulation of life with reference to a power above us felt to have a Providence over the world in which we live has an almost inevitable reaction on health and will lead to better things. The sincere pursuit of good conduct as an end in life under a Providence that is recognized will almost necessarily lead to better knowledge of our relations to the higher powers, and also of our relations to ourselves and the world around us.

With these preliminaries we are ready to consider religion and health and their mutual influence, but the inevitable question that suggests itself is, "Is religion a living force in our time? Has not science given it its death blow? While it walks the earth as yet, is it not only as the ghost of an outworn phase of human interest? Is it any more than merely a superstition in the sense once suggested as the etymology of this word by James Russell Lowell as if derived from *superstes*, a survivor, representing, as all superstitions do, a survival from a previous state of thinking, the reasons for which have disappeared, though the mental inertia of human beings still keeps them in vogue?" A good many people in our time, including not a few of those who are rather prone to consider themselves above the rest of the world, have not hesitated to express the view that it is only old fogies and especially those ignorant of modern science who continue to think that religion can still be taken seriously. Some few of them have the best of good will in the world and appreciate how much of benefit was derived from religious belief, benefit which they confess did good both for the mind and the body of man; and they are even ready to express sorrow that it has outlived its usefulness, but they feel that they must insist that religion is now only the wraith of its former self, a misty congeries of old-fashioned beliefs which the ignorant alone reverence, accepting it very much as they do ghost stories in general.

President Schurman of Cornell in an address before the Liberal Club of Buffalo thirty years ago,[1] reminded us that there are a number of people who are always ready to proclaim the end of religion and to weep for it. Religion continues to be as living a force and as lively as ever in spite of their proclamations, and this has been true generation after generation practically since the beginning of Christianity. President Schurman said:

[1] "Agnosticism," Scribners, New York, 1895.

"Every now and then we hear the requiem of religion chanted alike by the spirits who mock and by the pious souls who have 'no language but a cry.' I suppose we shall always have professional mourners. But it is greatly to be desired that their services should not be prematurely given. If there is anything in the world that is alive and active, it is just this religious spirit, for whose demise certain mourners go about the streets. The body of religion changes, the spirit and the life abide forever. To the assertion that religion is defunct, I reply by pointing to the intense interest wh'ch men to-day everywhere feel in religion. It was recently stated by a Massachusetts Judge — Burke observed truly that we Americans like to appeal to the law — that there is nothing in the world perennially interesting but religion. The ground of this dictum is to be found in the constitution of humanity; for the human soul which the things of sense fail to satisfy can attain its true home and its complete self-realization only in conscious communion with the Spirit behind the veil."

The recent death of Mrs. Humphry Ward recalled the experience with regard to her book "Robert Elsmere." In a certain narrow circle of intellectuals it was supposed that this novel represented a veritable death blow to a series of compromises which had permitted people familiar with modern progress and science, and especially with the higher criticism, to continue to practice their religion in peace in spite of the fact that belief had long since departed. How amusing it is now and indeed how almost incomprehensible to learn that Mrs. Humphry Ward's husband, a well-known English critic, suggested shortly after its publication that her novel had "shaken the very pillars of Christianity." It is surprising indeed how often the foundations of religion are supposed to have been completely undermined, and yet the edifice itself continues to stand and to be the shelter for the vast majority of mankind from the buffetings of a world that without it would be almost shelterless for them and a place of trial too hard to bear.

Men are incurably religious, and just as no tribe has been found, however low in the scale of savagery, which has not formulated for itself some system of worship of a higher power and definite feelings of dependence on it, so even those whose minds under the influence of certain phases of intellectual development lead them away from formal religion find deep in their hearts the belief and appreciation of their relations to a power that makes for good, even though it may be difficult to understand the mystery of it. Long ago the Scriptural expression was formulated that only the fool who thinketh not in his heart says there is no God. Due acknowledgment of the thought in practice, however imperfect it may be, is religion.

Religion has been with us for all the period that we know anything about man, for the very cave man buried his dead with manifest confidence in a hereafter, and there seems no doubt that it will be with us until this stage of mundane affairs has passed. It affects the body as well as the mind, as indeed do all the great modes of thought, and it deserves to be cultivated, not only for its effect on the soul but also on the mind and heart and the bodily powers. There is no doubt at all that it means very much, and there is only the question of facing its significance for the whole man candidly and straightforwardly.

CHAPTER I

CAN WE STILL BELIEVE?

There is no doubt that man's quite instinctive attitude toward the mystery which surrounds him, out of which he came and into which he goes, has always so influenced his attitude of mind toward his body and its processes as to affect them deeply. The medicine man with his appeal to the religious as well as the superstitious feelings of man always had a potent influence over the most primitive of mankind, but culture has not obliterated this source of special reaction in men. Even now, for the great majority of men it still remains true that no matter how vague their religious instinct may be, it continues to affect, to a notable extent, their physiological and psychological functions. An eclipse of the religious instinct is at the basis of the increase in suicide and also undoubtedly of insanity in our day. The lack of an abiding faith in Providence is the source of many dreads and worries that affect health. Every physician is sure to know of highly educated patients whose ills reflect their mental relation to the mystery of life and whose symptoms take on or lose significance, according to their religious feelings.

The question that in our time, however, is coming insistently into a great many minds is, Can we, as intelligent human beings, reasonably in touch with man's recent progress in science, be fair with ourselves and still continue to believe in the great religious truths that affected our ancestors so deeply? While we may realize all the depth of the mystery in the midst of which we are, can we, with our little minds, hope to fathom any of it? This is the questioning feeling that will not down for a certain number of those who have had educational advantages. Must we not just confess our inability to know anything definite in reality with regard to it, and feel that those who have thought that they held the key of the mystery were deluding themselves or allowing themselves to be caught by pseudo-knowledge, an inheritance from unthinking generations, instead of realities?

Has not the modern advance in science made it very clear to us that all we can hope to say of man's origin and man's destiny is that we do not know just what all this mystery that surrounds us is about? Will not this very rational attitude of mind preclude at least the educated intelligent people of our generation from having their health affected in any way by their religion? Above all, if religion is to influence health, must there not be some regular practice of it, and have not the scientists of the last generation made it quite clear that this is out of the question in any sincere and serious way for any one who knows enough of science and appreciates the present position of our knowledge of the facts of the relationship of man to the universe?

For a large and growing number of people, as the result of the prevalence of this impression, the practice of religion seems to be an interesting but entirely worn-out relic of an older generation when folk were more easily satisfied with regard to such things than we are in our enlightened scientific era. Religion is surely not something that our contemporaries, with their broader outlook on the meaning of life, can be brought to conform to very readily. The question "Can We Still Believe?" would seem then to have for answer in our time at best, "Speculatively, perhaps yes! but practically, no!"

We may still feel the religious instinct, but we can scarcely be expected to acknowledge religious obligations in any such strictness as would demand in our already overstrenuous daily life with its many duties the devotion of time to religious exercises. We surely cannot be expected to assume any additional obligations or rebind ourselves to a divinity who seems to be getting farther away from us.

Almost needless to say, if all this be true, then religion can have, in our time, only a very slight and quite negligible influence on health. Men may be incurably religious in the mass, as yet, but this instinct is manifestly passing, for the educated at least, and for sensible people is now without any significance for physical processes, though it may at times even yet affect psychological states.

There is only one fair and practical way to reply to this question "Can We Still Believe?" especially for those who think that modern science has obscured the answer, and that is to turn to the lives of the men who made our modern science and see how they answered it in their definite relations to religion. The surprise is to find that while so many people, and not a few of them professors in colleges and even universities, are of the very often expressed opinion that science makes men irreligious or at least unreligious, that is not true at all of our greatest scientists. Most of the men who have done the great work of modern science have been deeply religious, and a great many of them have practiced their religion very faithfully. It is true that not a few of the lesser lights in science have been carried away by the impression that science was just about to explain everything, and there was no longer any need of a creator or creation or of Providence, but that is only because of their own limitations. Francis Bacon, himself a distinguished thinker in science, declared some three hundred years ago that his own feeling was that a little philosophy takes men away from God, but a sufficiency of philosophy brings them back. His opinion has often been reached by our deepest thinkers in the modern time, and it is just as true for natural philosophy as it was for the metaphysical philosophy of the older time, for Bacon's aphorism had been more than once anticipated in the early days of Christianity, notably by St. Augustine, and it would not be hard to find quotations from Greek thinkers along the same line. The Scriptures said very emphatically, "Only the fool who thinketh not in his heart says there is no God."

While young scientists then are so prone to feel that science and religion are in opposition, and a certain number of scientific workers never seem to outgrow their youthfulness in this regard, it must not be forgotten that the greatest scientists of the nineteenth and twentieth centuries have practically all been firm believers in religion. Lord Kelvin, at the beginning of the twentieth century, at the moment when he was looked up to by all the world as the greatest of living physical scientists, did not hesitate to say that "science demonstrates the existence of a Creator." As president of the British Association for the Advancement of Science he declared: "But strong, overpowering proofs of intelligent and benevolent design lie all around us; and if ever perplexities, whether metaphysical or scientific occur, they turn us away with irresistible force, showing to us, through nature, the influence of free will, and teaching us that all living beings depend on one ever-acting Creator and Ruler."

Once when particularly disgusted with the materialistic views of those who, while denying the existence of the Creator, attributed the wonders of nature, animate and inanimate, to the potency of a fortuitous concourse of atoms, Lord Kelvin wrote to Liebig, the great chemist, asking him if a leaf or a flower could be formed or even made to grow by chemical forces, and received the emphatic reply, "I would more readily believe that a book on chemistry or on botany could grow out of dead matter by chemical processes."

Expressions similar to those of Lord Kelvin and Liebig are commonplaces in the history of science. Sir Humphry Davy declared, "The true chemist sees God in all the manifold forms of the external world." Linnæus, to whom the modern world confesses that it owes so much in the organization of botanical science, once exclaimed in what has well been called a spirit of rapture:

"I have traced God's footprints in the works of His creation; and in all of them, even in the least, and in those that border on nothingness, what power, what wisdom, what ineffable perfection!"

It would be very easy to make a long list of extremely great scientists who were firm believers. Clerk Maxwell once said to a friend, "I have read up many queer religions; there is nothing like the old one after all; and I have looked into most philosophical systems, and I have seen that none will work without a God." Pasteur declared in his address before the French Academy, when admitted as a member, "Blessed is the man who has an ideal of the virtues of the Gospel and obeys it." He had once said, impatient at the pretensions of pseudo-scientists: "Posterity will one day laugh at the sublime foolishness of the modern materialistic philosophy. The more I study nature, the more I stand amazed at the work of the Creator. I pray while I am engaged at my work in the laboratory."

Kepler, the great astronomer to whom we owe so many significant basic discoveries, once said:

"The day is near at hand when one shall know the truth in the book of nature as in the Holy Scriptures, and when one shall rejoice in the harmony of both revelations."

Sir Isaac Newton, whose modesty was equaled only by the magnitude of his discoveries, was so impressed with his own littleness in the contemplation of the wonderful works of God that he declared, a short time before his death, "I seem to have been only like a boy playing on the seashore, and diverting myself in now and then finding a smoother pebble or a prettier shell than ordinary, while the great ocean of truth lay all undiscovered before me."

Dumas, the great French chemist, for many years the secretary of the French Academy of Sciences, once suggested the great difference there is in the matter of religious belief between the original worker in science and those who know their science only at second-hand. Those who have acquired their knowledge of science easily have no idea of the difficulties which the original investigator had to encounter and how deep are the mysteries which he knows lie all around him. The second-hand scientist becomes conceited over his knowledge, but the original investigator becomes humble. Dumas said:

"People who only exploit the discoveries of others, and who never make any themselves, greatly exaggerate their importance, because they have never run against the mysteries of science which have checked real savants. Hence their irreligion and their infatuation. It is quite different with people who have made discoveries themselves. They know by experience how limited their field is, and they find themselves at every step arrested by the incomprehensible. Hence their religion and their modesty. Faith and respect for mysteries is easy for them. The more progress they make in science, the more they are confounded by the infinite."

Professor P. G. Tait, professor of natural philosophy at Edinburgh University for the last forty years of the nineteenth century, and who was the co-author with Lord Kelvin of Thomson's and Tait's "Natural Philosophy" (the well-known T+T) summed up the question of the supposed conflict of religion and science rather strikingly and in a way that makes it easy to comprehend many modern misunderstandings. He said:

"The assumed incompatibility of Religion and Science has been so often confidently asserted in recent times that it has come to be taken for granted by writers of leading articles, etc., and it is, of course, perpetually thrust by them broadcast before their too trusting readers.

"But the whole thing is a mistake, and a mistake so grave that no true scientific man (unless indeed he be literally a specialist — such as a pure mathematician, or a mycologist or entomologist) runs, in Britain at least, the smallest risk of making it.

"When we ask of any competent authority who are the

'advanced', the best, and the ablest scientific thinkers of the immediate past (in Britain), we cannot but receive for answer such names as Brewster, Faraday, Forbes, Graham, Rowan Hamilton, Herschel, and Talbot. This must be the case unless we use the word 'science' in a perverted sense. Which of these great men gave up the idea that Nature evidences a Designing Mind?"

Lord Rayleigh, the physicist and mathematician, professor of experimental physics at Cambridge and then Tyndall's successor as professor of natural philosophy at the Royal Institution, who, after having been secretary of the Royal Society for some ten years, was elected to what has been called the highest official position in the scientific world — the presidency of the Royal Society — wrote in answer to a question:[1] "I am not able to write you at length, but I may say that in my opinion true Science and true Religion neither are nor could be opposed.

"A large number of 'leading scientists' are not irreligious or anti-Christian. Witness: Faraday, Maxwell, Stokes, Kelvin, and a large number of others less distinguished."

Practically all the men whose names are connected with the evolution of electricity in the nineteenth century were thorough-going believers in revealed religion. Galvani, Volta, Coulomb, Ohm, Ampère, Oersted, Faraday, Sir Humphry Davy, and many others are among the believers. Faraday once declared when the dark shadow of death was creeping over him, "I bow before Him who is the Lord of all, and hope to be kept waiting patiently for His time and mode of releasing me, accord-

[1] I owe this and a number of other quotations in this chapter to Tabrum "Religious Beliefs of Scientists," London, 1911.

ing to His divine word and the great and precious promises whereby His people are made partakers of the divine nature."

Earlier in life, in the very maturity of the intellectual powers which made him immortal in science, lest perhaps some one should suggest that he had lost his mental grasp toward the end, he said: "When I consider the multitude of associate forces which are diffused through nature; when I think of that calm and tranquil balancing of their energies which enables elements, most powerful in themselves, most destructive to the world's creatures and economy, to dwell associated together and be made subservient to the wants of creation, I rise from the contemplation more than ever impressed with the wisdom, the beneficence, and grandeur beyond our language to express, of the Great Disposer of all!"

It would be easy to multiply quotations such as this from the great original workers in modern electricity. Hans Christian Oersted, for instance, the great Danish scientist, to whom we owe the discovery of the "magnetic effect" of the electric current, the demonstration of the intimate relationship between magnetism and electricity, whose name all Europe rang with in the early part of the nineteenth century, was a man of really great genius and scientific penetration and yet of deeply fervent piety. He did not hesitate to say that genuine knowledge of science necessarily produced a feeling of religious piety towards the Creator. Lord Kelvin once quoted some words of his in this regard on a memorable occasion, which are particularly to our purpose here:

"If my purpose here was merely to show that science necessarily engenders piety, I should appeal to the great truth everywhere recognized, that the essence of all religion consists in love toward God. The conclusion would then be easy, that love of Him from whom all truth proceeds must create the desire to acknowledge truth in all her paths; but as we desire here to recognize science herself as a religious duty, it will be requisite for us to penetrate deeper into its nature. It is obvious, therefore, that the searching eye of man, whether he regards his own inward being or the creation surrounding him, is always led to the eternal source of all things. In all inquiry, the ultimate aim is to discover that which really exists and to contemplate it in its pure light apart from all that deceives the careless observer by only a seeming existence. The philosopher will then comprehend what, amidst ceaseless change, is the Constant and Uncreated, which is hidden behind unnumbered creations, the bond of union which keeps things together in spite of their manifold divisions and separations. He must soon acknowledge that the independent can only be the constant and the constant the independent, and that true unity is inseparable from either of these. And thus it is in the nature of thought that it finds no quiet resting place, no pause, except in the invariable, eternal, uncaused, all causing, all comprehensive Omniscience.

"But, if this one-sided view does not satisfy him, if he seeks to examine the world with the eye of experience, he perceives that all those things of whose reality the multitude feels most assured never have an enduring existence, but are always on the road between birth and death. If he now properly comprehends the whole array of nature, he perceives that it is not merely an idea of an abstract notion, as it is called; but that reason and the power to which everything is indebted for its essential nature are only the revelation of a self-sustained Being. How can he, when he sees this, be otherwise animated than by the deepest feeling of humility, of devotion and of love? If any one has learned a different lesson from his observation of nature, it could only be because he lost his way amidst the dispersion and variety of creation and had not looked upwards to the eternal unity of truth."

The great contemporary and colleague of Oersted in the demonstration of the intimate relations between magnetism and electricity who was quite as outspoken as the Danish scientist in his recognition of the relations of science and religion, was the Frenchman Ampère, whose name was chosen as a term for one of the units of electrical science, because of his great original work in extending our knowledge of electricity. This choice of his name was made by an international congress of scientists who felt that he deserved this very great honor. Ozanam, to whose thoroughly practical Christianity while he was professor of foreign literatures at the University of Paris we owe the foundation of the Conferences of St. Vincent de Paul, which so long anticipated the "settlement work" of the modern time and have done so much for the poor in large cities ever since, who was very close to Ampère and indeed lived with him for a while, said that, no matter where conversations with him began, they always led up to God. The great French scientist and philosopher used to take his broad forehead between his hands after he had been discussing some specially deep question of science or philosophy and say: "How great is God, Ozanam; How great is God and how little is our knowledge." Of course this has been the feeling of most profound thinkers at all times. St. Augustine's famous vision of the angel standing by the sea emptying it out with a teaspoon, which has been rendered so living for most of us by Botticelli's great picture, is but an earlier example of the same thing. One of Ampère's greatest contemporaries, Laplace, reëchoed the same sentiment, perhaps in less striking terms, when he declared that "What we know is but little; while what we do not know is infinite."

Writing of Ampère after his death Ozanam, who knew him best, brought out this extremely interesting union of intellectual qualities, his science, his faith, his charity to the poor which was proverbial, and the charming geniality of his character, as well as his manifold human interests, in a passage that serves very well to sum up the meaning of the great Frenchman's life.

"In addition to his scientific achievements this brilliant genius has other claims upon our admiration and affection. . . . It was religion which guided the labors of his mind and illuminated his contemplations; he judged all things, science itself, by the exalted standard of religion. . . . This venerable head which was crowned by achievements and honors, bowed without reserve before the mysteries of faith, down even below the line which the Church has marked for us. He prayed before the same altars before which Descartes and Pascal had knelt; beside the poor widow and the small child who may have been less humble in mind than he was. Nobody observed the regulations of the Church more conscientiously, regulations which are so hard on nature and yet so sweet in the habit. Above all things, however, it is beautiful to see what sublime things Christianity wrought in his great soul; this admirable simplicity, the unassumingness of a mind that recognized everything except its own genius; this high rectitude in matters of science, now so rare, seeking nothing but the truth and never rewards and distinction; the pleasant and ungrudging amiability; and lastly, the kindness with which he met every one, especially young people. I can say that those who know only the intelligence of the man, know only the less perfect part. If he thought much, he loved more."

Ohm, after whom another of the units of electricity is named, was another of the scientists who realized very clearly the existence of Providence and in one very disappointing circumstance in life, when he found that some of his work at which he had spent much time was completely anticipated by a Norwegian investigator, he said very simply, "Man proposes but God disposes"; and he chronicled the fact that without the bait of this discovery which he vaguely foresaw at the beginning he would not have taken up the work, and yet during the time when he was at it "A number of things of which I had no hint at all at the beginning of my researches have come to take the place of my original purpose and compensate for it." When he undertook his next work he foresaw that he might not be able to finish it; he had hoped against hope that he would, and in the preface to the first volume he declared that he would devote himself to it at every possible opportunity and that he hoped and prayed that "God would spare him to complete it." This simplicity of confidence in the Almighty is indeed a striking characteristic of the man of whose discovery of the law of electricity Lord Kelvin declared that it was such an extremely simple expression of a great truth that its significance is probably not confined to that department of physical phenomena, but it is a law of nature in some much broader way. Professor George Chrystal of Edinburgh in his article on electricity in the "Encyclopædia Britannica" (IX Edition) says that

Ohm's law must now be allowed to rank with the law of gravitation and the elementary laws of statical electricity as a *law of nature* in the strictest sense.

Volta, whom the international congress of electricity so deservedly honored by giving his name to one of the units of electricity, is the genius who first constructed an instrument which would give a continuous flow of electricity. The Voltaic pile is a very great invention. Volta was much more, however, than merely an ingenious inventor. He was a great scientist who made discoveries not only in electricity but in various other branches of physical science. He was one of the eight foreign members of the French Institute, Knight Commander of the Legion of Honor, one of the first members of the Italian Academy and the gold medalist of the French Academy. There was nothing he touched in his work that he did not illuminate.

His was typically the mind of the genius, ever reaching out beyond the boundaries of the known, — an abundant source of leading and light for others. Far from being a doubter in matters religious, his scientific greatness seemed only to make him readier to submit to what are sometimes spoken of as the shackles of faith, though to him belief appealed as a completion of knowledge of things beyond the domain of sense or the ordinary powers of intellectual acquisition.

In Volta's time as in our own some of the less important workers in science had their faith disturbed by their knowledge of science and attributed that result to science rather than to the limitations of their own minds. One of them declared that though Volta continued to practice his religion, this was more because he did not want to offend friends and did not care to scandalize his neighbors and especially the poor folk around him in his country home, whom he did not want to be led by his example into giving up what he knew to be the most fruitful source of consolation in the trials of life, rather than because of sincere conviction. Volta, having heard this report, deliberately wrote out his confession of faith, so that all the world of his own and the after time might know it. When he wrote it he was just approaching his sixtieth year and was in the full maturity of his powers. He lived for twelve years afterwards, looked up to as one of the great thinkers of Europe and as one of the most important men of Italy in his time.

"If some of my faults and negligences may have by chance given occasion to some one to suspect me of infidelity, I am ready, as some reparation for this and for any other good purpose, to declare to such a one and to every other person and on every occasion and under all circumstances that I have always held, and hold now, the Holy Catholic Religion as the only true and infallible one, thanking without end the good God for having gifted me with such a faith, in which I firmly propose to live and die, in the lively hope of attaining eternal life. I recognize my faith as a gift of God, a supernatural faith. I have not, on this account, however, neglected to use all human means that could confirm me more and more in it and that might drive away any doubt which could arise to tempt me in matters of faith. I have studied my faith with attention as to its foundations, reading for this purpose books of apologetics as well as those written with a contrary purpose, and trying to appreciate the arguments pro and contra. I have tried to realize from what sources spring the strongest arguments which render faith most credible to natural reason and such as cannot fail to make every well-balanced mind which has not been perverted by vice or passion embrace it and love it. May this protest of mine, which I have deliberately drawn up and which I leave to posterity, subscribed with my own hand and which shows to all and every one that I do not blush at the Gospel — may it, as I have said, produce some good fruit.

"Signed at Milan, January 6, 1815, Alessandro Volta."

Silvio Pellico, whose volume, "My Ten Years' Imprisonment", is one of the precious little books of literature that seem destined to enduring interest, had doubted in the midst of his trials and hardships the presence of Providence in the world and the existence of a hereafter. In the midst of his doubts he turned to Volta.

"In thy old age, O Volta!" said Pellico, "the hand of Providence placed in thy pathway a young man gone astray. 'Oh! thou,' said I to the ancient seer, 'who hast plunged deeper than others into the secrets of the Creator, teach me the road that will lead me to the light.' And the old man made answer: 'I too have doubted, but I have sought. The great scandal of my youth was to behold the teachers of those days lay hold of science to combat religion. For me to-day I see only God everywhere.'"

In spite of traditions to the contrary great physicians in their relation to faith are like the great discoverers in electricity. As a rule the greater they are as original workers in the medical sciences the more emphatic their expressions of their belief in religion and its efficacy in the relief of human ills. The opinions of a few of our greatest physicians in the modern era of medicine are quoted here as examples of their attitude of mind.

Sir Richard Owen, probably the greatest anatomist of

the nineteenth century, was a convinced Christian and saw nothing in scientific truth inimical to the Christian faith. In an address before the Young Men's Christian Association, he asked his "fellow Christians":

"Has aught that is essentially Christian suffered — have its truths ceased to spread and operate in mankind — since physical doctrines, supposed or 'declared contrary to Holy Writ', have been established?

"Allay, then, your fears, and trust in the Author of all truth, who has decreed that it shall never perish; who has given a power to man to acquire that most precious of his possessions with an intellectual nature that will ultimately rest upon due demonstrative evidence."

Sir James Paget, sometime president of the Royal College of Surgeons of England and vice-chancellor of London University, looked upon as one of the most distinguished of medical scientists in his time, after whom a special disease described by him has been named, in answer to the question as to the attitude of scientists toward religion said: "You will find among scientific men very few who attack either theology or religion. The attacks imputed to them are made, for the most part, by those who, with a very scanty knowledge of science, use, not its facts, but its most distant inferences, as they do whatever else they can get from any source, for the overthrow of religious beliefs."

Sir Samuel Wilks, another of the presidents of the Royal College of Physicians and distinguished in many other ways among the physicians of Great Britain, in his Harveian Oration expressed himself very definitely in this matter of the relations of science and religion, and his quotation from our own Oliver Wendell Holmes adds to the interest of what he has to say.

"Hear what a learned professor of anatomy, Wendell Holmes, can say: 'Science represents the thought of God discovered by man; by learning the natural laws he attaches effects to their first cause, the will of the Creator', or in the poetic language of Goethe: 'Nature is the living garment of God.'

"Science conducts us through infinite paths; it is a fruitful pursuit for the most poetic imagination. We take the world as we find it and endeavor to unravel its mysteries; but the Alpha and Omega we know not. Enough for us to look at what is lying around us; it is a part we see and not the whole, but we can say with the poet, 'We doubt not, through the ages one increasing purpose runs.'"

Professor Sims Woodhead, well known as one of the distinguished contributors to pathology in the nineteenth century and who was, before being professor of pathology at Cambridge the director of the Laboratories of the Conjoint Board of the Royal College of Physicians (London) and Surgeons (England) may very well be taken as a representative of the medical scientists of the last generation of the nineteenth century. It has been said that where there are three physicians there are two atheists, and perhaps this may be true among the smaller fry of the profession, but it certainly is not among the most distinguished members of it. Such men as Pasteur, Lord Lister, Robert Graves, Corrigan, Laënnec, Claude Bernard, Johannes Müller, are the outspoken contradiction of it. Pathology and anatomy, in both of which subjects Professor Woodhead was a teacher, are often said to be rather serious in their inroads on the faith of the men who pursue them closely. Professor Woodhead is on record categorically with regard to this subject of the relations of the Bible and religion, and science and religion, and his words are well worth while quoting here.

"As regards the statement that 'recent scientific research has shown the Bible and Religion to be untrue', nothing is further from the real fact; the more the Bible is tested the more it is found to be made up of historical documents. Moreover, it is recognized that the Bible, as a record of truths, never falls foul of Science in its search after truth, and scientific men are too true to themselves to take the stand that they will not accept truth of any kind.

"I agree with you that certain theories put forward in the name of Science may be opposed to certain theological dogmas; but men are certainly coming to see that between the facts of Science and the essential teachings of the Christian religion there is never any real opposition; and by the 'Christian Religion' I mean the religion of Christ, not what some people have wished to read into it; and by 'science' I mean a search for truth and knowledge, and by 'men of science' I mean men engaged in that search."

Professor John W. Taylor, one of the distinguished physicians of Great Britain and president of the British Gynecological Society, summed up the answer to the question "Can We Still Believe?" in words that show how devout a great medical scientist can be:

"What can we 'hold by' as Christians? We can hold by the Faith of the early Apostles as enunciated in the Apostles' and the Nicene Creeds, and plainly foreshadowed in 1 Cor. xv. This was written within thirty years of our Lord's crucifixion and must have been 'received' by St. Paul immediately on his conversion." Any one who will turn to that chapter of First Corinthians will find that it contains all the essentials of Christian faith, yet here is a great modern physician finding in it the expression of his own mental attitude toward religion in our time.

Biologists, in spite of popular impressions to the contrary, have paralleled physicians in this regard. To cite but one or two:

Professor George Romanes, who was considered not alone one of the leaders of scientific thought in England, but one of the foremost naturalists of modern times, after expressions as a younger man that showed his deep and even devout belief in religion, wrote somewhat later a defense of atheism on scientific grounds. Some years afterwards, in the maturity of his powers, he prepared a thorough-going recantation of this in the shape of a work designed to show the fallacy of his former atheistic views, in which he said:

"It is a general, if not a universal rule that those who reject Christianity with contempt are those who care not for religion of any kind. 'Depart from me' has always been the sentiment of such. On the other hand, those in whom the religious sentiment is intact, but who have rejected Christianity on intellectual grounds, still almost deify Christ. These facts are remarkable."

"Unbelief," Professor Romanes concluded, "is usually due to indolence, often to prejudice, and never a thing to be proud of."

In every department of science one finds the representatives of the various branches of scientific study in harmony on this subject of religion and science. Professor George Boulger, whose work has been mainly done in botany and who was a fellow of a number of the scientific societies of England and vice-president of the Selborne

Society, has some very direct expressions in the matter that add to the significance of what has been said by others.

"In philosophy, in physics, and in astronomy I am content to place myself on the side of Bacon, of Newton, of Napoleon. I believe, with Bacon, that 'a little Philosophy inclineth Man's Minde to Atheisme; but depth in Philosophy bringeth Men's Mindes about to Religion.' With Newton I am content to 'seem to have been only like a boy playing on the seashore, and diverting myself in now and then finding a smoother pebble or a prettier shell than ordinary, whilst the great ocean of truth lay all undiscovered before me.' With Napoleon — not a man of science but a man of the world, a man of action — I would say to our neo-Epicureans as he did to his sceptical officers, pointing to the stars, 'Gentlemen, you may talk all night, but who made all these?'"

He recognized how many difficulties there might be for the scientist, but felt, as Cardinal Newman once said, that hundreds of difficulties may not make a single doubt. Professor Boulger has dealt with some of these cruder difficulties with trenchant directness.

"I am perfectly aware of the temptation of the physiological laboratory, when one is face to face with the facts of the localisation of brain-functions and the influence of purely physical conditions upon mentality, until one is almost led to Buchner's gross misstatement that 'the brain secretes thought as the liver secretes bile'; but here, as ever, it is at the very base of the problem that the unsolved mystery shows itself insoluble. Force, Matter, Life, Thought, Will, — what are they, whence come they? Science deals with their phenomena, their manifestations. With John Ray I would term the study of nature a pious duty, one suited to a Sabbath day and not improbably one of the main occupations of the endless Sabbaths hereafter. . . . But true science will never presume to say that it can deal with anything beyond these phenomena. As I am as convinced that the Christian Faith is a Divine revelation as I am that 'Nature' is the creation of the Divine First Cause, it is, of course, to me unthinkable that there could be any conflict between them."

Not only the scientists themselves but the philosophic students of the whole range of modern thought who took the information imparted by the specialists and coördinated it for the purpose of finding the philosophic conclusions to be drawn from it all as to man's life and destiny and the meaning of it all have recognized the place of religion in Life and its significance for humanity.

Mr. Frederic Harrison, the well-known English apostle of Comte, whose Positivism might possibly have been expected to lead him away from such ideas, did not hesitate in the midst of that wave of skepticism which spread over Europe shortly after the "silly seventies" when so many even of the well-informed thought that natural selection was going to explain everything for us and solve all the mysteries, to utter some very strong words on the subject that well deserve to be recalled. In his book, "The Creed of a Layman", he said, for instance:

"I believe that before all things, needful beyond all else, is true religion. This only can give wisdom, happiness and goodness to men and a nobler life to mankind. Nothing but this can sustain, guide and satisfy all lives, control all characters and unite all men. True religion must rule in every heart, brain and will, over every people of the whole earth; inspire every thought, hallow every emotion and be the guide of every act."

And by what he termed the true religion Mr. Harrison did not mean merely some vague deism or some shadowy belief in a vaguer power that made for righteousness, but a very definite personal relationship to a personal God who was not only to be looked up to and reverenced but who was to be loved.

"The paramount importance to Man of Religion — at once dominant over brain and heart — a living reality and working power — the necessity for this has not only never left me at any time but year by year has grown deeper as a conviction and more familiar as a rule of life. But as the indispensable need of true religion grew stronger in my mind, I more and more came to feel that religion would end in vague sentimentality unless it has an object of devotion distinctly grasped by the intellect and able to kindle ardent emotions. The nature — if not the name — of the Supreme Being is in truth decisive. Unless the Supreme Power be felt to be in sympathy with the believer, be akin to the believer, be in active touch with his life and heart, such a religion is merely a dogma; it cannot be a guide of life in the spring of action — the object of love."

Agnosticism, so fashionable in educational circles at the end of the nineteenth century, has practically disappeared, or at least has suffered such an eclipse that its adherents are comparatively few. There was a time in the generation that is still alive when a great many educators who felt that they were the leaders of thought in our time were quite sure that agnosticism would be the only mode of intellectual reaction which the educated man could possibly think of allowing to take place in him by the time the year of grace 1920 had come. Instead agnosticism, like so many other movements of similar kind founded on human thinking, in accord with the fashion of the moment, has dwindled into insignificance. Fortunately there were some educators who even twenty-five years ago recognized the real portent of it and stated their opinions so emphatically as to keep the educational world of their time from being entirely run away with. President Schurman of Cornell said:

"Agnosticism is the apotheosis of skepticism. It is skepticism as a creed, as a system, as an ultimate resting-place. Those who proclaim it strangely misread the processes and the conditions of our spiritual life. *They make the aimless gropings of the youthful intellect an ideal for the thinking of mature men.* Only, instead of the awful earnestness of the inquiring youth, they often affect an indifference to the great problems which oppress him. As though we could be indifferent to the highest interests of the human spirit! So long as life lasts, so long must we strive to grasp the ultimate truth of things. To shut our eyes to problems is an ostrich policy. Man is called by an inner voice to strive, and strive, and strive, and not to yield. Agnosticism would eradicate this noble endeavor. Its only justification, so far as I can see, is that men never attain the absolute truth, but only make successive approximations to it."

Such men seem to forget the great lesson that the differential calculus has taught us. It represents one of the greatest developments of modern mathematics. It does not solve problems by absolute solutions but by such approximations as make the answer which cannot be reached very clear. It has been of immense value in adding to the knowledge of mankind and in giving science particularly a command over principles that would otherwise seem impossible. Religion requires faith to complete it. Knowledge can never more than approximate conclusions with regard to many religious questions. Such approximations, however, like the answers in differential calculus, represent real advances on the road to knowledge that are of great value in directing men toward what is best in life.

Mr. Frederic Harrison has answered this question "Can We Still Believe?" by insisting that belief in the hereafter is the most precious heritage that man has, to be fostered above all else. He said:

"The great truth of a life beyond the grave is indeed one of the best possessions of Man, the fondest of all noble, living and working doctrines on earth. When Paul first preached it in that sublime song of triumph over death, which has so often thrilled us to the marrow as we stood round the coffined dead, he gave the human race a new and imperishable hope to last while the planet endures. . . . Let us cherish and hold fast this glad tiding of good things."

Any one who faces the question of religion seriously realizes that not only it is not a thing of the past but that the rationalistic tendencies of the later nineteenth century have had their usual inevitable reaction emphasized by the Great War, so that men are readier to be swayed by religious influences than ever before. The more one studies the problems of health of mind and of body connected with religion, and the strong factor that it is for the making of character, the shaping of destiny and the cultivation of happiness, the more one realizes the truth of Napoleon's expression that if religion were to disappear we should have to reinvent it, because of the immense benefit that it represents for mankind.

CHAPTER II

PRAYER

In spite of a very prevalent impression in the matter, the all-important element of religion is not attendance at church or the public exercise of religious functions, or even the joining in religious celebrations, for all these may be accomplished by routine without an element of real devotion to the Creator in them. They may even be gone through with hypocritically while all the time one is thinking of merely worldly things, or even of the effect that one is producing on others by the show of devotion, though with such slight advertence as to make the devotions of extremely little value or even a sort of insult to the Almighty if the negligent attitude of mind is assumed deliberately. Bodily participation in worship is a necessary adjunct of the expression of religious feeling, but it is of course of just so much less importance than the mental worship of the Creator as the body is less important than the mind. Mental adoration of the Deity is accomplished through prayer, which is the all-important personal element of religion.

Prayer in the words of the old Christian teachers is "A raising up of the mind to God asking for help, begging for forgiveness for past errors and thanking Him for all that He has done for us." Real prayer is no mere formula of words, and some very fervent prayers are made without being formulated into words at all. I remember once suggesting in a medical meeting that prayer was an extremely valuable adjunct to the treatment for certain milder forms of disturbed mentality and for the dreads and obsessions that haunt men and women, that is, in general for that very important class of diseases which in our day are grouped under the term psychoneuroses. A physician friend, in discussing the suggestion, said that no words that he knew would dispel or be of the slightest help in any of these conditions as they came under his observation. Prayer is not, however, a formula of words, but an act of the mind and the heart and the will, for to be genuine, it should contain acknowledgment, affection and resolve. My colleague's failure to appreciate the true meaning of prayer and his apparent persuasion that the words were the all-important element in prayer are not surprising, for rather frequently it happens that the personal experience of the professional classes as to prayer is not calculated to be really enlightening.

Professor James confesses that unfortunately comparatively few educated people have the real power of prayer; those who have, however, possess a magnificent source of renewed energy that can be of the greatest possible service to them. He says:

"Relatively few medical men and scientific men, I fancy, can pray. Few can carry on any living commerce with 'God.' Yet many of us are well aware of how much freer and abler our lives would be, were such important forms of energizing not sealed up by the critical atmosphere in which we have been reared. There are in every one potential forms of activity that actually are shunted out from use. Part of the imperfect vitality under which we labor can thus be easily explained. One part of our mind dams up — even *damns* up! — the other parts."

Manifestly the well-known professor of psychology envied those who lived lives of prayer and felt that he was missing something in life from not possessing the developed faculty to enjoy their privileges. Like so many other of the good things of life, prayer, to be really efficient for all the good it can produce, must be a habit and must be practiced as a rule from very early years. Otherwise it is hard to make it such a factor in living as is significant for the best, and professional men commonly have not given enough time to the practice in their earlier years to make it of potency when it may be needed.

It is of course not long vocal prayers — though many people find not only consolation, but strength for their work and the added capacity to bear their trials in these — but the frequent raising up of the heart and mind to the Power above us, striving to put our intentions in line with His in the hope to do our work so that it will not be unworthy of the best aspirations that He has put in our hearts, that counts. Many of the saints have suggested that all our work should be a prayer begun with the right intention, pursued, no matter how difficult it may be, with the feeling that this is what we ought to do here and now, and finished with the offering of it to the Creator who has lent us the energy to accomplish it. *Ora et Labora,* pray and work, was the motto which Benedict, who revolutionized the social conditions of Europe by bringing back the dignity of labor and lifting men's minds out of the rut of the cult of their bodies, into which they had fallen at the close of the Roman Empire, gave to the members of his order. It was really not two things but one that he meant. What his sons accomplished as the result of his great motto we are only just beginning to recognize. They saved the old classics for us, kept the torch of education burning when barbarism might have quenched it, passed it on to the new generation, yet at the same time saved and developed agriculture so that, as President Goodell of the Massachusetts Agricultural College said, they made some of the best agricultural schools, in the best sense of that term, that have ever been made, and organized health and happiness for the country people as they have never been made possible before or since, except in the very modern time.

In the chapter on longevity there are some statistics which might very well and easily have been increased in numbers with regard to the effect of St. Benedict's foundation on the length of life that men have lived. Even now, in the midst of all our improvement in sanitation which has so lowered the death rate among mankind, we find that nearly fifteen hundred years after Benedict's work was first begun, his direction to make life a compend of work and prayer is having its effect in prolonging existence for the followers of his rule to-day. He himself would probably have said that it was the combination of these two that proved so effective in this important matter of lengthening life. We find that people outside the monasteries work enough, however, but fail to pray, so it would seem that prayer is a particularly important factor for monastic longevity, at least. Length of life comes, however, from a healthy mind in a healthy body, and nothing so conduces to the possession of a healthy mind as the habit of prayer, since it enables man to throw off to some extent at least — and the deeper the prayer habit the more it will do it — the solicitudes and anxieties with regard to the past and the present and the future which disturb so many people. As Ignatius Loyola, the wise founder of the Jesuits, said: "Pray as if everything depended on God; work as if everything depended on you; but leave everything to the Almighty, for you might as well since His Will will surely be accomplished anyhow."

It would be very easy to think that such habits of prayer in the midst of work would only be possible if the work that one was engaged at was not very interesting or was not taken very seriously and was being accomplished in more or less of a routine. In particular many scientific students, and especially those who are interested in psychology, would probably feel quite sure that very great results could not be accomplished in any important work if distractions of this kind were allowed and above all encouraged.

It is interesting then to take some of the examples of men who are known to have formed and maintained such habits and yet accomplished very great work for mankind. The list might be made a very long one; we shall mention only a few of the most distinguished. Almost in our own time Pasteur said, as we have already quoted: "The more I study nature the more I stand amazed at the work of the Creator. I pray while I am engaged at work in the laboratory." A distinguished contemporary of his in France in his earlier years was Leverrier. There is no doubt at all about his power of concentration; he is the scientist who discovered the planet Neptune by mathematics alone without the aid of a telescope. He constantly kept a crucifix in his observatory and used to turn his eyes to it frequently for recollection and then go on with his calculations. There is a well-known picture of Vesalius, who so well deserves the title of Father of Modern Anatomy, at work in his anatomical rooms with a crucifix before him. The composition is founded on the tradition that the great anatomist was a devout man who prayed as he worked. He made a pilgrimage to the Holy Land in his older years in expiation for a fault committed.

In spite of traditions to the contrary, a great many of our scientists of the last two centuries whose work has meant most for modern medicine have been men to whom prayer meant very much. There are traditions of Morgagni, the distinguished father of modern pathology, as Virchow hailed him, which show that never a day passed without his raising his heart in prayer. Volta and Galvani, whose names have become so familiar in modern electricity, were both of them well known for their devotion to the practice of daily religious duties. French scientists were not less devout. Laënnec, a Breton by birth, lost none of the devoutness of his early years so characteristic of the Bretons even when he was in the midst of the great work which enabled him to write the greatest medical book in modern times. Ozanam has told us that when he himself felt thoroughly discouraged and ready to think religion something that any one who wanted to keep up with modern thought would have to give up, he wandered into a church, hoping that prayer might help him to dispel his doubts and difficulties and found there praying before the altar devoutly his great professor of science, Ampère.

Deep thinkers, whether of scientific temper of mind or not, have recognized the value of prayer. Vesalius' great contemporary, Michelangelo, who is perhaps the greatest intellectual and artistic genius that the world has ever known — sculptor, architect, painter, poet, and unsurpassed in all these modes of human expression at their highest — was another for whom his crucifix meant much and who frequently turned to it. One of his greatest sonnets is dedicated to the Crucified One. Of Leonardo da Vinci's private life we know less, but on his death bed he left a sum of money to be used to provide candles to burn before the altar of the little village church at which he had prayed as a boy, so that evidently something of that old fervor of spirit was his at the end. Leonardo da Vinci's mind was one of the most acute in the whole history of mankind. He was a great painter, sculptor, architect, and also a great engineer, a great scientific discoverer, an inventor of all sorts of useful appliances and a veritable marvel of comprehensive appreciation of the significance of even the most obscure things. He is a founder in half a dozen sciences, paleontology, biology, anatomy, physics and mechanics, and nothing makes one feel the smallness of the ordinary man like reading a sketch of Leonardo's achievements.

Of course the clergymen scientists have been men of prayer, but few people realize how many of them have made distinguished contributions to the domain of science. Poggendorf's "Biographical Lexicon" contains the names of nearly a thousand clergymen who have made such contributions to science as deserve that their fame should be thus enshrined among the scientists of history. One of the greatest astronomers of the nineteenth century was Father Secchi, a Jesuit, some of whose work was done for a time in America. Among the most distinguished names in modern science are Abbé Breuil and Father Obermaier, who have taught the world so much about the cave man. Both of them are well known for their faithful performance of their religious duties in the midst of their scientific work.

Raising up the heart and mind in the midst of work, instead of increasing distractions, rather helps to control them. Distractions will come and may prove seriously wasteful of time, but are caught in the habit of lifting up the mind occasionally, and then the original work is taken up with renewed energy. Above all, such a habit of prayer keeps people from getting into a state of irritable haste about their work in which they consume a lot of energy without getting much done and wear out their nervous systems by the feeling of nervousness that comes over them. To do anything under a sense of pressure is nearly always to disturb the best efforts of the mind and skimp the work. Doing things in this way leads to that bane of modern existence, nervous breakdown, which has become ever so much commoner since men forgot that it is not labor for ourselves that counts so much as labor for others, and that an over-anxiety to get things done for selfish reasons burns up nervous energy faster than anything else. Fussy, irritable effort to work gets on the nerves sooner than any amount of calm effort would. Prayer as I have described would be the cure for it. St. Theresa's well-known prayer is the antidote.[1]

When the life of the late Cardinal Vaughan of London appeared, one of the most surprising things in it was the story of the distinguished English Cardinal's habit of prayer. Almost needless to say he was an extremely busy man. Important problems in the administration

[1] Let nothing disturb thee,
Let nothing affright thee,
All things are passing,
God never changeth.
Who God possesseth
In nothing is wanting,
Alone God sufficeth.
(Longfellow translation.)

of his immense archdiocese and in the relationship of the English Catholics to their fellow citizens came before him every day. He had to carry the heavy burden of responsibility and make his decisions promptly and thoroughly, for a great many details necessarily devolved on him. Somehow he found time for hours of prayer during the day, and those who knew him best felt sure he would have declared that so far from distracting him in his work or taking time from it in any real sense of the word, it would have been quite impossible for him to accomplish all he did without this habit of prayer. It was this which enabled him to keep a placid mind and make his decisions easily and firmly in the midst of his work. He himself would undoubtedly have added that he felt he actually derived help from the Infinite through prayer, which enabled him to do his work ever so much better than would have been possible by his own unaided effort. There have been many others, and not a few of them who were not churchmen, who have felt this same way even in our strenuous times.

A whole series of the generals in command of important departments of the French army were men who never let a day pass without prayer and who often raised their hearts and minds up to the Power above them for help in their work and also for resignation that the will of the Most High might be accomplished. General Pau, for instance, was one of these. When, during the war, he was presented with flowers by the children of villages through which he passed, he would say, "These must be for the altar," and then he would ask the children to pray for the success of the French army and would insist that for victory "we must pray very much." General de Castelnau was another of these men who found a resource and a real help in prayer. He felt that the prayers of others helped him. That is the index of real recognition of the value of prayer. "I beg you to implore Him especially to give me light and courage; there is no position where one is more completely in His hands than that which I hold." He wrote to Monsignor Ricard, Archbishop of Auch, "More than ever I find by experience the all-importance in war, as elsewhere, of the 'imponderables' and these 'imponderables' are manifestly in His hands Who knows all and guides all."

We might go on with such examples. For instance, Marshal Pétain, who at the end of the war was in command of the French troops, was another of these strong men of prayer. Earlier in the Great War he had been in command at Verdun, transferred there just as it seemed almost impossible to believe that the Germans could be kept from taking the place. The words of his first order issued the day of his arrival — "They shall not pass" — show the character of the man. He was almost reckless in his bravery when it was necessary to impress his troops with the need to go on, no matter what it cost. Alone and on foot he led his troops under a rain of German shells at Saint Bon; after that he could ask anything of his men. General Gouraud, whose masterly defense of the Allied line when the Germans made their great final unsuccessful attack stamps him as one of the greatest military leaders of the day, had been wounded a number of times before this, but refused to give up, and when, early in the war, one of his arms had to be amputated and the surgeons were afraid that he would object, he said very simply, "Go on, if you think it necessary; I offer it to God for France." His recovery from his several wounds at that time seemed almost impossible, so in gratitude for it he hung an *ex-voto* in white marble at the shrine of Our Lady of Victories in Paris. General Fayolle is another striking example of prayerfulness in a practical man. He had intended to spend a year of his retirement, which came just before the war opened, in following the footsteps of St. Paul's missionary voyages. He offered himself for service and proved a great leader, yet a simple, kindly man whom his soldiers called Père Fayolle. A letter of his directed to the Mayor of Mainz showed very clearly that while he remembered and realized all the cruelty of the German occupation of Belgium and France, there was no fear of reprisals from the French, just though they might be. He is a man of deep knowledge of his religion as well as of firm piety, and he is famous for his matter-of-fact common sense. He has all the qualities which some people, because they have had so little experience in the matter, assume are not to be found in a man who believes thoroughly in and practices prayer.

A good deal has been said in recent years about the practice of "going into the silence" and finding there renewal of self. Like so many other new modes of expression, this is merely a new formula for that very old religious custom, meditation, and some of the old writers on spiritual subjects, not only generations ago but actually many hundreds of years before modern history began, laid down the rules for it rather carefully. Meditation can be a source of some of the most valuable suggestive, helpful consolation as well as profound enlightenment in difficult problems that human nature has. Above all it generates a calm that makes for peace of mind and, therefore, health of body. John Boyle O'Reilly recognized its deeper meanings a generation ago when he wrote:

"The infinite always is silent:
It is only the finite that speaks.
Our words are the idle wave-caps
On the deep that never breaks.
We may question with wand of science,
Explain, decide, and discuss;
But only in meditation
The Mystery speaks to us."

Most of the religious orders, and it is in them particularly that the effect of religion on health and happiness and efficiency and increase of the power to achieve, under the influence of profoundly religious motives, can be studied, require by rule that their members shall spend at least half an hour in meditation each morning; and with many of them, of course, an hour or more is required. They prepare for it the night before by reading some passage in the life of Christ, or by taking some special lesson from His teaching; the next morning they reflect how this can be exemplified in their own daily lives and proceed to make certain practical applications of it to the everyday concerns with which they are occupied.

It is surprising how efficient in living up to their very best during the day this makes a great many of the members. There are exceptions, of course, who fail to derive the proper benefit from the practice because they do not devote themselves to it with sufficient earnestness to secure its advantages, but most of them, as the result of this daily period of morning prayer, are rendered capable of going through a monotonous round of hard daily work and succeed in getting excellent results and in keeping cheerful and light-hearted in the midst of what might otherwise seem a very trivial mode of life. The motives thus imparted to them often make even the trifles of life of great interest and significant import.

As a result of their life of prayer, members of religious orders have ever so many less complaints than people who live under corresponding circumstances, largely within doors amid a rather monotonous round of existence. It is extremely rare to find religious devotees who "enjoy poor health" as so many of the laity do. Having less complaints they suffer less from disease, for after all discomfort depends on two factors, — one the irritation and the other the mode of its reception. An irritable person will suffer tortures, though under the same circumstances a placid, composed person will be but very little disturbed. Whenever there is much reaction, there is always an increase of the pain that has to be borne. Whenever much attention is paid to discomfort, the concentration of mind on it multiplies by the law of avalanche the number of cells in the brain affected, and this multiplies the actual discomfort felt. A few thousand cells may be affected by a particular focus of irritation, but if all the other cells of the brain are concentrated on this sensation, each of them, and there are many millions of them, will share something at least of the discomfort. Besides, concentration of attention sends more blood or rather opens the blood vessels in the irritated neighborhood somewhat in the way that a blush opens them up on the cheeks, and this hyperemia increases the sensitiveness of the part. The individual, then, who by the help of prayer lessens his complaints actually lessens his discomfort. To stand a thing patiently for a high motive actually makes the pain suffered less than it otherwise would be.

When a man can look calmly forward to the future and say wholeheartedly, "Thy Will be done on earth as it is in heaven," a great many things are easier to bear because of the recognition of the fact that they are the will of a Providence who oversees everything that is being accomplished, and that somehow, somewhere, all is to be for the best. When men recall to themselves the words, "Forgive us our debts as we forgive our debtors," or "Forgive us our trespasses as we forgive those who trespass against us," word it as you will, they are reminded of how much they owe to the Father in heaven, and, therefore, how much they ought to be willing to pay back, not only for what they have been given but also for all the failures that they have made, to say nothing of serious faults. Suffering then comes to have a real meaning that any one, even the least intellectual, can understand, and by that very fact it becomes easier to bear.

I have often found that I could do a great deal for nervous patients by suggesting that they adopt some morning practice of prayer. Usually the best thing for my Catholic patients was to advise them to go to Mass. For this they had to get up at a definite hour, dress promptly, and usually be some blocks away from home by eight o'clock. Some such duty as this, requiring promptitude and taking the mind off oneself and the little troubles that often loom so large in the morning, is an excellent thing for neurotic patients. The great characteristic of the neuroses is that they make people feel depressed when they first awake. They often feel tired and incapable and find it hard to begin the day well; and beginning the day well often means more than anything else in dispelling nervous symptoms and dreads and inhibitions. Most nervous people realize that when they have to get up promptly at about seven o'clock, as for instance after a night on a train, they have almost none of the feelings of oppression that greet their arising when they can turn over in bed and drowse a little longer and let the troubles which have awakened ever so much more promptly than their incentives to do things soak in and take possession of them. To get up and accomplish a duty that gives some satisfaction soon proves to be a wide-open gate of escape from these early morning "blue devils" of which so many of the nervous complain so bitterly.

The differential diagnosis between merely nervous symptoms and the feelings of tiredness and incapacity which come from organic disease can often be made from the early morning symptoms. Nervous patients feel their worst in the very early morning. They often wonder how they will be able to get through the day without breaking down. After an hour or two they begin to feel somewhat better, though life still looks blue enough. On towards ten o'clock they think that the sun may shine for them again. By noon, especially if they have done something in the meantime, they feel much better, and after their lunch in the early afternoon they begin to be quite chipper; toward evening they usually are persuaded that after all life may be worth living, and by the time they are ready to go to bed — and unfortunately they are tempted to put off going to bed until rather late because they do feel so well — they are inclined to wonder how it is possible that they felt so depressed in the morning. The sufferer from organic disease, however, always feels best in the early morning and begins to get tired toward noon; the evening is his time of least enjoyment, and he is quite ready to get to bed rather early. For the neurotic patient waking to a sense of his troubles at once, nothing is better than a prompt lifting up of his mind to God to offer Him the new day that He has given, no matter how it may turn out, and a readiness to take things as they come so that His will may be fulfilled.

In nervous patients one would almost have the feeling that their wills did not wake up nearly so soon as their memories, or even quite so soon as their intellects, such as they have. Their wills need to be aroused. For men setting-up exercises of various kinds are particularly valuable because the will has got to be used in doing them; many a young soldier who during the war was waked up at the unearthly hour of five o'clock and had perforce to get out of bed, found himself full of pains and aches not only of body, but of mind, and wondered how he could stand it. After ten minutes of setting-up exercises, with the blood coursing through his muscles and deep breaths of outdoor air to oxygenate sluggish tissues, he felt like another man. The days seemed nothing to endure then. For a good many nervous women the exercise of getting to church after prompt rising and dressing and then the occupation of mind with deep, serious thoughts of prayer, will do very much what the setting-up exercises did for the young soldiers during the war. I have tried this so often on patients that I know whereof I speak, and I can think of nothing that does them more good than to have some such enlivening incident that satisfies their hearts and minds and starts them at once doing something that will help them throw off the fear thoughts so prone to crowd in.

It is surprising often to learn what things are accomplished by people who find an unfailing resource for their powers physical and mental in prayer. I had the privilege of knowing a frail little woman whose life seemed to be one long prayer, so entirely was every action guided by what she felt God would like her to do at any particular time; and during very nearly sixty years she directed the destinies of a community of women who did more for the charities and education of an important State than any other single factor that I know. She organized hospitals, multiplied schools, built homes for the care of orphans, established an academy with excellent standards in the days when educational criteria were low, and put a climax to her work by building a college for women in which hundreds of young women are now being educated in the best sense of that word, — that is, not only having their minds stuffed with knowledge, but having their thinking powers aroused and, in Huxley's expressive phrase, having their "passions trained to come to heel by a vigorous will, the servant of a tender conscience." I am sure that Huxley's further words might be used of the graduates, — that they have "learned to love all beauty, whether of nature or of art, to hate all vileness and respect others as themselves." The little woman who did all this, frail little thing she often seemed, would have said, I feel certain, that she derived the energy to do it all from prayer.

Some years ago I wrote a sketch of another one of these women of prayer, a little Italian noblewoman who, touched by the condition of the poor Italians in America — only by America she meant both Americas — came over here to help them. She organized Columbus hospitals in New York, Chicago, Seattle and Denver. She established literally hundreds of schools. She gathered around her a band of several thousand young women who devoted themselves to the accomplishment of anything and everything that would help the Italians in this country. They were not all Italians themselves, but they were won to the work by the ardent enthusiasm and the marvelously charming personality of this little woman. The United States would seem to be field large enough for her zeal or for that of any one, but she did not think so, so she went down to South America and organized to similar good purpose down there, having herself carried on one occasion across the Cordilleras in a hamper on muleback. It seemed almost impossible that any one could have all the energy that she had and the initiative, and yet with it charming tact, winning ways and the prudence that enabled her to find her path in some of the most difficult circumstances. She said over and over again that she owed her power to prayer. Many times when she was told that she must rest, she just prayed and went on.

Sometimes the stories of these old-fashioned, prayerful women of our time will be told properly. They hid themselves from publicity as sedulously as most people seek it. I think it one of the most precious privileges of life to have known a score of such women, East and West. Some of them actually seemed to achieve the impossible and even ventured to get up from sick beds to do what they felt they must do, yet they pushed through successfully. Not infrequently they had to stand all sorts of hardships. Over and over again I have heard the story of pioneer work in the midst of privations that would surely seem must break down health; yet many of these women lived to be well beyond seventy and sometimes even beyond eighty years of age. They were strengthened, consoled, held up in trial by prayer, and it enabled them to tap layers of energy in their physical beings which they themselves scarcely knew they possessed and concerning which other people were so dubious that they felt sure the workers would die young of exhausted vitality. Many wondered why some of them did not suffer from nervous prostration. Men and women of prayer seldom suffer from nervous prostration in the ordinary sense of the word, and what is called that in them is very often the manifestation of some organic ailment which has not been recognized.

As to the power of prayer to enable people to stand suffering and pain, that is discussed in the chapters on these special subjects. Raising the mind and heart to God will do more to make even the extremity of pain bearable than anything else in the world. I have known a man under an engine, almost literally cooking to death from the steam that was escaping near him, in poignant agony, take on a quiet, peaceful look after a priest had crawled under the engine to give him the last rites of the Church; and though his groans would still escape from him involuntarily, it was mainly words of prayer that came and he was evidently in a very different state of mind from that which governed him but a few moments before when only the physical side of his case was occupying his mind. Many a soldier during the war found that when a dread came over him, and he feared that his courage might leave him, especially when men were falling thick and fast all around, a little prayer would lift him up and give him new courage; and when he was so tired that it seemed as though he could not go on any farther it would enable him to tap a new level of energy and get his second wind, as it were, and "carry on."

There are a great many people nowadays, and unfortunately they are ever so much more frequent among the educated classes than among those who have not had the benefit of an education, who seem to think that prayer is a confession of weakness. When a man or a woman has recourse to prayer they would be inclined to say that it is because he or she has not the strength of character and personality that enables them to stand up under the trials of life and to face difficulties valiantly and hopefully. Impressions like this have been rather fostered among the modern intellectual classes who, it must be recalled, are not always intelligent.

We saw in the first chapter that while there is a very prevalent impression that somehow science is opposed to religion and that scientists find it utterly impossible to accept religious beliefs seriously and indeed can only pity those who continue to cherish such outworn superstitions, practically all the greatest scientists of modern times have been deep believers.

What is true with regard to scientists and belief in religion is true also with regard to the strongest characters of the world and prayer. The greatest moral force of the war, the man who stood as Horace long ago said the perfect man, *totus teres atque rotundus*, should stand, unmoved, even though the world is falling in pieces around him, was Cardinal Mercier. When they asked him at the luncheon given to him in New York by some two thousand of our most prominent commercial representatives how he, a bishop, "brought up in the peace and quiet of a university, should stand unmoved in the presence of the greatest military power on earth and insist on the rights of his country and his people", his very simple reply was, "As a bishop, there was nothing else that it occurred to me for the moment to do."

Some of Cardinal Mercier's favorite maxims show how deeply he feels whence comes his strength. He said, for instance, that "the ideal of life is a clear sense of duty." His favorite quotation is from St. Theresa, that well-known expression, "whenever conscience commands anything, there is only one thing to fear and that is fear." His maxim for daily life was "The whole duty of man consists in doing God's will to-day. I care to have no vain regrets with regard to the past and no idle dreams as to the future, but I shall be quite satisfied if God gives me His grace to accomplish His Holy Will to-day." It is easy to see from these that the Cardinal feels his utter dependence on a Higher Power and the necessity for keeping as closely in touch with that Higher Power by prayer as possible. There is no doubt at all about his supreme strength of character and his placid, yet unbending resolution to accomplish what he sees as duty. There is no doubt, also, that he feels that he draws his strength to accomplish whatever he can from prayer. His daily recourse to it, far from being a sign of weakness in any sense, simply represents the man's own feeling of his inadequacy to accomplish what his conscience dictates unless he is strengthened from on High.

Perhaps it is to be expected that a churchman would find his strength in prayer, but it must not be forgotten that the greatest military leader of this war, who because of the immense armies that he had to lead must be considered one of the greatest military geniuses of all time, confesses also that the source of whatever power he had came from prayer. Over and over again during the time while he was the commander-in-chief of the Allied armies, Marshal Foch was discovered at prayer in some quiet chapel, manifestly absorbed in communion with God. When congratulated on what he had accomplished, he said at once, "Do not thank me, but thank the Author of all good to whom the victory is due." He was often known to ask for prayers and when on the morning of the first battle of the Marne he met the chaplain of one of his regiments, he said to him, "Pray for us, father; we advance from here or die here to-day."

There is a story that comes from his own headquarters that when sometimes he was thought to be asleep he was found at prayer. When his first decision as commander-in-chief of the Allied armies had to be made, and he had to determine whether Amiens should be surrendered to the enemy and a defense made on lines behind that city, both Haig, in immediate command of the British forces, as well as Pétain, the French commander, are said to have advised retirement. Foch listened patiently to their reasons and then asked for twenty minutes by himself before making his decision, declaring that he would give it in that time. He spent those minutes walking up and down the garden in the slight rain that was falling, very much in the concentrated manner that he was known to assume when praying. At the end of twenty minutes he declared that Amiens was to be held at all cost, — and it was. This was the first great step in the breaking of the enemy morale. When three months later, on the 18th of July — after the Germans had tried for three days to come through his lines and had practically succeeded and then, lacking in men and munitions had to stop — Marshal Foch launched his counter-offensive which represented the beginning of the end of the war, it was easy to understand the strain through which he had just passed and the immensity of the responsibility of the decision that he had to make. After the orders for the counter-offensive had been sent out he said, "Now I must rest." As can readily be imagined he had slept but little on any of the three preceding nights. Half an hour after he retired there came a dispatch which the high staff decided must be communicated to the general-in-chief. They hesitated for some time to wake him, but there was nothing else for it. His adjutant found him on his knees.

The practice of prayer, then, instead of being an index of weakness of character, is on the contrary a note that is found exemplified in a great many men who are distinguished for their strength of character. It is the strong man above all who knows his own weakness and realizes how incapable he is of doing very great things of himself. It is the conceited man who is confident that he can accomplish anything that he wants out of his own strength and often fails. Great generals almost as a rule have been men who turned aside from the immense calls made upon them by their military responsibilities to gain consolation and strength from the Most High. It is surprising often to find how devoutly they turn to the Higher Power in their trials. Field Marshal Lord Wolseley carried a copy of Thomas à Kempis' "Imitation of Christ" with him always and read in it every day. When they found Chinese Gordon dead at Khartum there was a little copy of Newman's "Dream of Gerontius" in which he had been reading and making some annotations during the days before the end. For him, too, the "Imitation of Christ" was favorite reading, as it was for Stanley the explorer and many another thoroughly practical, intensely brave and strong man whom the world has come to appreciate for his strength of character.

In our time there has been noted an extreme lack of delicacy and a diminution of that reticence which characterized human beings at their best. There has been a pouring out of the story of their woes and ills by men and women seeking sympathy which not only does them no good but which tends to break down their own character. It was Nietzsche who said, in one of these striking aphorisms of his, "Sympathy only makes us feel bad and the person for whom we sympathize feel worse than before." In an older time when there was more faith and the practice of prayer was commoner, the habit of prayer replaced this pouring out of the heart to others. People let God know about it and in that way brought themselves into the mental attitude that somehow, somewhere, all was well, for God's in His world and all is right with it. This proved an antidote to that sympathy-seeking self-pity which is not only so fatal to character development, but which actually makes the trials and sufferings of life harder to bear than they would otherwise be and will sometimes lift the little discomforts that are almost inevitably associated with living up to a plane of superconsciousness on which they seem to be torments. Prayer is often its own reward, though any one who practices it in reality knows that there are other and much higher effects than this psychological influence which can of itself, however, neutralize many of the lesser disturbances of life that may be so readily exaggerated.

To many people in our time prayer seems a useless exercise except in so far as the state of mind which it engenders reacts upon the individual to console and strengthen him in trials and to hearten him for difficulties that lie ahead. Even if it had no other effect than this, prayer would still be a very valuable factor for health in the midst of the difficulties and above all the dreads of humanity which are so likely to disturb the proper functioning of organic life. If this were all that it meant, however, prayer would not be a religious but a psychotherapeutic exercise. As a matter of belief, however, prayer is much more than this and, to the mind of the believer at least, leads to help from on High that may prove of immense consequence in the development of individual life. Many people feel that it would be idle to think that prayer can alter the ordinary course of natural events and that these are rigidly connected with the causal elements which lead up to them and cannot be modified, once the chain of causes has been set to work.

It is curiously interesting to realize that not a few of those who urge this inevitability of causation are just those who refuse to acknowledge the principle of causation as necessarily leading to the demonstration that there must be a first cause As suggested by Sir Bertram Windle, president of University College, Cork, in his volume "The Church in Science" which has recently been awarded one of the Bridgewater prizes in England, it is not difficult to realize "that the world is by no means so rigidly predetermined as many enthusiastic votaries of science would have us believe"; he adds:

"There is room for free play; chance has a real objective significance, viz., the intercrossing of independent causal chains, and is not a mere cloak for ignorance. Not alone is a large part of natural occurrences within our own control, but there is opportunity for God's special direction of events without any contravention of the laws of science. We cannot see far ahead; for aught we know, a small change of present plans may result in far-reaching future consequences. And many present realities were once frail possibilities hanging on slender causal threads; did not England's present mineral wealth and insular position originate in some chance-formed heterogeneity in a nebula? All these life-histories of countries and individuals stand spread out to God's eternal gaze. At each stage He sees the possibilities foreclosed or initiated; He influences development by the primal distribution in the past and by direction and inspiration in the present."

CHAPTER III

SACRIFICE

The essence of religion is sacrifice. St. Paul summed it up in his own inimitable fashion when he said, "I beseech you therefore, brethren, by the mercies of God, that ye present your bodies a living sacrifice, holy, acceptable unto God, which is your reasonable service." The supreme exercise of religious feeling is the readiness to make sacrifices because one feels that it is the will of the Deity that they should be made. The "Century Dictionary's" definition of sacrifice, "the giving up of some prized or desirable thing in behalf of a higher object", represents the state of mind that one must have if one is desirous of practicing religion sincerely. The tendency to make sacrifices seems almost to be ingrained in humanity and to be a sort of instinct. It is one of these precious manifestations of nature so difficult to understand and yet representing some great basic principle of humanity. The feeling of satisfaction that comes with it represents that compensation for the exercise of a natural function which so often accompanies natural processes and is sometimes supposed to be a feature only of the physical yet is so invariably found also in the moral order.

From the very earliest times men have made sacrifices in the spirit of religion. Now that the story of the cave man is known not by inference but by actual discovery of his remains in the caves of western France and northern Spain, we find that he was an artist who invented oil colors, grinding the oxides of manganese and of iron in mortars and mixing them with the rendered fat of animals and painting some of the most vivid pictures of animals that have ever been made on the walls of his cave in order to make his home beautiful. Instead of being just a little better than the beasts, he was an artist, and an artist is at all times the flower of our civilization, ahead of and not behind the rest of the race. In the tombs of the cave men finely made tools have been found buried with the bodies, demonstrating the belief in a hereafter and the readiness of those who were left behind to make sacrifices for their dead. For these tools had been produced at the cost of no little labor, and in the values of the time were precious. In order that their dead friend might be happy in another world they were quite willing to make these sacrifices and to devote other efforts to securing happiness for him. They devoted a good deal of care to the disposal of the body and even buried red coloring matter with the remains so that their dead friend might not look too pale in the next world and perhaps be the subject of remark, because of that. We rouge our corpses in our time again, but with the idea of making them presentable for this world.

This state of mind which prompts man to make a sacrifice is, almost needless to say, extremely valuable for health and for happiness, because it makes people ready to offer up their feelings in case of disappointment and even to be ready to accept trials that may come to them — and life is sure to have them — as representing opportunities for the making of sacrifices. If one has set one's heart on something and has devoted great efforts to getting it and then finds that owing to circumstances it cannot be secured, nothing is so effective as the deep religious feeling of sacrifice to aid in keeping the disappointment from affecting health and strength.

We need it at the present time sadly, and its eclipse through decadence of religion has been a great misfortune. Modern life has been very much disturbed by the fact that insanity and suicides are both on the increase to an almost alarming extent and that, sad to say, the average age at which they occur is steadily becoming earlier. Suicide happens at ever younger years just in proportion, it would seem, to the spread of popular education and the lessening of the influence of religion, while at the same time the necessity for restraint for insanity and of internments in asylums is also coming at a younger age. People used to go through with some of the very hard things of life before they were ready to give up struggling or broke down in mind, but now some of the minor trials of early life — a petty setback in school examinations or disappointment in a youthful love affair — may bring about a very serious breakdown in physical or mental health and may even lead to suicide.

We need ever so much more training in the discipline of sacrifice even from very earliest youth, but almost needless to say this can come practically only from religion, and religious influences are waning for a great many people. All young folks must be trained to give things up voluntarily so that when disappointment comes they are ready for it. They must be taught to stand some of the disagreeable things in life so that they may have the will power to endure even the hardest ones, if they should be called upon to do so. Such discipline, instead of being cruel, is really kind, for constituted as life is and with hardships and trials inevitable to the great majority of people, it is all-important that we should be prepared for them. It is the rôle of religion particularly to do this. It can accomplish it without producing unfortunate reactions, but on the contrary with personal satisfaction to the individual who has to be trained in endurance because of the feeling that the sacrifices have a worth beyond that of the merely material.

Whole-hearted sacrifice will lift a character up to heights of heroism that are supremely admirable and make life exemplary, though the failure to take the opportunities for sacrifice may lead to crushing of the spirit entirely. Almost inevitably this brings about disturbance of health as well as deterioration of character. The loss of children by death, particularly when there are but one or two children in a family, as is so frequent in modern times, often brings on a state of mental perturbation in which the health of mind and body, especially of women, may suffer severely. Religion, with its development of the spirit of sacrifice, whenever it is taken seriously, is the best possible sheet anchor in such cases, and the gradual diminution of religious feelings and abandonment of religious practice during the present generation have greatly multiplied the tendency to such severe breakdowns.

A distinguished scientist, Professor Whittaker, the Royal Astronomer of Ireland, dwelt on the scientific aspect of sacrifice for high purpose in a way that is illuminating and serves to make our generation understand better the enduring nature of sacrifice in creation and the place that it has in the up-building of what is best in life.

"Surrender to the will of God generally means the giving up of some of the delights of the world. Like the coral island built up on the accumulations of its own past life, the perfected kingdom is to be reached only by the sacrifice of countless generations of its own up-builders. But — and this is the greatest of all evidence of the divine life within humanity — in all ages men have left the pleasures of their former life to obey the inward call. The long procession that leads to the distant goal is re-united afresh in every generation: and to-day millions have found the joy of a life centered round the words of the Master, 'Repent', 'Follow Me.'"

A distinguished mathematician who is at the same time a very well-known physical scientist declared not long since that the formula for happiness may be expressed as follows:

$$h=\frac{g}{w}$$

In this, h stands for the amount of individual happiness and is equal to what the individual has got, g, divided by w, what he wants. If a man has a great deal but wants ever so much more, his fraction of happiness may be comparatively small. If he has got even a little but does not want much more, his fraction of happiness may approach an integer. If he has got anything in the world and does not want anything more, according to the terms of the formula, he is infinitely happy, for one divided by zero equals infinity $\left(\frac{1}{0}=\infty\right)$. What is important for men for their happiness then is not so much to try to increase the numerator by adding to or even multiplying their possessions, but to decrease the denominator by lessening their wants and by decreasing the number of things without which they feel that they cannot be happy.

Almost needless to say the one element above all in life which enables men to reduce their wants and to live in satisfaction with few things is religion. A great many men in the history of the race have for religious motives assumed the obligations of voluntary poverty and have greatly increased satisfaction in life and have found happiness thereby. The multiplication of material wants which after a time become needs that actually cannot be dispensed with without a feeling of serious deprivation leads to such preoccupation with mere bodily concerns that no time is left to live the life of the spirit and really to enjoy the things of the mind and the heart and the soul with the supreme satisfaction which their experience gives to us. The old pagan poet, Horace, suggested long ago that he hated the apparatus of luxury because it took away so much of the simple enjoyment of life and consumed so much time in idle concerns. Nothing is so helpful in enabling men to simplify life as religious motives. They learn to make the sacrifice of certain inclinations and feelings that would tempt them to rival other men and to be satisfied with a little for the sake of the lessened allurements to luxury that are thus secured for themselves and their children. Health comes as a by-product of this simplification of life as it is not likely to come under any other circumstances.

To all men there comes, sooner or later in life, the realization that the getting of things cannot bring happiness. Oscar Wilde said in one of his well-known caustic epigrams, "There are two tragedies in life; the one is not getting what you want and the other is getting it; and of the two the latter is the worse." Quite apart from the pessimism and the exaggeration of the apothegm which constitutes only part of the humor, there is a great deal of truth in the expression, as all men learn eventually. What Faust said to Mephistophcles was that "if ever a time shall come when I shall be willing to say to the passing moment 'stay you with me, for I shall be satisfied with you forever' then you may have my soul." All that the devil had to do was to make him happy, but that is impossible, for "man never is, but to be blessed." There is no lasting satisfaction in getting, for men increase their desires with everything they get.

Men come to realize, if they gather wisdom with the years, that the fruit of striving and the quest after anything in the world, be it riches or knowledge or honor or power, is of itself but dust and ashes in the mouth once the goal has been reached, for it is the quest and not the attainment, the hunt and not the capture that counts in life, and the only thing that can possibly give any genuine satisfaction to man is the cultivation of the spirit of sacrifice. Sacrifices made for a higher power give life a meaning that it would otherwise have lost. For those who have reached the years beyond middle life, the blessedness of giving rather than receiving, of making sacrifices rather than seeking satisfaction, means the renewal of life's hopes and aspirations.

It is making a virtue of necessity to cultivate the spirit of sacrifice, but then it was a great philosopher who said that "the only virtue worth while talking about is the virtue that is made out of necessity." Most of the things in life that are really worth while we have to do whether we want to or not, and it is the spirit in which they are done that lifts them out of the rut of commonplace, sordid, everyday actions into the realm of spiritual significance, because they are done for a great purpose. Each act of sacrifice may thus be made an act of worship of the Deity and have almost an infinite value. This makes even the minor acts of life produce a satisfaction not otherwise possible and gives a new significance to life when the novelty of living has worn off and when the *tædium vitæ*, the tiredness with life that comes to every one after a while, if mere human motives prevail, steals over us.

There is a passage in the Scriptures, the truth of which a good many people seem to doubt in the modern time, though the experience of centuries has confirmed it. "It is more blessed to give than to receive." Those who have experienced the delightful satisfaction of giving whole-heartedly, even when they did not have much to give, realize the truth of this. By comparison, the poor are the great givers among men, giving ever so much more in proportion to their means than do the rich, almost without exception, and it is to them particularly that these divine words have come home. They are ready to make all sorts of personal sacrifices to help those around them, almost as a rule, and they know the blessedness of giving. If the rich gave to others in anything like the proportion to what the poor so commonly do, there would be no suffering from poverty.

The sacrifices which they make bring with them a satisfaction that is eminently conducive to health. There is nothing like the sleep that comes with the consciousness of good accomplished for others, and the poor enjoy that just in proportion to the sacrifice that their doing of good has entailed. Giving up has often meant much for others, but it usually means more for oneself. The consciousness of having relieved the necessities of others is probably the best appetizer and somnifacient that we have. We talk of "sleeping the sleep of the just", and the just man is above all the one who thinks of others. Feelings of depression and melancholy, when not actually the consequence of organic disease or hereditary impairment of mentality, are probably better relieved by the consciousness of doing good to others than in any other way. This is particularly true when the doing of good entails some special sacrifice on the doer of it. Nervousness, in the broad general sense of that word, is at bottom very often a manifestation of selfishness, that is, oversolicitude about oneself and one's affairs, and nothing so serves to neutralize it as personal sacrifices made for others.

Sacrifice, moreover, is the fundamental element in most of the practices of religion. It represents the underlying factor of charity and fasting and mortification, for personal sacrifices have to be made of time and money and often of inclination and immediate personal satisfaction in order to accomplish these. As they are treated in separate chapters, they need only be mentioned here as representing component elements in that readiness to make sacrifices for the sake of others and oneself which Providence seems to demand.

Nothing requires so much sacrifice from men and women, even to the giving up of life itself, as war, and yet when whole-heartedly entered into, it becomes a magnificent discipline of humanity, affording satisfactions that are supreme and leaving memories that are the most precious for the race. Above all, men learn in time of war that there are things in life that are worth more than life itself, and there is no knowledge in the world that is so precious for mankind as this.

How much war's sacrifices may mean for the development of character Professor William James has emphasized in his essay on the "Moral Equivalent of War." He confesses the paradox, but he says:

"Ask all our millions, north and south, whether they would vote now (were such a thing possible) to have our war for the Union expunged from history, and the record of a peaceful transition to the present time substituted for that of its marches and battles, and probably hardly a handful of eccentrics would say yes. Those ancestors, those efforts, those memories and legends, are the most ideal part of what we now own together, a sacred spiritual possession worth more than all the blood poured out. Yet ask those same people whether they would be willing in cold blood to start another civil war now to gain another similar possession, and not one man or woman would vote for the proposition."

It must not be forgotten that strengthening of character, war's invariable effect on the man of moral aims, always diminishes the dreads of life. They mean ever so much not only for the development of the psychoneuroses and the whole domain of neurotic symptoms so common in our time, but also for the exaggeration of the symptoms of real physical disease which makes patients so uncomfortable, or full of complaints, and has led to so many useless operations in our generation.

Professor James even ventured to suggest that "the dread hammer (of war) is the welder of men into cohesive states, and nowhere but in such states can human nature adequately develop its capacity. The only alternative is degeneration." He adds that "the martial type of character can be bred without war", but only under very special circumstances and where men have been willing to give themselves up to a great cause. "Priests and medical men are in a fashion educated to it, and we should all feel some degree of it imperative if we were conscious of our work as an obligatory service to the State. We should be owned, as soldiers are by the army, and our pride would arise accordingly. We could be poor then without humiliation, as army officers now are."

Mr. H. G. Wells, in one of his paradoxical moods, has dwelt on how far the sacrifices needed for military life have lifted the life of the soldier above that of the civilian, in so far as its social value is concerned. "When the contemporary man steps from the street of clamorous insincere advertisement, push, adulteration, underselling and intermittent employment into the barrack-year, he steps on to a higher social plane, into an atmosphere of service and coöperation and of infinitely more honorable emulations. Here at least men are not flung out of employment to degenerate because there is no immediate work for them to do. They are fed and drilled and trained for better services. Here at least a man is supposed to win promotion by self-forgetfulness and not by self-seeking."

The war spirit with its necessary sacrifices serves to lift men above the dreads that wear away other lives and makes it very clear what the spirit of whole-hearted sacrifice can accomplish in keeping life from being disturbed by fear thoughts of many kinds. It might possibly be thought that the supreme call made upon nature's power to overcome such dreads, when combined with the extreme physical efforts that war often calls for and the draft upon nature's resources that the healing of wounds demands, would surely shorten the lives of military men, and that soldiers and officers, but above all these latter, would have on the average much less expectancy of life than the rest of mankind. Apart from actual fatal wounds, this is not true, however, but on the contrary men who have suffered severely from wounds, who have been placed under heavy burdens of responsibility and have gone through trials that would seem calculated to exhaust nature's powers, have lived far beyond the average length of life and even long beyond the vast majority of men. Lord Roberts, wounded over and over again, once shot almost to pieces, getting his Victoria Cross for bravery of the highest type, lived, still active, well past eighty and died from pneumonia behind the lines in the Great War quite as any man of the generation after his might have done. Sir Evelyn Wood is another typical instance of this living well beyond eighty in the enjoyment of health and strength and power to be of use to his country.

The spirit of sacrifice for a great patriotic purpose is like the spirit of sacrifice from religious motives which blesses while it furnishes the highest satisfactions that can come to a man. If men and women could be brought to exercise from religious motives in time of peace as much of the spirit of sacrifice as they do for war and patriotism, the world would be a very wonderful place in which to live. As it is, there are a great many who do so and whose lives have become veritable blessings for others and yet sources of supreme satisfaction to themselves. Their thoroughgoing faith and trust are examples to others that make life not only ever so much easier in the midst of hardships, but that give a new depth to the belief in immortality, because these others whose lives are so admirable have such a supreme faith in it that they direct all their actions to its reflection. As Professor Osler said in delivering the Ingersoll lecture on immortality at Harvard, a great many of us believe because there are around us persons, often those whom we love dearly, whose lives and faith mean so much to us that their confidence in immortality is imparted to us.

Religion is above all the motive of sacrifice that makes life more efficient and is productive of the healthy mind in the healthy body. It has quite equaled war in this regard, and the lives of missionaries, when lived under the most difficult circumstances, have often lasted long beyond even the Psalmist's limit of three-score years and ten. I have in mind as I write a dear old missionary who is still with us who spent twenty years with the Nez Percés Indians in the distant West, sharing all the hardships of the tribe and yet accomplishing very little in the matter of winning them to Christianity until at the end of that long time his leg was broken by a fall. The manly, uncomplaining courage with which he bore the accident won the hearts of the warriors, and they were ready to become Christians and to follow wholeheartedly the principles of religion which could make a white man so completely a man in every sense of the word as they had found their missionary. His health in the midst of all this had been excellent, and he is now in Alaska, past eighty, standing the climate and the trials of that country.

It is surprising how weak women, in the spirit of religious sacrifice, accomplish what seems almost the impossible and actually live healthier lives after they have given up everything and there is nothing more for them to dread. We have all heard of the story of Father Damien who so bravely went to Molokai in order to care for the lepers, but how many know that religious women have offered themselves for similar purposes, and not only at Molokai but at Tracadie in Canada and in Louisiana have given themselves up for life to the care of lepers? I know from records that some of these women, after having made the supreme sacrifice, were actually better in health living among the lepers than they had been when apparently living under much more favorable circumstances in their city homes. Some of them have lived to be very old, and none of them have contracted the disease.

The story of such a striking personal sacrifice as that of Father Damien among the lepers at Molokai, crowned by years of suffering and death, attracts sensational attention, but it must not be forgotten that he is only one of many who have given up all in similar spirit. There were many like him, though utterly unknown to the world, who in China, in distant India, in Central Africa, or among the Indians in our own country, have sacrificed everything that the world deems most satisfying just to give themselves to the care of their savage brothers. I shall never forget dropping off years ago one day in the West at the then little station of Missoula in Montana to meet an old teacher of mine who had been famous for his knowledge of Greek and of the Aristotelian philosophy and who was then engaged in taking care of Indians, where none of these special intellectual acquirements were of any service, but where his hearty good cheer made him the best of missionaries. He had made his sacrifice; he said there were plenty of others who could do the teaching of Greek and philosophy, and he felt the call to do something for others who needed his personal services. He was in better health than he had been in years and in better spirits, and there was a look about him which indicated that some of the hundredfold promised to those who give to the Lord was already coming back to him.

Many a man and woman in this country and in England has been lifted out of the depths, even out of the very "slough of despond" where dreads abound and a healthy mind in a healthy body is almost impossible of attainment, by reading about the work of Doctor Wilfred Grenfell, who has so nobly given himself and his professional services to the care of the poor fishermen on the Labrador coast. Their sufferings are often so severe as to be almost unbearable, especially during the winter time, and yet they cling to their little homes on the rugged coast, ready to bear through successive winters the vicissitudes of a climate and the bitter struggle for existence which seem almost beyond the endurance of human nature and where they need so much the sympathy and kindliness which have been extended to them by Doctor Grenfell. Any one who has come in contact with him personally learns that this spirit of sacrifice so finely exemplified and exercised to high achievement has made him a charmingly sympathetic man whom everybody who comes to know is sure to like, and who exhibits the best traits of the race in some of their highest forms of expression. Withal he is a very practical, common-sense individual grafted on the lofty idealist. His sacrifices have done him good, and the example of them has stimulated and helped an immense number of other people besides the special objects of his devotion on the Labrador coast.

What marvelous examples men can give in this way, examples which fairly quicken life in other and weaker brethren and set them at their tasks whole-heartedly to accomplish whatever they can when otherwise they would have been discouraged and downcast and apt to find excuses in poor health or weakness, is well illustrated by Doctor Grenfell's life and also by that of many others in our own day. I count it as one of the privileges of life to have been a close friend for some precious years of the man of whom one of those who came in contact with him has told the story which I shall quote. His example was all the more striking because it had for background that flagrant exhibition of the selfishness of men which a rush to new gold fields always presents. He was engaged in quite a different quest that for him seemed much more important, and he went on with his work in the midst of the excitement as calmly as if men all around him were not exhausting all their natural powers to the limit for a fancied prize which they were sure would make them happy.

"All of us can remember the mad rush for gold to the Klondyke, out on the northern edge of the world. Nature has pushed her ice barriers far to the south of it and fringed them for leagues with impenetrable forest and towering mountain and treacherous river, as though to guard her treasure. Men, lured by the golden gleams, essayed to break through. In tens of thousands they plunged into the unknown wilderness, pushing in frenzied haste through forest and cañon and river.

"By thousands they fell and died, and but a remnant crept out on the deadly Yukon plain, every step on which was a fight for life.

"Some of the first of these hardy adventurers were making their way across the frozen Alaskan waste when they saw ahead something moving that stood out black against the blinding white of the snow. Stumbling through snowdrifts, waist-deep in ice hollows, jumping treacherous crevasses, they pushed on, and the dark spot gradually took shape. It was a loaded dog-sledge, and in front, hauling laboriously, were a man and a dog. He was alone, and they stared in wonder at him, as if to ask what manner of man was this, so contentedly traveling in this land of dreadful silence, — a land that seemed to be the tomb of all living things that ventured into it. He gave them cheery greeting as they passed by, stopping not, for here the race was to the swift and strong, and wished them good fortune. Their guide knew him, and they learned with astonishment that it was not love of gold that had made him risk his life on that frozen tundra. That gray-haired man with the kindly face, buffeted by the icy wind that cut like a whiplash, and bent low under the sledge rope, was the best-known man in the Klondyke. His sledge was loaded with medicine and food for poor sick miners, 'his boys', as he called them, whom he kindly cared for in a hospital that with his own hands he had helped to build in the town in the valley of gold. They saw him next day, as he came down the street, still harnessed to the sledge; they saw the crowds that rushed from the canvas buildings on either side and pressed forward to shake his hand, and laughingly take the sledge from him, and swing along the street, filling it from side to side, to where at the far end stood his hospital; they saw him enter, and when they heard the shout of joy that burst forth from the inmates, at the sight of the only man that stood between them and death, tears sprang to their eyes, and they too pressed forward to exchange a word with and press the hand of a hero. Too soon there came a day when the axe and the sledge rope fell from the once strong hands, and he lay, dead, among the boys whom he loved. They buried him in the frozen earth between his hospital and his church."

The making of sacrifices for religious motives, that is,

from a religious sense of duty, is often followed by some of the most satisfying rewards of life. Physicians frequently have this brought home to them when they encounter people who, because of unwillingness to make what seemed to be sacrifices in their earlier years, have to go through some rather serious conditions later on in life. The woman who, having had opportunities to marry, has refused them because she fears the cares of family life and dreads the dangers of maternity, will very often suffer ever so much more during the years of involution and obsolescence in the second half of life as the result of the loneliness that will come to her and the lack of any heart interest in life which will leave her without the resources and satisfaction which come to the woman whose children are around her and whose grandchildren bless her. The man who has remained a bachelor will very often, unless, perhaps, some of his brothers and sisters have married and taken the trouble and had the joy of raising children, be even more pitiable in his solitary old age. This may not seem to mean much for health and happiness, and there may appear more sentimentality than reality in it, but the statistics of suicide and insanity among the unmarried, which are ever so much higher than among the married, demonstrate how much of hopeless discouragement and mental discomfort comes to those who have given no hostages to fortune and no pledges for the future, by the sacrifice of some of the passing pleasures and selfish satisfactions of youth.

Nearly the same thing is true of the married folk who have only a child or two in the family. The children are almost inevitably spoiled. A careful study of the single child in the family has shown very clearly how nervous and selfish the solitary child is likely to be and how much unhappiness the mother prepares for her child by refusing to give it the normal companionship of brothers and sisters. The real kindergarten of life should be the family of five [1] or six children raised together and learning to bear with each other and yield to each other and take care of each other as the highest kind of training in unselfishness. Even when there are two children in the family, especially if these are of opposite sexes, the boy and girl are likely to grow up with entirely wrong notions as regards their importance in life. The whole household is centered around them, and they learn how to impose on father and mother. Nearly always the parents prepare unhappiness for themselves as well as their children, though there is usually the excuse that they will be better able to provide for fewer children, afford them a better education, and bring them up so as to secure for them more opportunities in life.

The sacrifices of social pleasures and of passing ease and comfort in order to bear and raise four or more children in the family are, as a rule of nature, amply rewarded in the health and strength of both the children and the mother. In my book on "Health through Will Power", in the chapter on Feminine Ills and the Will, I have pointed out that in spite of the tradition which assumes that a woman's health is hurt if she has more than

[1] Dr. Karl Pearson, of London, the well-known authority on eugenics, has investigated rather carefully the health of children in large and small families, and has demonstrated that children are healthiest when there are five to eight children in the family. On the average, first and second children are not as healthy as those who come later in the family, and those who are in the best condition physically and mentally for life come after the fourth. The early children in the family are more liable to epilepsy and certain serious nervous diseases, and are often of unstable nervous equilibrium, while the later children are more gifted and are likely to live longer.

two or three children, the women of the older time, when families were larger, were healthier on the average than they are now, in spite of all the progress that medicine and surgery have since made in relieving serious ills. Above all, it was typically the mother of numerous children who lived long and in good health to be a blessing to those around her, and not the old maids or the childless wives, for longevity is not a special trait of these latter classes of women. The modern dread of deterioration of vitality as the result of frequent child-bearing is quite without foundation in the realities of human experience.

Some rather carefully made statistics demonstrate that the old tradition in the matter is not merely an impression but a veritable truth as to human nature's reaction to a great natural call. While the mothers of large families born in the slums, with all the handicaps of poverty as well as hard work against them, die on the average much younger than the generality of women in the population, careful study of the admirable vital statistics of New South Wales shows that the mothers who lived longest were those who under reasonably good conditions bore from five to seven children. Here in America, a study of more favored families shows that the healthiest children come from the large families, and it is in the small families particularly that the delicate, neurotic and generally weakly children are found. Alexander Graham Bell, in his investigation of the Hyde family here in America, discovered that the greatest longevity occurred in the families of ten or more children. So far from mothers being exhausted by the number of children that were born, and thus endowing their children with less vitality than if they had fewer children, it was to the numerous offspring that the highest vitality and physical fitness were given. One special consequence of these is longevity.

The spirit of sacrifice brings its own reward. The realization from a religious standpoint that it is better to give than to receive is one of the greatest blessings that a man can have. Nothing is so disturbing to health and happiness — and real happiness always reacts on health — as selfishness, the contradiction of the spirit of sacrifice. All the great writers on the spiritual life have emphasized the fact that nervousness is at bottom selfishness. Conceit is the root of a great deal of unhappiness and consequent disturbance of the health of mind and body.

CHAPTER IV

CHARITY

CHARITY is usually looked upon as a cure for social, not personal ills. Its activities, while recognized as supremely effective in fostering the health of people who have to live on inadequate means, are not ordinarily considered as reacting to benefit the health of the individual who practices the virtue. Any such outlook is, however, very partial. Religion has always taught that the benefiting of others invariably served to bring down blessings on those who took up the precious duty of helpfulness, blessings which are not reserved merely for the hereafter, but are felt also in this world, which affect not only the spirit but the mind of man. "Blessed are the merciful, for they shall obtain mercy" are the words of the Sermon on the Mount, and it must not be forgotten that that dear old-fashioned word, mercy, which is so often limited to forgiveness in our day, meant in the old time acts of benevolence — "works of mercy", as they were called — and in Luke it is stated that the "neighbor unto him that fell among thieves" was "he that showed mercy on him."

The personal satisfaction which comes from the performance of these works of mercy represents one of the most active factors that we have for good health and especially for the creation of that background of contentment with life on which good health is commonly developed. The merciful garner some of their reward here in the shape of a less troubled life, so far at least as their own worries might be sources of trouble, and a fuller, heartier existence in the consciousness of helpfulness for others. The words encouragement, discouragement, in Saxon English heartening and disheartening, putting heart into or taking heart out of people, have a literal physical as well as metaphysical significance that all physicians have come to appreciate rather thoroughly.

Charity is a cure not only for the ills of the social body, but it is also an extremely valuable remedy for the personal ills of those who devote themselves to doing their duty towards others. Vincent de Paul, that great organizer of charity, or as we would call his work in our time, social service — for during and after the great wars in France in the early seventeenth century he organized relief for literally thousands of people in the war zone and afterwards continued his great social work, which was quite as much needed then as our post-war work is now, in the large cities and towns of France — once used an expression in this regard that deserves to be repeated here because it emphasizes this reactionary effect of charity which means so much for health. Vincent said that "Unless the charity we do does as much good for the doer as it does for the one for whom it is done, there is something wrong with the charity." Here is a phase of charity that has been forgotten only too often in the modern time. It emphasizes the fact that the most important remedy for that very serious affection *tædium vitæ*, that sense of the unsatisfactoriness of life which comes to everybody at some time or other, is the doing of things for other people with a whole-hearted feeling of helpfulness.

It has been suggested that the doing of good for others, with all the good effects which flow from it for the active participants, may very well be accomplished without any appeal to religion, and that sympathy alone suffices as a foundation. Sir W. Thistleton-Dyer, in reviewing Huxley's position in this matter in a critique of Clodd's "Life of Huxley", suggests that the mystery would still remain as to how the sympathy is to be infused. He adds: "My experience of human nature inclines me to think that it requires a more powerful appeal to the imagination than is afforded by a mere academic council of perfection of this sort." As a matter of fact Altruism, as it has been called, is a very different thing from charity in its effect upon the doer. The deep feeling of the brotherhood of man and the fatherhood of God with which true charity is associated makes a profoundly impressive suggestion, with a favorable emotional tendency which serves to give almost as a rule and quite naturally a sense of well-being. The practice of charity from religious motives becomes, then, a very different thing from any mere feeling of sympathy with others founded, as it is so likely to be, on the selfish feeling of how painful it would be for us to be in like case, or tinged at least with the consciousness of condescension toward those below us which vitiates most of the good motives of doing for others on any human grounds.

For those who feel that the new Altruism may fully replace the old charity, and that people can derive just as much good from the stirring of their sympathies from merely humanitarian motives as they can from religious love of their neighbor, President Schurman of Cornell said some things that are very interesting:

"It is a blessed characteristic of our own age that

religion has come to express itself so nobly in practical well-doing. But beneficence is not piety. To make the love of man the essence of religion is to misread the latter and to divest the former of its supreme spiritual dynamic. If the religious man is a benediction to earth, it is because his soul is bathed in the dews of heaven."

The relief of the serious physical sufferings of those around us, together with the glimpse so often afforded while engaged in that work of the patience with which real ills are borne by others, is the best possible dispeller of the dreads which are the source of so many psycho-neuroses and the neurotic symptoms which complicate other diseases of modern times. These represent a much larger proportion of the ills of mankind than we were inclined to think. The Great War proved a revelation in this regard, for one third of all the dismissions from the English army, apart from the wounded, were made because of neurotic affections. Manifestly they must occupy an important place also in civil life. Those who practice charity, that is, those who not merely supply material aid to be distributed through agents or almoners, but give their personal service for those in need, have the chance to be impressed with the thought of how much worse things might be with themselves than they actually are, and how thankful they should be for their own conditions. The best practical definition of contentment still continues to be the conviction that things might be worse than they actually are. Indeed, it is this very satisfaction that comes from doing good that tempts people, humanly speaking, to do more and more of it, and the personal service habit, once formed, is as hard to break as almost any other habit that a man can contract.

The word charity has come to have in many minds a very unfortunate innuendo. It is associated with the thought of doling out alms, of pauperizing people and of making them dependent on others instead of arousing their power to help themselves. There are a good many people who seem to think that never until our time did the question of organizing charity, or social service as it is called, come into men's minds in such a way as to prevent these unfortunate abuses of charity which do so much more harm than good. The history of social service does not begin in our time, however, but goes back over all the centuries in the history of Christianity. Religion has always furnished the incentive to do good, but the Church and common sense have helped people to regulate their charity in such a way as to make it really useful to men. During the Middle Ages there were many legal regulations against "sturdy vagrants" who imposed on people and took the charity out of the mouths of those who deserved it and who abused the opportunities for treatment in hospitals or for lodging in places provided for the poor. Human nature has not changed much, and the tramp and the wanderer have always been with us, as well as the man who is willing to "give up", and let others take care of him.

Charity, as its Latin etymology suggests, means the dearness of others to us. It is our personal interest in them that constitutes its essence and not at all the mere giving of something or even the doing of something in order to be relieved from the necessity of thinking about them. Dear old Sir Thomas Browne, in his "Religio Medici", put the whole question of charity very succinctly when he said, "this I think charity, to love God for Himself and our neighbor for God." Milton summed up the complete quintessence of religion in the single word charity quite as Doctor Browne did, though with less aphoristic effectiveness. "Our whole practical dutie in religion is contained in charitie, or the love of God and our neighbor." Charity in this sense is a development of Christianity, and the personal service idea is almost unknown in ancient times. Lecky, in his history of European morals, says that "the active, habitual and detailed charity of private persons, which is so conspicuous a feature in all Christian societies, was scarcely known in antiquity, and there are not more than two or three moralists who have noticed it."

It is the love or affection that goes with whatever is done that is the real essence of charity. It is this quality especially which makes the charity of benefit to the doer. This helps him and above all her to eliminate that superconscious preoccupation with self which has become the bane of existence in modern times. It is at the root of more serious physical and mental symptoms than any other single factor that we have in pathology. Anything that will take people out of themselves, that will interest them in others and keep them from thinking about themselves, will do an immense amount of good in helping to maintain their good health, but above all will keep people from exaggerating feelings of all kinds, some of them scarcely more than normal, a great many of them merely physiological, into symptoms which seem to indicate serious disease and sometimes to portend extremely serious consequences. Charity that really touches the heart is a panacea for more ills than any remedy we have. It will make even those who are sufferers from genuine disease often of severe or almost fatal character ever so much more comfortable, and it has furnished some invalids with such occupation of mind and heart as has enabled them to do a great deal of good in the world. A great many of us know of one bedridden lady, utterly unable to sit up, who has succeeded in organizing throughout the country branches of an extremely valuable organization which helps the poor to provide proper clothing for their infants and has saved many lives and made many homes happier.

There are a great many people who are afraid lest they should do harm by their charity and who apparently fail to realize that it is their own selfishness which takes refuge in the excuse that doing things for others may possibly pauperize the objects of their beneficence. As John Ruskin reminded us in "Sesame and Lilies", it is extremely important not to let ourselves be deceived by any of the very common talk of "indiscriminate charity." He adds, in one of those passages of his that only he could write and that are so full of the meat of thought for those who care to think about such subjects:

"The order to us is not to feed the deserving hungry, nor the industrious hungry, nor the amiable and well-intentioned hungry, but simply to feed the hungry. It is quite true, infallibly true, that if any man will not work, neither should he eat — think of that, and every time you sit down to your dinner, ladies and gentlemen, say solemnly, before you ask a blessing, 'How much work have I done to-day for my dinner?' But the proper way to enforce that order on those below you, as well as on yourselves, is not to leave vagabonds and honest people to starve together, but very distinctly to discern and seize your vagabond; and shut your vagabond up out of honest people's way, and very sternly then see that, until he has worked, he does not eat."

Works of charity under religious impulses have always constituted an excellent resource for people inclined to be overoccupied with themselves and who need the stimulus of contact with those in suffering to make them realize that their own troubles are largely the result of too much preoccupation with trifling discomforts of various kinds or even with symptoms of various affections which must be borne and which will cause much less suffering and general disturbance of health if there is the distraction of sincere and deep interest in others. Anything that will act as a brake on the working of the Law of Avalanche which is discussed in the chapter on Pain and which serves to increase all suffering through subjective influences will do human beings a great deal of good. As a rule nothing is so effective in this direction as preoccupation with the much severer ills of other people.

The seven corporal works of mercy, as they were called, that is, the seven modes of succoring those in need which St. Paul suggested every Christian should practice, are particularly valuable for the neurotic individuals whom, like the poor and needy, we have always with us, but who have multiplied so much more in this generation because a great many people have not enough to occupy their time properly, but above all have not enough exercise of their heart impulses and their affections to satisfy this imperative need of humanity. Women particularly must be afforded, as a rule, the opportunity to mother somebody who requires their care. If they have no children of their own, and with the loosening of the bonds of religion more and more of them have not, then they will seldom be happy unless the chance is provided for them to devote the emotional side of their natures to other human beings who need them and whose needs constitute the best possible opportunity for the exercise of the spiritual side of this precious function.

The seven corporal works of mercy are: (1) To feed the hungry; (2) To give drink to the thirsty; (3) To clothe the naked; (4) To harbor the harborless; (5) To visit and ransom the captive; (6) To visit the sick; and (7) To bury the dead. These represented a list of very definite duties which children were taught to repeat from memory when they were young; and they were told very simply that if they did not take the opportunity to perform them they were really not doing their Christian duty. To visit the sick, for instance, meant not only to spend an hour or two with a sick relative, but to seek out those who were sick and poor and had no one to care for them and make some provision for them. Some of the old hospital visiting customs in this regard are extremely interesting, inasmuch as they reveal the resource that this must have been to people who are usually thought of as being occupied solely with social duties in the much narrower sense of the term. Martin Luther tells in one of his letters that during his visit to Italy about four hundred years ago, one of the things that proved a great source of edification to him was the fact that the ladies of the nobility in the Italian cities made it a custom to visit the hospitals regularly and to spend hours at a time there and do things for the patients with their own hands. Some of them wore veils while they were performing this beautiful service in order that they might not be recognized, lest what they did should come to be talked about, and they did not want to practice their charity for the sake of publicity. The people of the old time were often as intent on avoiding publicity as our generation, as a rule, seems to be intent on securing it. Almost needless to say ostentatious philanthropy is not charity and has none of the reactionary good effects for the doer to be found in real charity.

It must not be forgotten that whenever hospitals are visited regularly thus by the better-to-do classes there is very little likelihood of serious abuses creeping into them. The care of even the very poor patients is kept at a high standard because these visitors see the beginnings of abuses and either bring about their correction at once, or else devote themselves to some modification of hospital routine that will prevent the recurrence of such unfortunate conditions. Religion thus proved a stimulus to the better care of the ailing poor that was a distinct benefit to the health of the community. It was when hospitals ceased to be the object of such attention on the part of the better-to-do people that they ran down into the awful condition which prevailed so generally in them even less than a century ago.

Burdett in his "History of Hospitals" has not hesitated to say that hospitals placed in the midst of cities and visited regularly by the well-to-do represent a great social instrument for the betterment of all sorts of social conditions. The wealthy are kept from being selfish, the poor from being envious, the classes of the community are not so separated that they fail to understand each other, and both of them are greatly benefited by the experiences which bring them together.

Burdett has gone even further and insisted that the support of hospitals by the State, because it removes opportunities for charity, is an unfortunate development in modern times. Those who are well able to help the poor and the ailing get the feeling that due provision is made for them out of the taxes, and that, therefore, no further obligation rests upon them and the needs and requirements of the poor are no concern of theirs. As a consequence, he says, "an increasing number of people are being brought up on a wrong principle and are thus led to forget the privilege and to ignore the duty of giving toward the support of those who are unable to help themselves."

Besides pointing out how much is lost of social value and social stimulus when private charitable institutions are replaced by State institutions, Burdett emphasizes not only how much of social good is accomplished by voluntary charity, but also how much of personal relief is afforded to some of the trials of life that often prove the source of unfortunate pathological conditions. He said: "Apart from the evils we have briefly referred to, there is a loss to the whole community in the lessened moral sense which State institutions create. The voluntary charities afford an opening for the encouragement and expression of the best of all human feelings, — sympathy between man and man. They give to the rich an opening for the display of consideration toward the poor which is fruitful in results. They create a feeling of widespread sympathy with those who suffer and impress on the population the duty of almsgiving to an extent which no other charity can do. They constitute a neutral platform whereon all classes and sects can meet with unanimity and good feeling. They provide a field of labor wherein some of the most devoted and best members of society can cultivate the higher feelings of humanity and learn to bear their own sufferings and afflictions with resignation and patience."

I have made it a practice for years, now, when women

who were without children and without any special outlet for their affections suffered from neurotic symptoms, to prescribe that they get in touch with the ailing poor in some way. Especially for those trying patients who complain of inability to sleep well, a feeling of depression when they awake, a lack of appetite, but also a lack of incentive to do anything and a tendency to stay much in the house and by themselves, a condition which not infrequently develops in childless women shortly before and after what is called "the change of life", no prescription is so valuable as hospital visiting, or where that is impossible for some reason, at least to make it a rule to visit sick friends regularly. I have seen women suffering severely from neurotic symptoms that made life miserable for them become not only quite reconciled to existence, sleep better and eat better, but actually find some of their first real satisfaction in life as the result of discovering that they could visit the orthopedic ward of a hospital regularly, tell stories to the crippled children and bring them little toys, help to make Easter and the Fourth of July and Thanksgiving Day and Christmas and New Year's happier for them. I have known women who thought after some serious domestic affliction that they could never be happy again, to find, if not happiness, at least satisfaction in life after they had visited a cancer home regularly for some time and had seen with what cheerfulness patients could face the inevitably fatal affection which they knew was gradually sapping life and carrying them day by day into the shadow of death. No therapeusis that I know is so valuable for the stony grief without tears that some women exhibit after a great loss as the ward for crippled children or some regular visiting of incurable patients.

To visit and ransom the captives, that is, to visit prisoners and help them in any way possible, is a work of mercy that comparatively few people in our day seem to think they are under any obligations to do merely because they are Christians. They took this duty very seriously in the older time, however, and the result was excellent for the prisoners as well as for those who visited them. When condemned to serve a sentence and then left to wear out prison existence for years as best he can, seeing only his fellow prisoners and his keepers, a prisoner is very likely to grow bitter. In not a few of the prisoners, health of body and even of mind gives way under these hard conditions. If the prisoners were visited at definite intervals by some one willing to listen a little patiently to their story, for there is always another side to every story — even though the other side may not be very true — and who would occasionally bring them little things like tobacco as a solace or reading matter to occupy idle hours, and who would promise to interest himself in securing any favors that were possible and to see that they were given advantage of every benefit allowed them by the law, they would have less of the feeling that they were outcasts of society. It is because the corporal works of mercy as representing serious Christian duties somehow have come to be neglected that we have had this rather disturbing social problem of the bitter-minded prisoner so likely to get into prison again thrust upon us. But it is also because of the lack of such a fine human interest as is afforded by contact with prisoners who show some hope of reform that many an overoccupied business man suffers from such profound weariness of life that rest cures and special vacations have to be prescribed for him.

I once had a bachelor friend whom I had known for many years come to me as a patient, and though he had been a model of common sense, whom I had been accustomed to think of as utterly without nerves, I was surprised to find how many neurotic symptoms were gradually developing in him. He had lost his sister who had made a home life and a heart interest for him, and he had no near relatives; he had nothing but his business to occupy him; he had no hobby and no interest in that direction that seemed likely to develop, and I wondered what I should advise him to occupy himself with to keep him from getting further on his own nerves. He had an extremely important and correspondingly difficult position involving the carrying of a heavy burden of responsibility for a great many rather complex details of a huge business. A chance remark of his own in pity for a young fellow whom his corporation had found cheating and had felt itself compelled to prosecute — for example's sake — led me to suggest the visiting of prisoners. For years that man spent several hours on two or three Sundays of every month visiting the prisoners of a large city. He gathered around him a group of men who found a good deal of satisfaction in that work. He himself began to sleep better and wiped off the slate of life a series of dreads and obsessions that he was beginning to foster. Men often talk of "the blue devils" getting hold of them, but it is often just a case of the devil finding work not for idle hands but for idle hearts. Especially at Christmas and Easter he used to have as good a time, in the best sense of that expression, with his "little brothers" of the prison as any father and mother ever had with a house full of children. He once told me some of his experiences in a way that revealed his tactfulness in the handling of these sensitive fellow mortals that was one of the most interesting revelations of the Christian gentleman I think I have ever had given me.

To harbor the harborless as a work of mercy, when stated in this form, seemed to me as a child, when I learned it in the catechism, some wonderful exhibition of charity for shipwrecked mariners. I could not help but think that it must be harborless sailors who needed to be harbored. Stories of even two or three generations ago here in America show how seriously this Christian duty of the old-fashioned words was taken. There are still many country places, in the mountains of Kentucky and Tennessee particularly, where a family will take in a stranger for the night if he happens to be in their neighborhood. They will give him his supper and breakfast too — or they would a few years ago — and likely would be insulted if he offered to pay for them. They have performed a simple duty of hospitality which comes down to them by tradition from the older time. A man who is still alive told me that when he was young, and two or three of his brothers slept in the bed with him, occasionally they would find, when they woke in the morning, that father had taken in a stranger during the night, and since there was no other place for him than the children's big bed on the floor, the children had been crowded over and room had been made for him with them. This happened not in the south, but in Pennsylvania. I know that my old grandmother long ago, living in a one-roomed house with an attic, used to take in the "greenhorns" from Ireland in this manner and give the men shelter and food until they could get a job; and give the girls who came a lodging and a chance to learn something about plain American cooking and the care of a house until they would be ready to take a place in service.

Almost needless to say, this exercise of hospitality proved a very interesting diversion for people whose lives were rather monotonous. I feel sure that it must have meant much for the relief of that dissatisfaction with life because it lacks variety which is so often the first symptom of a neurosis. The stranger brought the news from a distance; the "greenhorns" brought news from Ireland, and many things were talked over while they ate their meals or sat around the fire in the evening, and it proved real entertainment. This was not the motive for which the charity was offered, for that was, as a rule, as Christian as it could be, but it represented that reward which is so often — it cannot but be divinely — attached to a good deed and which brings so much satisfaction with it.

Our entertainment of guests, as a rule, is very different. Above all it entails no personal effort. Even when people are invited to dinner nowadays, hostesses seem to consider it necessary to ask somebody to entertain them, for if they should be permitted to entertain themselves or be asked to make an effort to make their own conversation entertaining, they would probably be almost bored to death. Is it any wonder that our fulfilment of so-called social duties often proves nerve-racking and a season of it must be followed by a rest cure while old-fashioned hospitality did good to the doer and the recipient? Ours is the selfish striving of social aspirations; theirs was an exercise of real charity, an external expression of the dearness of fellow mortals.

Above all, the presence in a household of an occasional guest who is not a relative is good for family life. It relieves the monotony, often relaxes domestic tension, gives a new zest to living and cements personal friendships.

To feed the hungry, to give drink to the thirsty and to clothe the naked were, in the Christian ritual of corporal works of mercy, not obligations to be accomplished by writing one's name on a piece of bank paper and passing it over to a social service society of some kind, nor by handing a few bills to some almoner who distributes condescendingly your dole to the poor. Some one has very well said that the only action calling for any reward in such activities is the effort required to write one's signature or reach into the pocket for the money. The rest of the transaction is only a matter of debit and credit on a bank balance and makes practically no difference in most cases to the individual who gives it. The most compelling motive for charity in our time is that you might as well give up to fifteen per cent of your income, for if you do not the government will take it anyhow. So have the satisfaction of getting ahead of Uncle Sam.

Charity in the older time was thought to be actual, personal work for others. It is this personal service which carries its reward with it, often by provision of needed physical exercise, always by happy occupation of mind, affording the opportunity for the satisfaction of heart inpulses with the many other personal reactions which enter into true charity.

Religious teaching furnishes an abundance of examples of even kings and queens and the higher nobility and of wealthy merchants and their wives who devoted themselves to personal service in the performance of these works of mercy. St. Louis of France, St. Ferdinand of Castille, St. Catherine of Siena, though she was only a dyer's daughter in this group of notabilities, St. Elizabeth of Hungary, St. Margaret of Scotland and the good Queen Maud her daughter, Dick Whittington (of the cat), Lord Mayor of London and many others, — all these were held up as symbols of what people ought to do in the matter of personal service.

There is often the feeling at the present time that when people give to charity it is not infrequently because they have heard some recent harrowing reports of the condition of the poor or have been brought in contact with some particularly pitiable case, and that the memory of these is likely to recur to them and intrude on their social satisfactions unless they can do something to make them feel that they have at least tried to fulfill their duty in the way of affording relief. A merchant on the way home from business who meets a beggar on the streets knows that as a rule, if he gives money, it will do harm rather than good, but he knows too that when he is comfortably seated after dinner before the fire, with his coffee and his cigar before him, if the thought of the beggar that he refused comes to him, it will make him uncomfortable. To give with the idea of avoiding such discomforts is, of course, not charity, but refined selfishness, and it is no wonder that it lacks the surpassing sense of satisfaction which helps so much in making life more full of the feeling of usefulness. This is not the charity that does as much good for the doer as for the receiver of it.

In our time settlement work, neighborhood houses and the like have represented this personal service which religion in the older time listed under the various titles of the corporal works of mercy. Many physicians have learned that young women particularly who had not very much to do, indeed perhaps no definite duties and yet had an abundance of vital energy which had to be expended in some way, found very interesting and satisfying occupation of mind in connection with settlement work. Above all they secured an opportunity for the exercise of the heart impulses, so natural to women, and which must almost as necessarily be expended on something as the physical energies which they develop every day must be employed in some sort of labor if they are not to be short-circuited and make them miserable. It is perfectly possible and even easy to pervert heart impulses which might be the source of good for self and others, into sexuality of various kinds, whether that be exhibited in philanderings with the male dancers employed by the hotels to make *thés dansants* interesting for feminine youth — and also idle middle age — or in love affairs with the family chauffeur. They will find an issue some way almost inevitably. It may be that writing notes to the latest matinée idol or even letting one's feelings be properly harrowed up at performances of sex-problem plays may prove sufficient for a time, but something more will be demanded before long, and there must be something real to satisfy natural cravings.

There is probably no better safeguard against the tendency of the young heart to overflow on unworthy objects than to give it the opportunity to exercise itself on unselfish aims which lead up to the fine satisfactions to be derived from helpfulness for others. Settlement work and cognate personal activities have so organized the opportunity for this that young women do not have to travel in perilous neighborhoods except under such circumstances as reasonably assure their safety from insult or aggression of any kind. The charity that prompts occupation with such activities often leads to a development of character, while at the same time affording such exercise of body and mind as greatly promotes that eminently desirable end, — the possession of a healthy mind in a healthy body. There is much discussion at the present time over sex dangers for young people, but it must not be forgotten that these are mainly due to the sexual incitements which we are fostering in the dance hall and the theater and the cabaret supper room, while the best possible corrective for sexual erethism is to be found in contact with some of the misery of the world. The remedy is at hand, but unfortunately it is not made use of as a rule, and we wonder why evils increase as selfishness becomes more rampant.

John Ruskin summed up the situation with regard to the young women of our time in his address on The Mystery of Life and its Arts ("Sesame and Lilies"), in words that deserve to be in the notebook of every one who hopes to be able to help the young over some of the difficult parts of their path through life in our time.

"You may see continually girls who have never been taught to do a single useful thing thoroughly; who cannot sew, who cannot cook, who cannot cast an account, nor prepare a medicine, whose whole life has been passed either in play or in pride; you will find girls like these, when they are earnest-hearted, cast all their innate passion of religious spirit, which was meant by God to support them through the irksomeness of daily toil, into grievous and vain meditation over the meaning of the great Book, of which no syllable was ever yet to be understood but through a deed; all the instinctive wisdom and mercy of their womanhood made vain, and the glory of their pure consciences warped into fruitless agony concerning questions which the laws of common, serviceable life would have either solved for them in an instant, or kept out of their way. Give such a girl any true work that will make her active in the dawn and weary at night, with the consciousness that her fellow creatures have indeed been the better for her day, and the powerless sorrow of her enthusiasm will transform itself into a majesty of radiant and beneficent peace."

The friendly visiting of the poor is an old-fashioned Christian practice which had lapsed, unfortunately, until it was restored to some extent at least by the great work of Frederick Ozanam of Paris. The conferences of St. Vincent de Paul organized by him in Paris while he was professor of the university there about one hundred years ago had for their principal object the visitation of the poor, not so much for the purpose of giving them alms as of helping them with advice, making them feel that there are people interested in them, and giving them a new sense of human dignity; though also providing them with such necessaries as they might be in immediate want of and, above all, securing them occupations whenever they were needed. I have known many men who have developed a new and vigorous sense of life as a consequence of learning that they could be so useful to others as the Ozanam organization permitted them to be.

For a great many men some such escape from the sordid routine of daily business life is needed. This is particularly true when they have passed a little beyond middle age, which for me is not beyond fifty, as so many people seem to think, but thirty-five, the period indicated by Dante in the first line of his "Divine Comedy" as marking the mid-point of existence. After forty, particularly, most men who take life seriously and do not merely try to make money and kill the intervening time that hangs heavily on their hands in any way that they can, as a rule lose their interest in reading novels and do not care for the trivial plays of our time. They need diversion. They are not likely to get it at the opera unless they are very musically inclined. Card-playing may prove an excellent diversion and one that personally I think ever so much better than the reading of trivial novels, but there are a great many men to whom it has no appeal. If they stay at home they are likely to fall asleep in their chairs over the evening paper or a current magazine, and nothing in the world makes one feel so uncomfortable or so spoils an evening as to go to sleep in that way.

If they are particularly occupied with business affairs these may intrude themselves on their evening hours, but they very soon learn the lesson that it is dangerous to take business home with them. They need some serious occupation of mind quite different from what occupies them during the day. Professional men find something of this in the meetings of professional societies, but they too need a heart interest, a sympathy interest for their fellow man quite as well as the women. Many of them find it with their children as these grow up around them, and family life will help very much. But as the children grow older and have their own interests in the evenings, father is more and more likely to be left by himself, and then he needs something that will occupy him in some broad, human way. A good hobby of any kind would be a saving grace, but hobbies, to be effective, should be cultivated from early in life. One cannot be created easily at need after forty.

For such men friendly visiting of the poor, for it is only in the evenings that the man of the house can be seen, since he is always at work during the day, will often prove a most valuable resource. In a number of instances I have suggested to men who were beginning to get on their own nerves that they interest themselves in this way and have been rather well satisfied with the results when they took the advice seriously. In a few cases I have seen really wonderful results when it seemed almost inevitable that men were drifting into dangerous neurotic conditions because they were living lives too narrow in their interests and above all so self-centered that they were dwelling on slight discomforts and exaggerating them into symptoms of disease. Contact with the suffering that one sees among the city poor is a wonderful remedy for neurotic tendencies to make too much of one's own feelings, for the poor almost as a rule face the real ills of life with a simplicity and a courage that inevitably causes any one who is brought close to them to admire them and to feel that his own trials are trifles compared to what these people undergo with very little whimpering.

There is another phase of charity, probably unintentional in its activity and almost unconscious, that is extremely interesting and has a very definite place in a discussion of health and religion. Some men who have made a success in life far beyond their neighbors have preferred to continue dwelling in their old home rather than move into the quarter of the city to which their changed circumstances would have permitted them to go. Such families represent the very best possible kind of settlements in the poorer quarters of the city and help more than anything else to keep a neighborhood from running down in such a way as to make life harder for the poor who dwell there. The old walled cities are often said to have been almost intolerably unhealthy because of the inevitable crowding of the population which they compelled, and undoubtedly they were a fruitful source of disease and ills of many kinds for the population; and yet it is doubtful whether any old-time city was ever so insanitary as the slums of our modern crowded cities were a generation ago or are even in many places at the present time.

There was one feature of the old cities whose obliteration one cannot help but regret. The better-to-do families often lived on the front part of a city lot while the less well-to-do, often indeed the men who worked for the proprietor of the house in front, lived on the back of it. This was true particularly in many foreign cities and continued until a few generations ago.

This arrangement kept the conditions of living, so far as regards the middle class of the poor, from being so markedly indifferent as they are at the present time. Those who lived in the rear knew all the happenings, the births and deaths among their employers, while the family in the front took an interest in the events, the births and deaths and illnesses in the families in the rear. This proved to be valuable for social reasons, and it kept conditions of health among the poor from degenerating in anything like the way that has happened in modern times. The mutual personal interests did a great deal more to make life more satisfactory and more full of good feeling than the relationships of classes to each other do in our time, and this reacted to make a state of mind much more conducive to health than would otherwise have been the case.

Such associations would seem to be almost impossible in modern days, and yet the late Mr. Thomas Mulry, president of the Immigrants Savings Bank, at a time when, I believe, it was the largest savings bank in the world, continued to live down among the poorer folk to whom so much of his life was devoted for years after families of his standing in the financial world had long moved out. Our present governor of New York has declared his intention of continuing his residence among his friends in the old Seventh Ward, and undoubtedly his presence there will mean much not only for the health of those around him, but also for the health of his family because of the simple life which is so likely to be perpetuated in these surroundings.

For such social work as this, religious motives are probably the most efficient impulses. Nothing is quite so direct a denial of the brotherhood of man that religion teaches as the tendency for people to move away from old neighbors into the better quarters of the cities just as soon as they are any way able. Such reasoning may seem idealistic and impractical, but then religion is the typically ideal and impractical thing in life which teaches that self-advantage is not so important as advantage for all those around one, and that man's principal duty in life is to love his neighbor as himself.

How often has it happened that the building of the new house in a new neighborhood proves the last straw which serves to make an end of the good health and heartiness of life which the head of the family had enjoyed up to this time. The new habits that are necessitated, the interference with the active life which had been customary up to this time and above all the more luxurious living, very often with less exercise, which come under the new conditions bring about deterioration of health. The move is made for the sake of the young people, but it takes the old folks out of the precious, simple habits of a life-time which meant much for the preservation of health, so that it is no wonder that many a physician has had a patient whose breakdown in health followed not long after the move to a new and handsome house that carried people away from their old associations and their old neighbors and left them without those heart resources which are so important for the preservation of a healthy mind in a healthy body. It is men, not things, that count in life, though that lesson is hard for many to learn.

For a while, toward the end of the nineteenth century, owing to a misunderstanding of the significance of the struggle for existence, there came to be the feeling that sympathy and helpfulness for others was somehow contrary to modern scientific principles and that it represented at best a sentimentality that could scarcely hope to be effective and was indeed sure to fail in the long run because it was in opposition, though to but a very slight degree, to nature's inevitable elimination of the weak. Further investigations in biology, however, have revealed the fact that while the struggle for existence is an important factor in whatever evolution takes place, mutual aid is another factor of scarcely less importance in general and of supreme significance within the species. While one species preys on another, the members of the same species usually possess certain deep-seated instincts of helpfulness. Only at times when there is famine or when a mother is seeking food for her young do members of the same species seriously interfere with each other's activities, or injure each other, while a great many of them have mutually helpful instincts that are extremely precious for personal as well as generic developments.

The smaller living things, as the insects, dwell together in communities and perform their duties constantly with the community benefit rather than personal satisfaction in view. It might be said perhaps that these small creatures would have to be gifted in some such way to secure their preservation in the struggle for existence and their defense against their enemies. The larger animals, however, have the same helpful instincts. Wild horses run in droves and when attacked by a pack of wolves — the wolves hunting in packs because they can thus secure their prey better — the horses gather in a circle with their heads facing in and the young foals and the mares in the center, and only a battery of heels is presented to the attackers. Even such large animals as elephants travel in herds, with the huge bull elephants on the outskirts of the herd ready to hurl back any of the big cats, the lions or tigers who might spring to get one of those toothsome morsels, a baby elephant, traveling with its mother near the center of the herd. Smaller animals live in villages and groups of various kinds, and those of the same species are often helpful to each other in many ways.

Manifestly the great law of charity in a certain basic way at least pervades all nature. Nature may be "red in tooth and claw", but brother animals very often have by instinct a fellow feeling that is a factor in the preservation of the race. The idea that the discovery of the struggle for existence and the preservation of favorite races in that way has in any fashion neutralized the law of charity is entirely a mistake. Men in their selfishness have occasionally asserted this, and above all those who felt uncomfortable because their own selfish successes were, as they could plainly see, causing a great deal of discomfort and sometimes the ruin of others. It was once suggested that when the nurseryman wants to grow specially beautiful American Beauty roses he is careful to eliminate all except a few buds, so that these may have an opportunity to grow to the greatest possible perfection, and that this same policy pursued in human affairs led to the production of such great institutions as the Standard Oil Company. This was a particularly odorous comparison; it was made some twenty years ago. Almost needless to say every one sees the absurdity of it now, though at that time there were not a few who thought that the biological principle of the struggle for existence justified even the hurting of rivals in order to secure success. The Great War completed the elimination of such ideas. It was undertaken with the thought that any nation or people who could dominate the world was bound to do so, because that was manifest destiny for the benefit of the race. Just as it took our Civil War to end the defense of slavery in the United States, so it has taken the Great War to end such pretensions and bring out the fact that mutual aid, and above all charity undertaken out of real love for others through a divine motive must be the rule for men, while its symbol, mutual aid among the members of the various species, constitutes an important element for the preservation of the various races and the working out of the great laws that underlie all nature.

We in our generation were the inheritors of a philosophy of life which, for a time in what has now come to be called the "silly seventies", people thought could do away entirely with the necessity for a Creator and with the idea of a Providence because it seemed to them as though the suffering in the world around them contravened *their* notion of an all-wise Power capable of relieving suffering and yet not doing so. The doctrine of the survival of the fittest seemed to many a demonstration that victory was to the strongest or to the swiftest, and that the rest must simply go to the wall or lag behind in the race of life. The doctrine of the superman seemed to be the very latest discovery of science, but now, after having fought a great war to overthrow that doctrine, the world is much readier to go back and take up the thread of the philosophy of the race before the theory of the struggle for existence came to figure so largely in it. We have come to realize that everywhere in nature there is a great law of mutual aid within its species impressed upon all living things, and this is even more applicable to the human species than to those of the lower orders.

CHAPTER V

FASTING AND ABSTINENCE

Practically all religions have enjoined fasting as a part of their practice, either as a sacrifice made to higher powers or a recognition of the fact that occasional voluntary abstinence from food gave man a power of control over himself which represented a real religious gain in his relations with the deity. We have heard not a little in modern times of the evils to health consequent upon the abuse of fasting and of the limitation of food generally. Appetite must rule the quantity to be eaten, and this must not be interfered with by religious motives or health will suffer. Undoubtedly imprudent fasting, like the abuse of anything else, no matter how good in itself, has done no little harm. So much has been said, however, of the hysterical and neurotic conditions which resulted in women particularly, who out of an exaggerated sense of piety ate less than was necessary to support their bodies properly, that a rather violent prejudice has been created in many minds with regard to fasting as if it were an old-fashioned superstitious practice which our progress in knowledge and in the proper understanding of man, and his relations to the higher powers had enabled us to see the foolishness of and do away with for good and all.

Careful observations made in the course of the advance of modern scientific medicine have, however, made it very clear that periodical abstinences from food, or at least certain foods, especially among people who are accustomed to eat rather heartily, instead of being in any way a detriment to health, are practically always a distinct hygienic advantage. Physicians are not likely to take seriously such expressions as that most people dig their graves with their teeth or that eating too much is the bane of the race, but they appreciate very well that there are a great many people, especially among the better-to-do classes, who eat more than is good for them. It is just the people who have least exercise and need the least food who are tempted by the variety and tastiness of modern food to eat too much. Any practice that would limit this would undoubtedly be good. Fasting and abstinence, because periodic, would be especially valuable, for they are likely to do less harm than any continued limitation of food. The one phase of modern sanitation and hygiene, as made clear from the mortality records of the departments of health of our cities, that has been seriously disturbing in recent years, has been the increase in mortality among people above the age of fifty. We have been very properly proud of the fact that we have reduced municipal death rates and made the average length of life much longer than it used to be. We have done this, however, by saving more young children and by greatly lessening the infectious diseases among young adults, but the deaths from apoplexy, Bright's disease and heart disease, just when life is at its most valuable stage, have increased and not diminished. The tendencies to these serious degenerative diseases are due, it is well understood, ever so much more to overeating than to undereating. This is particularly true as regards the overeating of meat and other foods rich in proteid materials which have been the special subject of religious fasting regulation.

Religion then, by inculcating the practice of fasting and abstinence from flesh meat at certain times, has conferred a great benefit on the race. One fish day in the week, for instance, all the year round, has in the minds of a great many physicians given nearly as much rest to the digestive tract and certain of the more delicate metabolic processes of the body as Sunday freedom from labor has given to the mind and the body generally. The fact that a large part of our population will eat no meat on Friday and must have fish leads to a commercial provision of fresh fish on that day in the week, of which practically all the community, including those who feel no religious obligation in the matter, takes advantage.

Abstinence from meat, however, is quite a different thing from fasting, and Friday is a day of abstinence and not of fast. The fast days come at certain periods of the year, as in Advent and Lent, and certain days which are specially designated. The keeping of Lent, during which for forty days people are expected to eat one third less than they have been accustomed to, is a very valuable institution. I am not one of those who think that everybody eats too much and who like to be constantly insisting that people are destroying their lives by overeating, but I know very well that considerably more than half of humanity eat more than is good for them. I know, too, that about one fourth of humanity does not eat enough for its own good, and that unfortunately a good many of these are taking the warnings with regard to eating to heart, though those who need them most are neglecting them. Practically everybody who is overweight is eating too much and exercising too little. A good many people who are underweight are eating too little. Considerably more than one half of adult mankind, however, would be benefited by keeping rather strictly the regulations for the Lenten season. The fact that the Sundays are not in Lent and that good, hearty meals can be eaten on that day gives assurance that people are not likely to be hurt by the fast. I think that most of the physicians of the world would agree that the great majority of men and women would be benefited by the rest and change which their metabolic processes receive as a result of limitation of eating, and the observance of ecclesiastical regulations as to the modification of food.

The reduction in meat eating and the production to some extent of a taste for the white rather than the dark foods generally, for butter and eggs and creamed vegetables rather than the meat soups and meat sauces and the dark, heavy meats, so rich in the irritative extractives, is undoubtedly of distinct hygienic advantage. Of late years particularly, probably much more meat than is good for people has been eaten. The better-to-do classes have gradually come to the fashion of removing the fat, cutting off all the connective tissue portions of their meat and serving it or eating it in solid muscular masses, which is neither conducive to good digestion and elimination nor to the proper building up of the body. Too many irritant materials are thus consumed, and it is no wonder that that properly dreaded disease, arteriosclerosis, the hardening of the arteries, representing premature lessening of the elasticity of the tubes which convey the blood on which vital processes depend to so great a degree, has begun to be much more frequent than it used to be. There is agreement among physicians that a rich meat diet has much to do with this and that excessive meat eating is a growing evil in our time.

Only religion could accomplish a change in this tendency, for there is an allurement about meat which grows as more of it is taken. This can be noticed in children very readily, and human habits in civilized countries have unfortunately followed a direction in this matter that requires some profound influence to modify them. Not that meat is of itself a deleterious substance, nor one that should not be eaten, for there is no reason in nature for vegetarianism; but excess in eating it, like excess in anything else, may do serious harm. Nature, and when we use the word we mean nature's God, set an index that is infallible as to the variety of our diet when we were given cutting and tearing as well as grinding teeth. The presence of both these varieties of teeth, though the meat-eating animals have only the incisors and canines, while the plant-eating animals have only the molars or grinders, makes it clear beyond all doubt that human beings were meant to eat meat, but in this, as in everything else, excess must be avoided, and if it is not serious consequences follow.

A great many are inclined to think of abstinence as representing abstinence from food alone, but it must not be forgotten that as understood in connection with religion it represents abstinence from all the harmful things. For instance, it represents abstinence from sleep when that is being taken to excess, and as a rule any healthy human being above the age of twenty and under sixty who sleeps more than eight hours in the day needs to practice such abstinence. There is literally such a thing as oversleeping and thus accumulating more energy than one has use for. The surplus energy is then used up within the individual to the disturbance of functions of various kinds. Many a woman who has no children and who lives in an apartment hotel and has no duties that she has to get up for eats breakfast in bed, and does not rise until after eleven o'clock, after having gone to bed the night before sometime around midnight, and then wonders why she feels so miserable. Nothing would do her more good than to be out a little after eight in the morning briskly walking somewhere with the idea of helping some one else. She needs to practice abstinence of a very definite kind.

Then there are others who abstain too much from exercise. Whenever they go out they ride either in a trolley car or in a machine; the idea of walking a mile is disturbing to them and walking three or four miles seems utterly out of the question. Some of them are gaining in weight and are already overweight; they are wondering why they cannot bring themselves down and perhaps they are practicing abstinence of all kinds for that purpose. The famous English statesman, Lord Palmerston, who lived in good health to be a very old man and was for sixty years very prominent in English politics, was well known for the amount of exercise that he took. His maxim with regard to it should be very well known. He said, "Every other abstinence will not make up for abstinence from exercise." There are a great many people who are abstaining too much from exercise and need to abstain from rest. If they would do so for religious motives, and there are a number of people who keep themselves going when they are tired by these motives, they would not only accomplish a very great deal for their health, but they would at the same time make their religion mean ever so much more in a practical way in life.

The religious custom of setting a day of fasting before a feast day and of introducing three Ember Days before some of the larger feasts and at certain seasons of the year when, owing to the abundance of food provided for the day of rejoicing, people are likely to overeat, has been extremely beneficial as a simple matter of health conservation and prophylaxis against the effects of overeating. It has always been the custom to provide better and ampler meals on the feast days and if these are prepared for by a day of fasting, when one third less at least than usual is eaten, the stomach and digestive tract generally come to the full table much more ready for the feast. An old medical friend once suggested that the only things in the world worth while considering in matters of health are contrast and microbes. From the fast to the feast one gets the contrast and the variety in life distinctly makes for better resistance against microbic invasion. The Church believes in the satisfaction of reasonable appetites and encourages the feast days and their celebration by a larger provision of good things, but conserves health and disciplines the moral character at the same time by inserting the fast days before them. The occurrence of feast days at regular intervals so that a special gratification of the appetite is looked forward to has been declared by most physicians who have considered the subject to be an excellent thing for health. Monotony of diet begets sluggish digestion.

In some very serious diseases, as for instance occasionally in Bright's disease and rather more frequently in diabetes, fasting periods of short duration have been found particularly valuable as therapeutic measures. In certain forms of digestive disease fasting is also a valuable adjuvant, though it needs to be used under the direction of a physician, for people who prescribe their own fasting often fail to realize that they may weaken their digestive organs rather seriously by the process. The stomach has a very good habit of passing on to the other organs the nutritious materials that come to it and will sometimes drain itself of necessary nutrition in following out this good habit in this matter. People who are overweight particularly are often benefited by a fasting period, though here too care must be exercised.

Ecclesiastical regulations which have introduced fasting at intervals, but with proper interruptions on Sundays, even when there is a prolonged period of fasting, have certainly been beneficial to mankind. The loosening of the bonds of religion in modern times and the very general persuasion that somehow we are not capable of standing such abstinence from food as was insisted upon for the people of long ago are almost surely mistakes. All the nations of the world found during the war that their men could stand a great deal more than either they themselves or any one else thought they could. The soldiers taken out of the comforts of our cities lived in uncovered ditches in the open fields winter and summer, spring and fall, rain or shine, hail or snow, often with wet feet and clothes frozen upon them, with coarse food and not too much of it, taken at irregular intervals often in cold and unappetizing form, with interrupted sleep amid war's alarms and yet they actually came out of it in better health than they were before. We hear much of hurting human nature by deprivations, but it seems very probable that the old-fashioned habits of religious discipline with even fasting rigorously enforced, for all who are in normal health, would do good rather than harm. Not only could men stand them, though so many fear they could not, but they would be actually benefited by them. Nothing is so relaxing to the physical fiber of mankind as overindulgence, especially if continued persistently.

Undoubtedly the old-fashioned ecclesiastical regulations would do good to the moral as well as the physical side of man and also to his mental power. An overabundance of food sets up irritations of many kinds which make people restive in mind and body and adds fuel to passion. The expression in the Scripture is "My beloved waxed fat and kicked." The people who kick over the traces of the ordinary rules of conduct in life are much oftener well fed than underfed. I refer, of course, to the sins against self and others rather than to the sins against property. Fasting was always recognized as an extremely valuable adjunct in helping in the control of the passions. The practice of it made a man much more capable of controlling himself. The passions are all serious for health when permitted to get beyond bounds. Many a case of indigestion is dependent on that irritability of temper which so often develops in good feeders and then proceeds to form a vicious circle of influence, perpetuating itself. Irritability of tissues is often in direct ratio to irritability of temper, and not a few men owe both conditions to overindulgence in the pleasures of the table and failure to acquire, to some extent at least, such habits of self-control as the practice of fasting at intervals would help them to secure.

The bodily passions, especially those related to sex, are particularly likely to be influenced by overeating and to be brought under subjection by fasting, while at the same time the practice of this gives strength to the will in overcoming appetites which is a very valuable auxiliary for self-denial and self-control. All the authorities in the spiritual life, that is to say, to use a modern way of putting it, all the students of psychology in the olden time who devoted themselves to finding out how man could best regulate his instincts and train his will to self-control are agreed in declaring fasting particularly valuable for the proper regulation of certain very natural physical tendencies that may readily prove the source of serious temptations involving danger to health as well as to morals.

If fasting had done nothing else in the olden time but help men to control tendencies to sexual excess, religion, by its encouragement of the practice, would be a great creditor to health. One of the reasons why young folks, particularly nowadays, find it so hard and indeed some of them seem to think almost impossible — to control their sexual impulses, is that they have had no practice in building up habits of control of bodily appetites and no exercise of their will power to help them to suppress the natural tendencies, whenever these threaten their own good or that of those around them.

Perhaps modern hygiene may in the course of time find it advisable to reintroduce days of abstinence from certain foods and definite periods of fasting into the year for the sake of their mere physical benefit, just as holidays have been reintroduced in the last generation or so to replace the lost holydays of the older time. There are undoubtedly corresponding benefits for humanity in both movements. Some of these have been indicated more in detail in the chapters on Purity, Mortification and Suffering, so that the specific benefits of the practice of self-denial with regard to food and drink which religion has always encouraged may be seen in them. Religion has always counseled plain food for growing young folks, pointing out the dangers particularly of overeating, feeding the sex impulses, or at least making them extremely difficult to repress. This is particularly true as regards the richer foods specially prepared with condiments that tempt the appetite and lead to the accumulation of heat-forming materials for which there is no natural outlet except hard physical exercise. Sugar and the sweets generally are particularly undesirable in this respect, hence the benefit of the pious practice which makes many young folks abstain from candy during Lent.

CHAPTER VI

HOLYDAYS AND HOLIDAYS

If religion had done nothing else for mankind than insert holydays into the year, which came to be holidays in the best sense of the word, the health of mankind would have a great deal for which to thank it. Humanity is deeply indebted for the breaks in the routine of labor which came as the result of the institution of Church holydays of various kinds and especially for the Sundays. That every seventh day man should be free from labor was indeed a blessing. How few there are who realize that the Sundays, taken together, fifty-two of them, make seven weeks and a half of vacation in the year. Seven weeks of continuous vacation are usually too much for most people to enjoy properly; so long an interval palls on them. Coming once a week, however, the Sundays are probably the most wonderful aid to health and the conservation of strength and the keeping of people in good condition that we have.

One of the things for which we find it hardest to forgive the French Revolution is that when men tried to rule themselves by what they thought was pure reason, they changed the observance of Sunday every seventh day into a day of rest every tenth day. There seems to have been no other reason for that except that the French were introducing the decimal system, and ten seemed to be the number that appealed to them. Perhaps there was the feeling that seven was a sort of mystical number often mentioned in the Scriptures and deeply connected with religion. Their thoroughgoing reaction against the mystical made them reject it. Seven is, however, a much better number on which to regulate the day of rest than ten, and the seventh day has been extremely valuable for mankind.

Practically every one who has thought about the subject has recognized this, and yet it usually needs to be called particularly to their attention to have people generally appreciate it properly. Mr. Gladstone once emphasized the great benefits which he himself had derived from it and which he felt ought to be accorded to every workingman.

"Believing in the authority of the Lord's day as a religious institution, I must, as a matter of course, desire the recognition of that authority by others. But, over and above this, I have myself, in the course of a laborious life, signally experienced both its mental and its physical benefits. I can hardly overstate its value in this view; and for the interest of the working-men of this country, alike in these and other yet higher respects, there is nothing I more anxiously desire than that they should more and more highly appreciate the Christian Day of Rest."

Macaulay, the well-known English historian and essayist, emphasized particularly the fact that the rest of Sunday, instead of proving a detriment to mankind, was actually an advantage. During the war the British had to learn that lesson over again. Men and women in munition factories were at the beginning, owing to the high wages, but with the full approval of the government authorities, encouraged to labor in the factories on Sunday as well as on other days in the week. It was very soon found, however, that continuous labor, instead of enabling the operatives to keep up a greater production than before, was soon followed by a diminution in the power of production which sadly reduced the output. The restoration of the Sunday rest was promptly followed by an increased output, for nature seems to need such a rest, or after a while there comes a lassitude and relaxation of muscular power which actually prevents men and women from accomplishing their tasks with anything like the energy that they have under a regime of six working days followed by a day of rest. Only the most menial of routine labor, requiring no thought for its accomplishment, can be kept up without definite days of rest for relief and recuperation of forces.

Macaulay declared: "We are not poorer but richer because we have, through many ages, rested from our labour one day in seven. That day is not lost. While industry is suspended, while the plough lies in the furrow, while the exchange is silent, while no smoke ascends from the factory, a process is going on quite as important to the wealth of the nation as any process which is performed on more busy days. Man, the machine of machines — the machine compared with which all the contrivances of the Watts and Arkwrights are worthless — is repairing and winding-up, so that he returns to his labours on the Monday with clearer intellect, with livelier spirits, with renewed corporeal vigour."

During the ages when organized religion had the power to regulate human life much more than it has at the present time, there were many more days of rest than the Sundays. It is surprising now to find how many days in the year there were on which the Church forbade servile labor. All the Holydays of Obligation, so-called, were days of rest. From the very earliest time in Christianity there were at least two dozen of these in the year. The feast days of the Twelve Apostles, for instance, were twelve holydays of obligation with no work, and then there were of course nearly another dozen important celebrations in honor of the Lord. Christmas, and New Year, the Annunciation on March 25, Holy Thursday, Good Friday and usually two or three days in Easter week, Whitmonday and, as time went on, certain feast days in honor of the Mother of the Lord were added and then certain local saints' days in particular regions, as for instance the patron saint of the church of the place and often of the country. All together there were some thirty of these Holydays of Obligation, that is one extra day every two weeks and a little more than that was a holiday, on which no work was done. As the vigils of all first-class feasts were free from labor after the vesper hour, two in the afternoon, and as no work was done on Saturday afternoons after the same hour, there were actually well above one hundred days in the year free from labor.

One of the awful things that happened in the social order in modern history was the obliteration of these holydays shortly after the Reformation. We are engaged, now that we have waked up to the necessity of working people having days of recreation, in putting the holidays back into the year. We in this country have Lincoln's Day, Washington's Birthday, Decoration Day, Independence Day, Labor Day, and in most of the States Columbus Day, Election Day, and Thanksgiving Day as well as Christmas and New Year. In England, in order to make up for some of the holidays that have been lost, or rather so unwarrantably taken away from the working classes, they put in the bank holidays four times in the year, having them occur on Monday always, so that from Saturday afternoon until Tuesday morning people are free from the obligation of laboring. We know now how wise, from a human and merely natural as well as the divine and spiritual aspect was the insertion of holydays in the year. We must have more holidays; there should be at least one every month, and the old custom of having at least one every two weeks would be much better.

There are not a few people, especially in our strenuous time, deeply intent on human productiveness rather than on human life and happiness, who seem inclined to think that so many holidays in the year sadly hamper the power of humanity to get things done and, therefore, represent a very serious waste of time. Those who think that, however, are usually in quest of some personal advantage of some very sordid kind and are not interested in the real achievements of humanity. After all, human accomplishment, like personal advance, depends not on how much we get done but how well it is done. It is not from extremely tired, overwrought mortals, whose physical forces are always in tension because of the almost continuous strain to which they are subjected that we can ever expect to get any products that are really worth while. Slave labor may be exploited thus, and it is possible to build barracks and railroads and even pyramids in this way, but to erect structures of any noble kind which comprise in material form beautiful expressions of the artistic feelings of mankind, there can be no rush of tired human beings, but time must be taken.

The late Mr. Standish O'Grady of Dublin, to whom probably more than to any one else is due the modern revival in Irish literature which has been such an incentive for better poetry throughout the English-speaking world, once discussed this question of the achievement of mankind when men are released from the obligation of continuous labor and are free to think and have the opportunity to invite their souls and be inspired to higher things. It was at a dinner here in America, and he was remarking the fact that every one whom he met over here in this country was busy, *busy*, BUSY! They did not apologize for the fact, as a rule, but on the contrary seemed to be proud of it and to think that it must be the normal state of man to be so occupied with what he was about that he was ever deeply intent on it. He reminded his American audience that leisure was the foster-mother of nearly everything that mankind had ever done that was worth while, for the worth-while things must have thought in them, and thought requires time and leisure for its fulfillment.

Mr. O'Grady recalled the fact that twice in the world's history when men accomplished results so great that the world will never willingly let die the monuments then created, the most important feature of life was its leisure. Actually one third of the time of the men of Greece in the Periclean period, that Golden Age of achievement, was spent in the preparation for and the celebration of religious mysteries. Their greatest architectural monuments were their temples; their finest sculptures were the figures of the gods and goddesses, but what is not usually realized is that their literature was the product of the leisure afforded for competitions in their great religious festivals, and their painting had a similar origin. The

Greeks, like the medieval Christians, had a great many feast days during the year, and on these they held games and contests of various kinds, not only athletic but poetic, dramatic and literary of all kinds, for Herodotus read his great history before the assembled multitude in the celebration of a religious festival at Athens and was awarded a prize equivalent very probably to ten thousand dollars in our time.

What was true of the Greeks was true also, as has been said, of the Middle Ages. The generations which made the great Gothic cathedrals which we have come to look upon as such triumphs of construction, which built the magnificent abbeys and town halls and hospitals of the later Middle Ages, enduring monuments of their genius in construction, spent one third of their time in the celebration of and the preparation for religious festivals. Twice in the history of the world, once in the later Middle Ages and in the older days in Greece, dramatic literature originated anew in religious mystery and morality plays. The men who gave us Magna Charta and all the great charters of liberties that lie at the basis of modern rights and privileges in practically every country in Europe had the time to think out the solutions of their problems in the leisure afforded by the fifty-two Sundays and thirty Holydays of Obligation which they were accustomed to celebrate. The undying literature of the thirteenth century, the Cid in Spain, the Arthurian legends in England, the Nibelungen in Germany and Dante all came at a time when men set apart days for religious meditation and a contemplation of higher things than the sordid concerns of everyday life.

So far from one day of leisure in three interfering with human productivity in the best sense of that word, the custom actually added to it. Men who work continuously from day to day without intermission can make a quantity of trivial things, but they cannot make anything that would be enduringly interesting, for they have not the time. I have often said that I thought that the greatest expression in American literature is those famous words of Thoreau as to the relation of time and money. The Sage of Walden found that by working about one half a day in the week he could support himself, and he used the rest of the time for the study of nature around him and for inviting his soul in the woods and along the streams. He feared that the business of making a living might keep him from really living. It is easy to understand that his thrifty Yankee neighbors failed utterly to comprehend any such attitude toward what they conceived to be a workaday world. Especially at harvest time when they needed help it seemed a shame to see Thoreau wandering apparently lazily and aimlessly while they were working so hard and looking for workers whom they were willing to pay what they thought was very good wages. They stopped Thoreau and offered him better pay than they were usually accustomed to offer, but Thoreau replied very simply, "I have no time to make money." There seem to be a great many people in our day who apparently are of the opinion that the only reason for which time is given is to make money.

The Sundays and holydays, as arranged by the religious authorities, made excellent recreation days. After their morning spent in church, listening to a sermon by some favorite preacher, but having the eye and the ear and even the nose appealed to by the rest of the celebration, the people were then free for recreation. The old Church had no Puritanic scruples about people playing on the

Sabbath; there were sports of various kinds on the green in front of the church and their parish priest might be the referee; neighboring parishes held contests in archery or at bowls or in what the Irish call hurling and the English call shinney. At certain seasons the guilds offered prizes for these contests; the young were encouraged to go into training for them for weeks beforehand, and the prizes were conferred rather gloriously before all those whom the young folks most loved and respected.

These Church holidays were associated with various celebrations, such as May Day, the Feast of the Innocents or Fools; the beating of the bounds when in procession the parishioners on the Rogation Days walked round the various properties of the parish and asked the blessing of heaven on the crops; the carnival time when, before abuses crept in, the Church encouraged the celebration that would mark the beginning of Lent and make everybody ready to bid good-by to the pleasures of life for a while. Then the various fairs and markets were usually so timed that they immediately followed some important festival day in the year and afforded people an opportunity for a little vacation and an outing in connection with the feast, while at the same time they were able to buy what they needed.

Above all, religion insisted that some part of these days of recreation, the holydays of the years, should be spent not merely for one's own selfish pleasure, but in bringing pleasure to others. It was suggested, for instance, that there could be no better occupation for a portion of Christmas and Easter or of some Sunday afternoons than visiting the sick or prisoners or bringing consolation to those in need. Kings and queens washed the feet of the poor on Holy Thursday, and there were similar practices at other times in the ecclesiastical year. The people were encouraged to bury the dead reverently and then to keep their graves green and to visit them occasionally on the holydays as a sign that their memory had not faded, though also as a reminder of the fact that sometime they hoped to be with their dear friends in another world. This may seem a rather solemn occupation for recreation, but taken in the open air, while the children played around the graves and the old folks sat and talked, it was ever so much better than that unconquerable tendency to crowd together in hot, dusty places which afflicts people on our holidays. The old graveyards represented the parks in even the smallest towns, and the inhabitants had a pride in keeping them in order and found a pleasure in visiting them occasionally. In the unfortunately crowded conditions in which they often lived, the only lungs for some of their villages were to be found in the churchyard. There was scarcely a town in this country two generations ago that had anything approaching a public park, except its cemetery.

There is a constant tendency to encroach on the Sunday rest for commercial and industrial reasons of one kind or another, and only religious influences have saved the Sabbath for mankind. Even as it is, the decadence of religion in many countries has led more and more to neglect of the Sabbath-day rest, and in certain of the European countries particularly, Sunday, instead of being a day of rest for the small tradesman, is sometimes his busiest day. Here in this country religious influences were the only factors that kept the saloons more or less closed on Sunday and kept the rest day from being an orgy of dissipation for many people. Selfishness continues to encroach on the precious day of rest and various forms of trade try to present some necessity for their being open on the Sabbath. This has always been the way, and the religious sanction in the matter has been the most precious safeguard.

At the present time, there are a good many stores open for a while or for the whole day on Sunday for which it is hard to find any necessity. Some of the fresh food and milk stores have a certain justification, but why tobacco stores should be open, seeing that their product will keep perfectly and that any man can rather easily lay in a store to carry him over a day at least, is indeed hard to understand.[1]

Another abuse of the public confidence is the opening of all drug stores on Sunday. As a consequence hundreds of thousands of men are deprived of this day of rest in the week. Drugs are extremely important and should of course be available at all hours, but there is no more reason for all the drug stores to be open every Sunday than there is for all the drug stores to be open all night. Certain drug stores should be open, but as St. Antoninus suggested five hundred years ago, there is no good reason why there should not be an arrangement by which the drug stores should be open in rotation on Sundays, so that drugs would be always available and only the absolutely necessary articles needed for emergencies should be sold on that day. There is no reason at all why the modern department store annex of the large drug corporations which happens to have a small corner of its store space set off for the filling of prescriptions should

[1] There are probably several hundred thousand men in this country who have to work on Sunday because the tobacco stores are open. This is an abuse corresponding to that with regard to the saloon, which will almost surely bring about a reaction in the public mind against the traffic in tobacco generally.

do business on Sunday than for an immense department store to put in a prescription department and then sell goods all over the house because they have to keep their drug department open on Sundays. Only the religious element in life will save us from this commercial invasion, with the harm which it does in depriving so many people of their day of rest.

The future of the Sunday as a needed day of rest is dependent more on religion than on any other factor. The insidious selfish quest for money will find excuses for the violation of the day in one way or another. The institution and maintenance down the ages of the Sabbath day of rest is a wonderful example of what religion can accomplish for man in the face of the corroding power of selfishness and is the best demonstration of its living influence for the bodily as well as the spiritual and mental health of mankind.

CHAPTER VII

RECREATION AND DISSIPATION

As has been suggested in the last chapter on Holydays and Holidays, religious institutions have been the most effective organizers of recreations sane and safe for the mind as well as for the body of man, and recreation is one of the most important factors for the preservation of human health. The man who does not take the time for recreation and above all who does not know how to recreate is almost inevitably drifting toward a premature aging of tissues, or often is laying the foundation for an acute breakdown in health. Recreation is an absolute need of humanity, adding to health, strength, efficiency, length of life, and power of accomplishment. Instead of being a waste of time, it is a time saver and above all a saver of suffering, mental and physical, as the years roll on.

Dissipation is, however, the very opposite of recreation. What corresponds to these two words in human conduct is confounded in the minds of a great many people probably as often as the activities which respond to those other much abused words, liberty and license. Recreation, as the etymology indicates so clearly, means the building up of energy, while dissipation signifies the scattering of it, usually to no purpose. It is extremely easy for what is meant to be recreation to become dissipation, and religion has been the most important factor in life in controlling the tendency to dissipation which exists among men, not only from the moral but also from the intellectual aspect of life. Religious motives have succeeded better than any other factors in lessening this tendency and securing such genuine recreation as would serve to rebuild men's minds and bodies after they had been more or less worn out from work, and at the same time tend to keep them from immorality and afford such relief from the strain of serious occupation as would provide real reconstruction for them.

Unfortunately in our time, just in proportion as religion has lost its hold on men, recreation has become largely a matter of dissipation of mind when not also dissipation of body. More and more barbaric or merely bodily modes of recreation are preoccupying the leisure time that men have outside of their regular occupations in life. It must not be forgotten that the way a man or a generation spends its leisure is the best possible index of the character of the man or the generation. It is the way that a man spends the time that he is free to use any way that he wishes which reveals what he is. It was a great philosopher who said, "Tell me what a man does with his leisure, and I shall tell you what sort of a man he is." We all have to work a certain portion of our time, and often what we work at is not a matter of choice but necessity. What we do during our leisure, however, is dependent on ourselves and represents our tastes.

The recreation of our time reveals that people are ever so much more interested in their bodies than they are in their minds and hearts and souls. Very often the recreation of the older time consisted of hours spent with all the advantages of outdoor air, exercise, and fine satisfaction of mind, perhaps in visiting the poor or the prisons or the hospitals, or in encouraging the sports of children, or in arranging for outings of various kinds in which the pleasantest of social intercourse between friends and neighbors was associated with such recreation of body as gave a good healthy weariness after a day's outing. More and more these old-fashioned modes of recreation are passing, and sophistication has brought in occupation of mind with a lot of unworthy things.

Instead of taking an active part in what is supposed to recreate them people must now be amused. Whenever this happens and participants pay for the amusement, the character of the amusement degenerates because it must appeal to as great a number as possible. As a consequence, in our day recreation, especially for young folks who ought of course to be actively engaged in sport and not merely onlookers, consists in attendance at "shows" and games. The "shows" have an appeal merely to the senses, they have not an idea lost in them anywhere; the music is a caricature of real music founded on the fact — which the most primitive of savages have always discovered for themselves — that a rhythm appeals to men and gives them a certain bodily satisfaction, probably because of some ill-understood interaction with the heart beat. The main feature of appeal is really the sex element that enters into the show and produces feelings. The lyrics are, if that term for them were to be taken seriously, a crying shame, for the words of the songs usually mean absolutely nothing. The rule is to take certain words that rhyme, like kiss and bliss, and love and glove, and for the rest to talk about the moon and some sentimental twaddle. There is not a glimpse of poetry about them in any sense of the word.

The attendance at games of various kinds in which people watch other people exercise is a favorite occupation in our time, but it is only the shadow of recreation. It is usually associated with feelings aroused by the desire for one side to win, either because of betting or some other sentiment often entirely artificial. Whenever anything occurs to disappoint the desire, there is likely to be an exhibition of some of the ugliest feelings of mankind. Men invade the field, take up quarrels, and sometimes not only threaten but actually attempt bodily injury of the players and particularly of the umpire. Probably nothing could be more unworthy as recreation for human beings than this passive interest in the exercise that other people take, and the elevation of the contests of paid professionals into something to occupy men's minds seriously and even arouse their feelings deeply.

More and more bodily interests are drowning out higher interests, and prize fighting and wrestling command ever larger audiences, while the sums of money that are paid for such exhibitions grow in size, showing the importance of bodily interests to the general public. There is an old story of Cimabue's Madonna causing the stoppage of business in Florence in the old days, but the transport of no mere picture along the street, no matter how beautiful it might be, would have any such effect nowadays, though the arrival of a prize fighter who had just won a heavyweight contest, if his coming were announced beforehand, would almost surely interfere seriously with business for some time in the neighborhood of the station.

Just as in the days of Rome when the amphitheater was the center of attraction, recreation is becoming mere barbaric dissipation for a great many people. The cultured, intelligent Romans — at least many of them were educated — went to see gladiators fight with wild beasts or with each other unto the death, or to get a special thrill by seeing the Christians thrown to the lions. The other shows they attended were mainly the dancing of slave girls scantily dressed, whose actions were meant to excite sex feelings. At Rome the women had no virtue and the men no courage; they were interested in their bodies and degeneracy had come. No wonder the real barbarians came to replace their counterfeit presentments in the pseudo-refined Romans.

Even our mental occupations are very largely taken up with bodily interests. Reading is supposed to be an intellectual diversion, but it has become a matter of attention to sex and other bodily emotions. My friend, Doctor Austin O'Malley, suggests that one of the most important criteria of intelligence is contained in the rule "the book that you like is like you," to which may be added, of course, that the play that you like is like you and the magazine that you like is like you. If our generation is to be judged by its occupation of its leisure, the estimation will not be very high. Most of the leisure time of men is spent in reading the newspapers. Indeed, it may be said without exaggeration that the greater part of civilized mankind now spends the major portion of its hours of relaxation over the newspaper. News was defined by an old-fashioned editor succinctly as sin. The definition has enough of truth in it to give us pause when we consider that every one is occupied with the newspaper for an hour or more each day. We want to know the last details of the ugly sex crimes and the misfortunes of various kinds that have happened to people, perhaps with a feeling that things might be worse for us than they are, but the suggestive effect is almost the worst that could well be imagined, and the recreation of mind becomes a sad dissipation of mental energy.

Religion brought the holydays, which were in our modern sense holidays, into the year, but did ever so much more than this by suggesting, organizing and encouraging such occupation of them as afforded recreation for men and women in definite contradistinction from dissipation. On all the Sundays and holydays men rose to attend services and usually spent some hours in this occupation. Attendance at religious services in our time has become very largely a matter of duty, requiring considerable self-denial and control for its accomplishment. The religious ceremonials of the older time were, however, extremely interesting, and people looked forward to them. They had to attend them as a matter of duty, but the great majority of them found a pleasure in the duty because of the appeal that the Church ceremonial made.

Various societies associated with religion in one way or another organized the recreations for the afternoon of the holydays or for the vigils or eves of the great festivals, on which there was no work done after the vesper hour. The guilds, for instance, most of which received saints' names, and many of which built chapels of their own and were closely affiliated with the ecclesiastical authorities, offered prizes for athletic exercises among the young folks, both boys and girls, and arranged contests in archery, in the pitching of quoits, in the old-fashioned form of hockey and the like, between the inhabitants of neighboring villages, and then there were also individual athletic contests of various kinds. Banquets were held four times a year on the special feast days, to which a man was expected to bring either his wife or his sweetheart. They did not believe that it was good for men to be alone in their feasting, and realized that there was likely to be much less of excess and ever so much less of a tendency to quarrel if the women were present. The banquets were held in the afternoon, and there was dancing on the green afterward for the young folks and games of various kinds, all of which were meant to give the young particularly innocent enjoyment and bring them together for proper matchmaking.

Religious authorities have always recognized the necessity for recreation. Besides, they have always tried to keep recreation on that higher plane where it may do good and not harm. Dancing, for instance, has very often had a place in religious ceremonials. Rhythmic movements of the body can add to the significance of even the deepest thought. They may, of course, be reduced merely to the expression of sensuality or constitute an invitation to it. David danced before the Ark, and dancing has always had a place in the expression of religious feelings. The old Greeks employed dancing to great effect, even in their higher religious ceremonials. The great Greek dramatists wrote choric odes which are among the most beautiful lyric poems ever written. They were on such subjects as life and death and man and fate and all the other great mysteries with which man is confronted. The chorus, in singing them, danced, and the reason for the dance was that it added to the significance of the beautiful words that had been written. The Greek plays were staged as a part of the religious ceremonial in celebration of the festivals of Dionysus; his name has been translated by the supposed Latin equivalent Bacchus, but the Greeks meant the god of inspiration and not the god of intoxication.

Religion then proved a source of a great deal of genuine recreation. It emphasized the joys of existence rather than merely the pleasures of life. It encouraged family participation in everything and found a place for the children. There is a great distinction between joy and pleasure that is often missed when religion is in decay. Joy is a profound feeling usually associated with the performance of simple duties and rather easily attainable by every one. Pleasures are often expensive, frequently are followed by remorse, and more often than not do harm rather than good to those who indulge in them, especially to any excess. Joy, however, inspires human beings to the further accomplishment of duty, gives a supreme sense of well-being, brings light-hearted sleep and is very precious in the memory. Joys are usually associated with domestic duties and religious observances and the celebration in family groups of the great festivals. What religion did in bringing joy into life is one of the most precious factors for real recreation that we have.

The main feature of religion's work for recreation, however, consisted of the development of dramatics. Twice in the world's history, as I have noted in the chapter on Holydays and Holidays, dramatic literature has developed out of religious ceremonials. These ceremonials very naturally take on the dramatic form, and the evolution of this in the course of time led to additions to religious services which soon came to occupy so much attention as to deserve a place and time for themselves, and then they were transferred to the temple porch in the older time, or to the open space at the foot of the steps, or in the Middle Ages to the churchyard or the green in front of the church.

This encouragement of recreation with a deep appeal

to the emotions and the higher feelings which at the same time brought satisfaction for the intellect, proved of the greatest possible service for health. Men need to have thoroughgoing diversion of mind from their ordinary occupations. Such diversion of mind is, in my opinion, even more important than exercise of body. The effort in our time is concentrated on doing nothing with the mind, as a rest for it, or doing something that is so trivial that it is supposed to provide opportunity for mental recreation. Almost needless to say it is impossible to do nothing with the mind. The mind will keep right on thinking about something or other, and unless thought is diverted it is very inclined to recur to the last worries and troubles which the individual has experienced. The attempt to occupy the mind with trivial matters does not divert it. To read the newspaper or some popular magazine or a light novel will enable the person to kill time, but up through the print will always come obtruding itself the worry or anxiety that occupied it before. What is needed for true recreation is that the mind shall be interested in something very different from its ordinary occupation. This interest must be deep and abiding and holding, or it will not prove so successful as would otherwise be the case.

Some form of intellectual hobby makes the very best recreation, but not every one has either the time or the money and above all the intelligence to cultivate a hobby that will be absorbing in its appeal. Religion, then, with its universal appeal, its deep touching of the feelings, its sense of supreme satisfaction when people believed, its presentation of ceremonies that have even a sensory attraction, formed in the past a fine avenue of escape from the sordid considerations of life for a great many people and can still be an invaluable resource for those who take it seriously. In the midst of trials and hardships the folk of the older time learned to turn to religion as a consolation that occupied their minds and promised them divine help in their difficulties. Religion as organized in the later Middle Ages, with its great celebrations on the festival days in the beautiful Gothic churches, on the background of great art, served this purpose of diversion of mind extremely well. If that had been its only purpose it would have been quite unworthy of the great intellectual and artistic accomplishments which religion aroused. But as a secondary consideration this must not be forgotten, and the absence of an appeal of this kind makes for that tendency to dissipation of mind which is so unfortunate because so unworthy of human nature and at the same time proves so ineffective as providing any real recreation of mind.

In the old days when the Puritans went to a sermon two hours long, they listened with rapt attention to the preacher, and in so doing their minds were occupied with an entirely other subject from that which ordinarily attracted their attention. Such a diversion, even though it may seem to be pretty hard work, represents a real mental rest because the part of the brain that is usually occupied gets its rest, the blood being diverted to other parts of the brain. This may seem a paradox to some people until they are reminded that men who have lived very long lives have usually been men who turned from one form of mental work to another for diversion and rest. Gladstone, for instance, who was Prime Minister of Great Britain when past eighty years of age, was an intensely hard intellectual worker all his life, but found recreation from his political cares in the study and discussion of the problems of Greek literature. Leo XIII, who lived to be ninety-three, concerned to the very end with the administration of the Church — an immense task — found his recreation in the writing of Latin poetry, though that might seem to some people too hard work of itself to be classed as rest. For a great many of these hard-working, long-lived people, as was true of both Leo XIII and Gladstone, prayer was a recourse in time of trial that made anxiety less and took the edge off solicitude and occupied the mind with the profound thought of the Providence that overrules and somehow cares for us.

I have often said before medical societies, and in articles for medical journals, because the expression represents a definite medical conclusion in my mind, that the reason why nervous and mental diseases were growing commoner in our time was that men and women had no real mental recreation. They go to trivial shows of various kinds, vaudeville, musical comedy and the movies, and they laugh a little and feel a great deal, but think almost not at all. They try to forget their ordinary occupations and worries, and indeed plays and novels are now advertised as "the kind that make you forget", but they do not succeed very well in this effort and their minds are not really diverted. For diversion the mind should become occupied rather deeply with some other subject, so that the blood which has been going to a particular part of the brain in order to call up the memory of things associated with the special interests of the individual may be diverted to another part. This will give the portion of the brain previously occupied a rest as almost nothing else will. Doing nothing with the mind is impossible, though some people apparently come very near it. Doing very trivial things will not divert the current of attention so as to allow of real rest. Attention is probably a matter of increased blood circulation to a particular set of brain cells. These will go on working in spite of the wish to stop, unless the blood is actually diverted elsewhere in the cerebral tissues or the individual sleeps, with its accompanying brain anemia.

For believers religion has this deep appeal and strong interest which represents very definite diversion of mind. Of itself, then, it may afford genuine recreation, though so little associated with recreation in the modern sense of the term. It is the most cogent reliever of worries. It affords the best neutralization of such intense preoccupation with merely sordid concerns as may prove dangerous for health.

Religion has always insisted that idle dissipation of mental and physical energy was an extremely dangerous thing. The devil finds work for idle hands is an expression that has come from very early Christian times. While the Church has appreciated thoroughly the necessity for occupation of mind and enjoyment and amusement and has put the holydays into the year in large numbers and made true holidays of them, it has also recognized clearly the dangers there might be in recreations of various kinds. Fashion has often been strong enough to override religious counsels in the matter, but at least they have served to restrain to some extent, and they have always pointed out the dangers so that young folks have not gone into them unseeing and unthinking; thus a good many have been saved from grave risks and absolute moral and physical injuries which might have proved serious as the result of religious regulations and advice.

Dancing has always been one of the modes of recreation with regard to which religion has felt the need to exercise surveillance and inculcate the necessity for proper supervision. There has been no unthinking opposition to it and no mere bigoted intolerance. The dance has always been recognized as an excellent exercise of the body and a very definite mode of expressing beautiful thoughts in graceful postures and movements; the dance has actually been used in Church ceremonies, and its symbolism made to lend significance to the body's share in worship or in the expression of beautiful thoughts. When graceful dancing was to a great extent discarded and the essence of the dance came to be the intimate contact of two persons of opposite sex in the lively movements of modern dancing measures which were almost sure to arouse passion, no wonder that religion counseled prudence in order to prevent harmful developments which are often the source of so much danger for health of body as well as for holiness, that is wholeness of spirit. The restraint exercised in this way over the control of occasions that might lead to serious consequences makes religion an important factor for health.

It is quite true that religion does not often succeed in her well-meant efforts in controlling such tendencies to dissipation and sometimes seems utterly to fail, but that is largely because in recent years there has been an unfortunate decadence of religious influence, and people do not live up even to the principles of religion which they themselves hold. Among those who still maintain the religious life, the restraint exercised as regards many of these unfortunate dissipations means a very great deal for health of body and mind. Certainly social evils would be much worse only for the presence of a great conservative institution exercising restraint and calling on people to practice self-control and self-denial in these matters, no matter how alluring they might be nor how much they may have met with the approval of what is called society.

Probably the most important element for health in the modern time is the conservation of the distinction between recreation and dissipation. Almost inevitably recreation becomes dissipation; that is, the relaxation of mind and body so necessary for health becomes a dissolution of physical and mental forces to the serious detriment of the individual, unless there are strong, impelling motives to prevent the degeneration. Such motives may be drawn from human respect or from the desire to maintain the body in healthful vigor, but these lower motives very often fail of their purpose and at best apply only to a comparatively few among mankind. For the great majority of men, motives with a deeper appeal than mere self-respect or the respect of others or even the preservation of the body from impending disease are necessary. In youth particularly bodily degeneration seems a distant possibility, almost surely to be escaped without much difficulty, especially if one has any luck, and even if serious disease be incurred it will surely be cured rather easily by the means that science now has at her command. The general appeal that is necessary to give men a fixed point of support in maintaining recreation on a high level and not letting it slip down into dissipation is to be found in religion.

The reason why recreation and dissipation have so often come to be confounded in our time, or at least that recreation has sunk to a much lower level than it used to occupy, is the diminution of religious influence over a great many people. The old religious family life made it much easier to maintain such discipline in the lives of growing young folks as kept them from the tendencies to dissipation almost sure to develop unless there are strong safeguards in the household. Where the young folk themselves are firm believers in the great truths of religion, their control is much easier and is exercised much more by themselves than by any external measures. It is the having a fount of incentive to what is good and deterrents for what is evil within oneself that is the best possible auxiliary for the neutralization of tendencies to evil that are as natural as they can be and that represent one inexplicable phase of that mystery of evil by which we are surrounded in the world.

The only satisfactory explanation of that is to be found in faith, and it is from this that strength can be derived to prevent the lower nature of man which shares so many animal proclivities from governing the individual to the detriment of both sides of his being.

CHAPTER VIII

MORTIFICATION

MORTIFICATION is a word with an interesting etymology. It means literally the dying or more properly the putting to death of one part of an animal body while the rest is alive. From this it has come to mean, to quote the Century Dictionary, "The act of subduing the passions and appetites by penance, abstinence or painful severities inflicted on the body." It has had this signification from the very earliest times of Christianity, for the early Fathers spoke of dying to self to have a higher and a nobler life. It is used exactly in this sense in the old medieval Latin as well as by that first great prose writer in modern English, Sir Thomas More, for he spoke of "the mortification of the fleshly woorkes" in just this signification. After all our recent Poet Laureate, when in "In Memoriam" he summed up so much of the current thought of our time, expressed the same ideas as the earlier religious authorities when he said that "we rise on stepping stones of our dead selves to higher things."

It was a favorite idea of the Greeks of the classical period that the way to get most out of life was to repress the body and give the mind and soul a chance. Aristotle said, "The vanities of the world are a hindrance to the soul," and he paraphrased by anticipation that expression which came to mean so much during the war that our rising generation learned the precious lesson "that there are things in life worth more than life itself" when he said, "'T is better for the soul's sake to suffer death than to lose the soul for the love of this life." Socrates had said before him, "A wise man ought to look as carefully to his soul as to his body", and Plato, going straight to the point, declared, "Whoso desireth the life of his soul ought to mortify the body and give it trouble in this world." No one knew better than Plato that the desire of having things did more than aught else to make the higher life impossible. He did not hesitate to say, and the expression constitutes one of the most striking commentaries on our time that we could have, "the soul is lost that delighteth in covetousness." Pythagoras long before the group of the classical period had said, "Order thyself so that thy soul may always be in good estate; whatsoever become of thy body."

It would be easy to find almost as many expressions commending mortification among the old Greek philosophers as among the Fathers of the Church. Plato said, "He obeyeth many that obeyeth his body." And Aristotle said, "He that hath bound himself to follow his fleshly delights is more bound than any caitiff", which after all, is only another way of wording Plato's expression, "the worst bondage is to be subject to vices." Seneca, five centuries afterwards in Rome, declared, "Too much liberty turneth into bondage", doubtless imitating, as he did so often, Euripides, who declared, "Better is it to be free in heart and bond in name than to be free in name and bond in heart."

In spite of this very respectable ancient lineage which would indicate an agreement for many centuries among thoughtful people that mortification has a definite place in life, many in our time seem inclined to think that the idea underlying the word is a mistake, and that the virtue attributed to it does not actually work out in practice. Hence mortification is at present considered by a good many to be only one of the good old ways of life evolved in an earlier day when men were less capable of judging of the significance of things than they are now, but which humanity ought to set definitely back in the lumber room of discarded notions, now that an era of really rational development of humanity has come. The old-fashioned idea that in this way the passions can be controlled is looked upon as a sort of worn-out superstition, good enough for people who did not know as much as we do and who did not understand as we have come to understand the profounder psychology of humanity. We are apparently quite sure in our time that sweet reasonableness must be the only rule for mankind and that anything so crude as self-inflicted suffering is not needed by generations which have not sounded the depth of human nature as we have done.

Nothing is commoner than to read tirades of various kinds against the practices of mortification that were in vogue in the older times. A great many writers who think themselves well informed feel assured that the people of the olden time performed the most difficult acts of penance and inflicted intense self-suffering on themselves with no other purpose in view than to curry favor with the Almighty quite as if they felt that the Creator delighted in the suffering of His creatures. They do not seem to realize at all that the real reason why the older peoples thought such self-inflicted suffering might be looked upon with favor from on High was that the efforts required to perform these acts strengthened their wills so as to enable them to repress their passions and inordinate desires and to control the tendencies to do wrong which are in every nature and which require constant watching and subjection, or they prove extremely difficult to master.

Before the war, when the world generally was rather inclined to take a good deal of its psychology from Germany, the scoffing tone with regard to mortification was particularly rife in academic circles. While other nations as a rule did not adopt the German idea of the superman, they were usually much more tinctured with that teaching than they suspected. Nietzsche's great teaching was that a man must follow his instincts and develop his personality to the highest, regardless of the consequences to others. One of his famous parables is that of the soft coal and the diamond. The soft coal is heard complaining to the diamond, "We are brothers, why then do you scratch me?" and the diamond replies, "Since we are brothers how is it that I can scratch you; why are you not as hard as I am, and then all would be well between us?" and Nietzsche's conclusion was, "For I preach to you a new doctrine; be ye hard." As Germany had more professors of psychology than any other nation, it is easy to understand what far-reaching influence her teaching had. A very few were conservative, but most were radical, and the only consolation that we have now is to realize that the nation which had the most professors of psychology least understood the minds of men, as was demonstrated very clearly by the egregious blunders which the German government made with regard to the neutral nations during the course of the war.

The modern psychologists who have thought most deeply about human nature do not share at all the supercilious contempt for mortification and even the habit of performing frequent acts of self-repression, though they may cost effort and suffering, which so many thoughtless people are ready to express. Professor William James, who was surely not at all a medievally minded individual and who is recognized as one of the leaders of thought in modern psychology, did not hesitate to express his conclusions on this matter in a paragraph that should be very well known:

"As a fine practical maxim, relative to these habits of the will, we may, then, offer something like this: Keep the faculty of effort alive in you by a little gratuitous exercise every day. That is, be systematically ascetic or heroic in little unnecessary points; do every day or two something for no other reason than that you would rather not do it, so that when the hour of dire need draws nigh, it may find you not unnerved and untrained to stand the test. Asceticism of this sort is like the insurance which a man pays on his house and goods. The tax does him no good at the time and possibly may never bring him a return. But if the fire does come, his having paid it will be his salvation from ruin. So with the man who has daily inured himself to habits of concentrated attention, energetic volition, and self-denial in unnecessary things. He will stand like a tower when everything rocks around him, and when his softer fellow mortals are winnowed like chaff in the blast."

Above all in youth there is need of enduring hard things in order to form character and enable people to control themselves and deny themselves. This is sometimes supposed to be a medieval idea, but Goethe, with all his leaning toward the ways of the old Greeks and his liking even for the Olympian religion, did not hesitate to say that the most important thing in the world for a man was self-denial. *Entbehren sollst du, sollst entbehren.* "You must deny yourself, must deny yourself." There is only one way to do this, and that is to practice it by a succession of acts until it becomes habitual. The great world teacher of this practice is and has always been religion. Sacrifice has been preached as the very essence of Christianity.

To many people it may seem as though mortification, that is, the practice of doing a series of things that are hard to do and even painful to accomplish, in order to increase one's power over oneself may be beneficial and even necessary for weak characters; but that surely strong men and women can dispense with any such artificial support of their personalities. Such an expression must probably be considered an excuse that enables people to escape the difficulties and self-denial of practices of mortification, but not at all as a real reason. Some of the strongest men who have ever lived have recognized the necessity for the insurance policies of little acts of supererogation that require real will power to accomplish in order to keep their strength of character at its top notch of efficiency. Probably few men in history have ever had a stronger character than Sir Thomas More. All his life he was noted for the absolute purity of his motives and the thoroughgoing righteousness of his life. He is the only man in the history of England who ever cleared the docket of the Court of Chancery. He was the first lay Lord Chancellor that England ever had. The opportunities for using his high office for his own benefit are well illustrated by the expression of Lord Campbell, who declared of More in his lives of the Lord Chancellors: "I am indeed reluctant to take leave of Sir Thomas More, not only from his agreeable qualities and extraordinary merits, but from my abhorrence of the mean, sordid, unprincipled chancellors who succeeded him and made the latter half of the reign of Henry VIII the most disgraceful period in our annals."

Nearly a hundred years after More's death when Lord Bacon was impeached by the English Parliament, he made as the excuse for having taken bribes that he was the best Lord Chancellor that England had had for fifty years. Very probably he was; no one knew that better than he. Yet Sir Thomas More had gone unscathed through the fire of temptations such as these to which every Lord Chancellor for a hundred years afterward yielded; but More went farther, and when it was a question of conscience he died for what he felt was the right. It did not matter to him that others had been able to compound with their consciences; he even told the jury that condemned him that he hoped to meet them in heaven, but right was right and even death was not too high a price to pay for its fulfillment. One of More's practices at times during his life had been the wearing of a hair shirt; even when in prison — and God knows the Tower of London, with the shadow of the scaffold hanging over it, would seem to be mortification enough — he wore his hair shirt, and it was found among his possessions after his death.

I suppose to-day, after a generation of contemptuous scoffing at mortification, it may be necessary to explain to many people what a hair shirt is. It is a very coarse undergarment woven of hair to be worn next the skin, and the discomfort of the skin surface is so great that until one gets a little used to it one can scarcely think of anything else except the constant irritation. It was a very common practice to wear it in the Middle Ages, and we have the story of one mother who felt that perhaps nothing would do her boys more good than to learn to stand something like this in order that they might be able to withstand youth's temptations. She was Mabel Rich, the mother of Edmund of Canterbury, who has come to be looked upon as one of the great characters of English history. For years he suffered in exile rather than give up to the king the rights of his people and the Church; this great scholar, professor of Oxford that he was and leader among men, who might have had all sorts of favors from the king had he yielded, spent fifteen years in poverty and hardships rather than yield a point of conscience. He tells that when he and his elder brother went off to the university, where they were to be gone for four or five years, their mother packed with their clothes a hair shirt for each of them. She asked them to wear them occasionally for her sake and to remember that they had to stand many things in life in order to keep on the right path. This London tradesman's wife of the early thirteenth century knew as well as any city mother in modern times the dangers her boys were going to encounter and which they would have to go through successfully or lose health of soul and body. There is apt to be a feeling in many minds that these problems have only come to be realized in our day, but that is due only to failure to project our knowledge of human nature into the past. Mabel Rich, like a good sensible mother, did not make an hysterical appeal that might cause her boys to feel her fear that they could not keep right, but she asked them, partly for her sake but mainly for religious motives, to submit to voluntary sufferings sometimes so that they might have the strength to bear any temptation that came to them. Edmund of Canterbury declared, toward the end of his life, that he owed more to his mother and her example and training for whatever his character had enabled him to accomplish in life than to any other single factor.

In the chapter on Purity I have quoted distinguished authorities in psychology who insist that the one way to strengthen the young man and the young woman against the allurements of impurity and thus help them to avoid the extremely serious dangers to health involved in yielding to such temptations is to have them practice self-denial in little things. Mortifications of one kind or another are to be undertaken, and the young folks build up self-control by the doing of things which are hard, though not obligatory, with the one idea of enabling them to perform even harder things in self-control whenever it may be necessary. There are some who seem to think that such practices may weaken men's powers of accomplishment, as if personality might be impaired by self-control, but there is no reason to think that.

Foerster, the well-known German writer on ethics, knowing well how much contempt has been thrown on asceticism in recent years, did not hesitate to say that the fear of weakness is all due to a misunderstanding. The ascetic is not a stunted human being who has mutilated himself, or prevented his development lest by any chance he might wander so far away from the path to his heavenly home that he might not get back. Asceticism has for its derivation the Greek verb ἀσκεῶ which means to exercise, — that is, not to decrease but to increase power. The ascetic exercises his will power so that he will be able to follow the straight path that he wants to tread, no matter how many difficulties present themselves to him.

No matter how steep the hills, he will not turn aside to the pleasanter paths that lead so gently downward because he wants to "carry on." Professor Foerster said: "Asceticism should be regarded, not as a negation of nature nor as an attempt to extirpate natural forces, but as practice in the art of self-discipline. Its object should be to show humanity what the human will is capable of performing, to serve as an encouraging example of the conquest of the spirit over the animal self. The contempt which has been poured upon the idea of asceticism in recent times has contributed more than anything else towards effeminacy. Nothing could be more effective in bringing humanity back to the best traditions of manhood than a respect for the spiritual strength and conquest which is symbolised in ascetic lives."

With regard to that anxiety of mothers to help their boys and girls in the very serious matter of sex temptation which has become so prominent a social feature in recent years, Foerster has a passage that is well worth putting before every mother:

"There are plenty of modern mothers who are aware of the necessity for instruction in matters relating to sex, and who are perhaps anxiously awaiting the suitable moment: it is a great deal more important, however, that they should make their children acquainted with what Sailer called 'the strategy of the Holy War', that they should train them every now and then to deny themselves some favourite article of food, or to accomplish some heroic conquest of indolence, or to practise themselves in ignoring pain.

"The outstanding feature of sexual education should not be an explanation of the sex functions, but an introduction to the inexhaustible power of the human spirit and its capacity for dominating the animal nature and controlling its demands."

Joseph de Maistre once said: "Everything that hinders a man strengthens him. Many a man of thirty years of age is capable of successfully resisting the allurements of a beautiful woman because at the age of five or six he was taught voluntarily to give up a toy or a sweet!"

Mortification in little things seems to many people too trivial in its effects to be of any real significance. If there is anything in the world that has been brought home to us in medicine in the modern era it is that little things count immensely. Microbes so small that we not only cannot see them, but never hope to be able to increase the powers of the microscope in such a way as to be able to get a sight of them, may cause the most serious epidemics. One of these ultramicroscopic microbes is probably the cause of infantile paralysis, which we know to have been in existence over five thousand years, because the mummy of a princeling of one of the early dynasties in Egypt shows that its possessor suffered from it as a child. Another of the ultramicroscopic microbes is perhaps the cause of influenza which carried off in a few months more victims among young people than the greatest war in human history did in over four years. No wonder that little things count in the moral order then, since they may mean so much in the physical order. Whenever anything affects living beings, then it cannot be counted small.

Four hundred years ago Michelangelo declared that "trifles make perfection, but perfection is no trifle." No one had a better right to an opinion in the matter than he, for he was the greatest sculptor since the time of the Greeks, one of the greatest architects who ever lived, perhaps the greatest decorative artist in all history, as the Sistine Chapel demonstrates, and he wrote sonnets of the highest quality. If in the mind of so supreme an artist soul little things count so much in making a great work of art, surely they must count for a very great deal in making a moral masterpiece, or anything that approaches it.

Michelangelo himself recognized over and over again in life what bearing the trials and troubles of existence might have on building up character for him and bringing him other than an earthly reward. He once said to one of the popes, "If these fatigues which I endure do not benefit my soul I lose both time and labor." There is a famous sonnet of his in which he begs pardon of his Crucified God if he had ever attributed to himself any of the glory which he ought to have given to his Maker. If ever a man lived who had the right to have some conceit of himself it was Michelangelo. When we look around and see the little whippets who have monumental conceit and then think of Michelangelo's deprecation of himself, it is easy to understand how he must have suppressed — or, as they said in the older time, mortified — his pride in order to keep his humility and not let any self-exultation run away with him.

Mortification in its true sense is indeed much more a question of the mind and the heart than of the body. Cultivating detachment from the things around us means more than anything else. This mortification of the spirit of man so that material possessions are not allowed to crowd out the genuine good things of life is particularly important. Nowadays people are so afraid to be poor, or indeed to lack anything that their neighbors have, that the principal efforts of life are expended in "keeping up with the Smiths", or with some other utterly insignificant people who happen to be making a display. I suppose that every physician in a large city has known people who actually denied themselves some of the necessaries of life in order to wear a little better clothes, and of course every physician everywhere sees people who deform their feet and disturb their organic health in other ways trying to keep up with the fashions. The fear of being thought to have less than other people and of having to deny oneself something that happens to be fashionable is particularly rife in our time and plays sad havoc with mental equanimity and with such satisfaction with life as is the best safeguard of continued health.

There was a time centuries ago, under the Roman Empire, when money had come to be as much thought of as in our own time, when the wealthy went down to Naples in the winter, up to Como in the summer, had a house at Ostia as well as a palace in Rome. It is easy to understand that the people then as now failed to comprehend how any one could possibly *choose* to be poor, even though thus he succeeded in putting off the cares of wealth and gave himself an opportunity to live his life for the sake of higher things.

Religion raised up men who went into voluntary poverty and restored the dignity of labor, when manual work had become almost a disgrace, by deliberately electing to occupy themselves with it for a certain number of hours a day. Their example proved very precious, and as it was mainly the young men who did it, they influenced deeply a series of generations. The sons of the nobility as well as of professional classes were represented among these reformers who believed first in reforming themselves, but along with them were young men of all classes, and the barriers between the classes were thus lowered. The cultivation of religious poverty proved the greatest kind of blessing in the social order and has always meant much for the amelioration of social conditions which it brings with it.

I suppose that the greatest possible benefit for health that could be conferred on mankind at the present time would come from the eradication of the mad strife for the possession of money which has taken possession of so many men's minds. Our recent Great War was precipitated by the struggle for markets and favored nations among whom to distribute surplus industrial products so that certain nations might go on piling up money. This is so badly distributed that serious social disorders are impending. Men spend their lives getting money and then leave it to their children, to hurt them physically and morally. They take away incentive, and they provide the greatest possible facilities for temptations. Justice Hughes said some years ago, when governor of New York, "The main occupation of men in our time seems to be the raising of a corruption fund for their children."

We need some of that poverty of spirit which Christianity brought in with it when it was so sadly needed and which was cultivated with so much success during the later Middle Ages, when the great scholars and saintly characters who most deeply influenced the times were mainly members of the mendicant orders, that is, of associations of men who refused to own any possessions in order that they might have the time to devote themselves to higher things and who depended on the work of their hands and the beneficence of the public to enable them to continue their work. Their motto was plain living and high thinking, and it is surprising how much they accomplished. The spirit which made St. Francis of Assisi choose the Lady Poverty for his bride and delight to call himself *Il poverello di Dio*, "the little poor man of God", would seem to be entirely too impracticable and utterly idealistic to have any interest for our time, and yet literally more than a score of important lives of St. Francis have been written during our generation. We are beginning to wake up to the realization of the fact that "things are in the saddle and ride mankind", and that things seem ever so much more important than thoughts, though it requires no special intelligence to understand what an utter contradiction of real values any such state of mind represents.

What is now needed above all is such detachment from the things around us that we shall be poor in spirit. This is the element above all that religion supplies. In the Sermon on the Mount, that greatest sermon ever preached, the Master said, "Blessed are the poor in spirit, for theirs is the kingdom of heaven." Certainly there is no straighter road to heavenly peace than that, for a man may have great possessions and yet be poor in spirit because he is detached from them and has mortified his feelings with regard to them so that they do not puff him up and make him vain (what striking old Saxon words those are), so that he is able to use them not for himself alone but for the benefit of the community.

The expression "poor in spirit" is not popular in our time and has often been spoken of contemptuously. There are some who think that actual poverty, as well as poverty of spirit, has a paralyzing effect on human incentive, but it is well to realize that there are a good many serious thinkers in our generation who do not agree with this impression but on the contrary feel that detachment from temporal goods may well prove a source of the highest and best stimulation to the accomplishment of what is really worth while in life. Some of them express themselves rather strongly on the subject, and perhaps no one has stated his mind more emphatically with regard to it than Professor William James, who did not hesitate to declare just when money had come to be apparently the most important thing in modern life:

"Among us English-speaking peoples especially do the praises of poverty need once more to be boldly sung. We have grown literally afraid to be poor. We despise any one who elects to be poor in order to simplify and save his inner life. If he does not join the general scramble and pant with the money-making street, we deem him spiritless and lacking in ambition. We have lost the power even of imagining what the ancient idealization of poverty could have meant: the liberation from material attachments; the unbribed soul, the manlier indifference; the paying our way by what we are or do and not by what we have; the right to fling away our life at any moment irresponsibly — the more athletic trim, in short, the moral fighting shape. When we of the so-called better classes are scared as men were never scared in history at material ugliness and hardship; when we put off marriage until our house can be artistic, and quake at the thought of having a child without a bank account, it is time for thinking men to protest against so unmanly and irreligious a state of opinion. . . . I recommend this matter to your serious pondering, for it is certain that the prevalent fear of poverty among the educated classes is the worst moral disease from which our civilization suffers."

All the great religions have preached mortification. Some of them have made it apparently of value in itself as working merit, but this was practically always an abuse of the original idea that a man learned to control himself by practicing hard things. Our generation resents even the term "hard things" and does not like to hear "hard sayings", though even that gentlest of human beings, the Divine Master, felt that He had to use them. There can be no doubt at all, however, about the benefit to be derived from enduring hard things. Every trainer who hopes to have a winning team in any department of athletics knows that he has to put them through hard things in order to enable them to acquire power and make their energies available when they are needed. Somehow people do not seem to realize that exactly the same thing is necessary with regard to training of the will as for training of the muscles, and that indeed training of the muscles is of itself effective largely because of the training of the will connected with it which makes the nervous system capable of reacting according to the desires of the individual.

While we are so intent on making things easy for the young, let us not forget that the best authorities on the subject of man's development of his powers so as to make them available for life's purposes are practically all agreed that the most important element in the formation of character — and on character depends destiny — is the having to go through hard things when one is young. In the chapter on Suffering I have quoted Thucydides in this matter and its approval by Gladstone and John Morley in our own time. We hear much of a favorable environment for young folks but most of what is so called represents the worst possible set of influences for the development of character.

Professor Conklin of Princeton, in his volume on "Heredity and Environment," which consists of lectures delivered on the Harris Foundation of the Northwestern University and afterwards at Princeton, and which therefore must be taken to represent the scientific thought of our time, does not hesitate to say:

"How often is it said that the worthless sons of worthy parents are mysteries; with the best of heredity and environment they amount to nothing, whereas the sons of poor and ignorant farmers, blacksmiths, tanners and backwoodsmen, with few opportunities and with many hardships and disadvantages, become world figures. Probably the inheritance in these last-named cases was no better than in the former, but the environment was better. 'Good environment' usually means easy, pleasant, refined surroundings, 'all the opportunities that money can buy', but little responsibility and none of that self-discipline which reveals the hidden powers and which alone should be counted good environment. Many schools and colleges are making the same mistake as the fond parents; luxury, soft living, irresponsibility are not only allowed, but are encouraged and endowed — and by such means it is hoped to bring out that in men which can only be born in travail."

Above all, mortification, that is, the suppressing of the natural inclinations, must be practiced for health's sake as regards the bearing of ills that have to be suffered anyhow, and in the forbearance from passion when that would certainly prove physically disturbing. "Bear and forbear" has been sometimes set down as the most important formula for life, and it is certainly as valuable for the physical as for the moral side of humanity. The repression of the natural tendencies is an extremely valuable practice for the prevention of the many excesses which have so much to do with the undermining of health. The man who controls himself and compels his instincts to submit to correction and modification, even when that is unnecessary, so far as any serious consideration is concerned, will surely find himself in a position to resist natural proclivities to evil which may easily be serious from the standpoint of health, whenever they assert themselves.

Austerity is supposed to be old-fashioned and out of date, but all those who want to get anything really worth while done in the world know that they must deny themselves and their inclinations and work out their ideas in lonely vigil and by hard work. Nothing that is easy counts. When men do things that will be remembered they have devoted themselves whole-heartedly to them to the exclusion of more attractive occupations.

Matthew Arnold, in his splendid sonnet on Austerity as the poet must practice it, has brought this out very forcibly. He tells the story of Jaccpone da Todi, the author of the Stabat Mater, who, on his wedding day, saw his bride of the morning killed by the fall of a stand at a spectacle and found beneath her bridal robes a penitential garment. He was so deeply impressed that he became a Franciscan and subsequently the author of the famous hymn. Certainly pathos was never more wondrously expressed than by this man whose own austerities, initiated by the example of his beloved bride, made him ready to strip himself of every trivial interest in the cult of the eternal verities.

"That son of Italy who tried to blow,
Ere Dante came, the trump of sacred song,
In his light youth amid a festal throng
Sate with his bride to see a public show.
Fair was the bride, and on her front did glow
Youth like a star; and what to youth belong —
Gay raiment, sparkling gauds, elation strong.
A prop gave way! crash fell a platform! lo,
'Mid struggling sufferers, hurt to death, she lay!
Shuddering, they drew her garments off — and found
A robe of sackcloth next the smooth, white skin.
Such, poets, is your bride, the Muse! young, gay,
Radiant, adorn'd, outside; a hidden ground
Of thought and of austerity within."

So far from mortification being in any sense of the word an old-fashioned, worn-out practice, good enough for the foolish people of the dark ages who had nothing better to think of, it is, in so far as it brings about training of the will and exercise in self-denial and self-control, the most important element in education at all times. We have unfortunately been neglecting it, but that neglect is the real trouble with our modern education. Nearly every one who talks about education has some mental panacea for it; but the trouble lies deeper than that. It is the education of the will that has unfortunately been neglected and that requires, to cite once more the Century definition, the subduing of appetites, even though painful severities should have to be inflicted on the body.

Huxley, in his address on "A Liberal Education; and Where to Find It", delivered before the South London Workingmen's College, has a passage in which he brings this out very well. Almost needless to say Huxley was the farthest possible from being medievally minded, and yet he placed the essence of a liberal education in will power over self rather than in intellectual development, or above all the accumulation of information. He said:

"That man, I think, has had a liberal education who has been so trained in youth that his body is the ready servant of his will, and does with ease and pleasure all the work that, as a mechanism, it is capable of; whose intellect is a clear, cold, logic engine, with all its parts of equal strength and in smooth working order; ready, like a steam engine, to be turned to any kind of work and spin the gossamers as well as forge the anchors of the mind; whose mind is stored with a knowledge of the great and fundamental truths of nature and of the laws of her operations; one who, no stunted ascetic, is full of life and fire, but whose passions are trained to come to heel by a vigorous will, the servant of a tender conscience; who has learned to love all beauty, whether of nature or of art, to hate all vileness, and to respect others as himself.

"Such an one and no other, I conceive, has had a liberal education; for he is, as completely as a man can be, in harmony with nature."

CHAPTER IX

EXCESSES

THE most important rule of conduct for health is the avoidance of excesses of any and every kind. Men have recognized this fact for as long as the memory of the race runs. The instruction of Ptah Hotep, the letter of advice from a father to his son, written by the vizier of King Itosi in the fifth dynasty in Egypt, something over five thousand years ago, which is often called the oldest book in the world, emphasizes particularly the necessity for the avoidance of excess in all things. Self-control and self-denial are held up as the highest attributes of man. One of the seven wise men of Greece adopted as his contribution to the wisdom of mankind "avoid excess." A favorite maxim of the Romans was *ne quid nimis*, "let there be nothing too much"; and another favorite expression of theirs was *in medio tutissimus ibis*, "you will go most safely if you follow the mean" (and not either extreme).

The most powerful factor for securing the avoidance of excess among men has always been religion. The four cardinal virtues are prudence, justice, fortitude and temperance, and the last is considered by no means the least. Almost needless to say, by temperance was meant not only abstinence from excessive drinking and eating, but that moderation and self-control in all things which the ancients recognized as the most important factor in human life, and which religion, trying to perfect nature by grace, set forth as one of the cardinal or "hinge" qualities on which the whole of a good life swings. When reason and not impulse, when virtue and not passion, when strength of character and not weakness rule a man's life, the motives which impel him or, as we would rather say in our modern knowledge of psychology, stimulate him to action and enable him to accomplish what he desires in so important a matter are drawn much oftener from religion than from any other source.

Religion has done more than anything else to make people rational in their lives and not merely the sport of their impulses and instincts. Men are animals, but possessed of reason, though reason can be obscured to a great extent or even almost completely eclipsed by the impulses that arise from the lower nature of man. Religion has above all helped to make men think of others who are so often hurt by their unreason rather than themselves, and has helped to keep them from self-indulgence.

Abernethy, the distinguished surgeon who impressed himself so deeply on the history of medicine in London at the beginning of the nineteenth century, was accustomed to say that the two great killing powers in the world are stuff and fret, — in a word, eating too much and worrying about things, most of which will never happen. Satisfying the desires of mankind and fostering their dreads will do more to wear out life before its time than anything else. Religion represents the ever present signpost pointing away from travel in either of these directions. Men do not heed her warnings very often until they have gone so far on the road of life that some of their powers have been lost because of their neglect, but at least they can recognize then that the signposts are always in place, and that they saw them, and that it was their own fault if they did not follow them.

Homer, three thousand years ago, told the poetic story of the men who had been turned into swine by Circe and who, though swine, knew that they were men, but could not get back to the use of their reason. The similitude lies so close that it is perfectly clear that the idea behind the old myth of the goddess who invited men to share swinish pleasures and secured such control over them that they could not get back their reason again was the goddess of lubricity. Ulysses himself had to abstain from the indulgence that had captivated his men, and then he had to come to their assistance with the herb *moly* which, revealed to him by one of the gods, enabled him to turn Circe's victims back to men again. The old Fathers of the Church used to emphasize the fact that this herb *moly* represented grace, for without divine assistance it is almost impossible for men who have given themselves over to the pleasures of the body to win back self-control again. Men may recognize their unfortunate state yet be unable to set themselves right. No wonder the Church Fathers proclaimed the story as told by Homer to be one of the prefigurements of Christian symbol which showed that the old poet was, in a certain way at least, a messenger from celestial powers carrying on the tradition of Providence in the world.

It is a commonplace among physicians that the so-called pleasures of life indulged in to excess are much more prone to be followed by ill health than is the hard work of existence, no matter how apparently trying the work may be. We hear much of hard work shortening life and of bringing on states of exhaustion in which health is at a low ebb, but physicians find it very difficult to collect cases that illustrate any such effects of hard work. Some of our hardest workers, men who have devoted themselves to half a dozen different difficult tasks with an ardor that made other men wonder how they could possibly stand it, have lived to even advanced old age. I have personally known about a dozen physicians who lived to eighty-five or beyond, and all of them without exception had been very hard workers when they were young. Distinguished generals often live to a good old age; though not infrequently they have been shot to pieces when they were young, wounded a number of times during life, yet, like Lord Roberts, Sir Evelyn Wood and Von Moltke, they have lived well beyond eighty years of age, active and capable until the very end.

The ill-effect of hard work is a fetish created by people who are themselves afraid of hard work. Hard play has killed many more men than hard work. Concentrated efforts to compress into life all the possible pleasure that one can secure will break a man down sooner than anything else in the world. Such a breakdown is usually thorough and seldom is followed by complete and enduring recovery. Hard physical work, on the contrary, performed under any reasonably favorable circumstances, is a factor conducive to health and strength and long life, and this is particularly true if it is accomplished in the open. The devotee of pleasure is notably short-lived. Work, according to the Scriptural expression, was imposed as a curse on man, but it has been very well said, "if when the Lord curses they turn to blessings this way, what must it not be when He blesses?" No wonder that we say, "Blessed is the man who has found his work." The more experience a man has had, the more he recognizes this truth. Work is one of the most precious resources for men in the world, while pleasure, unless carefully guarded from excess, can be the worst of curses. Though so costly, so much sought after and so often even looked forward to as the reward for work, pleasure is but seldom satisfying and is often followed by remorse which proves disturbing to both mind and body. The deterioration of constitution brought about by the physical consequences of pleasures indulged in to excess must be counted among the most serious factors for ill health to which humanity is subject.

Doctor Carroll, in his "Mastery of Nervousness", says very well, "the danger of overwork is far less common than that of underwork. . . . Close observation brings the conviction that the great majority claiming overwork as the reason for their nervous deficiency are the victims not of earnest productive work itself but of defective methods of work discounted by haste, stress and strain, by impatience, worry and fear." In a word nervous breakdown, when it comes to a busy man or woman, is due ever so much more to the irritable state of mind into which they get in the midst of their press of work than to the work itself. The feeling of haste is ever so much more dangerous than the actual hurry. The mistakes that are made under these circumstances are great wasters of time and of energy and disturbers of morale, until a feeling of impotence grows on one and then becomes inveterate. As a matter of fact a great many people who break down do so not during the stress of work but afterwards, when they have the leisure to look back on it and think about it and wonder why they did not break down, and while their friends keep sympathizing with them and they have the chance to let their self-pity cause the crumpling of their character.

Premature old age, that is, the precocious hardening of the arteries, for "a man is as old as his arteries", came particularly, the older physicians used to say, to the devotees of the three pagan deities, Venus, Bacchus and Vulcan. That is, senility came before it was due in the order of nature to those who indulged in venery or in wine and its almost inevitable accompaniment, overeating, and then to the man who did such hard physical work as the blacksmith does, for Vulcan, it may be recalled, was the blacksmith among the gods. In this enumeration two out of three of the factors unfavorable for health come from the pleasures of life; but I think there is no doubt in the minds of physicians that if a comparison in the number of patients whose ailments were the consequences of the worship of the deities named were to be made, there would be found ten times as many men who became prematurely old or suffered from the development of organic affections because of wine and venereal disease as from hard physical labor.

Aneurysm is the one form of arterial degeneration to which the hard worker is particularly liable, and the more we have learned of that the more we have come to realize very clearly that while the hard work was the immediate occasion, the real underlying cause of the degeneration of arteries that led to the development of the aneurysm was to be found in some overindulgence. The French physicians sometimes said satirically that overwork of the heart much more than of the head or the hands laid the foundation on which aneurysm developed, for it occurs oftenest on a luetic basis.

Practically all the degenerative diseases affecting heart, arteries, kidneys and brain are due to excesses. The excesses of life are counted by religion among the deadly sins. Pride, anger, covetousness, lust, gluttony, envy and sloth, — all these represent indulgence in evil passions that very readily affect the body. Religion has constantly used all its influence to overcome them and has succeeded better than any other single factor in life. It is perfectly possible to have a veneer of religion and be a miser or a glutton or a very devil of pride, but real religion of the heart, while it does not eradicate the tendency that exists in human nature toward these unfortunate qualities, helps the possessor of them materially to control them and to keep his passions in subjection.

In this control of excesses religion has been an extremely important factor for health. It is true that many other factors, human respect, worldly consideration, preservation of one's own dignity and similar non-religious factors have had a like influence. Occasionally indeed it would seem as though mere respectability had more to do with preventing men and women from making exhibitions of themselves by the public commission of sin than even religion itself. This would appear to be surely true if different strata of society were compared with each other. If, for instance, the working classes who practice their religion and the better-to-do classes who perhaps neglect it were to be compared in these regards, the contrast would favor the latter as a rule, but any such comparison would be eminently odious. There is no doubt that mere human motives can be effective, but the value of religion should be gauged from its effect on people who are living in the same circumstance. The vast majority of the very poor have found religion a sheet anchor of veritable salvation under circumstances where sin would have been not only not a disadvantage but actually have proved of material benefit to them. While, on the other hand, many a well-to-do person lacking religion has fallen into sin in spite of the fact that every human motive spoke emphatically against their commission of it.

Religion has been particularly helpful in the neutralization of temptations to excess in the matter of alcoholic liquor. Father Matthew's great crusade in Ireland, England and this country enlisted millions of people under the banner of temperance and helped marvelously in enabling the world to understand that the serious evils connected with the liquor traffic were by no means inevitable, but could be repressed to a great extent by simple personal appeals which called to the manhood of men and made them understand their own power to throw off the shackles of what to them seemed an unconquerable habit by a serious act of the will. The immense amount of suffering that was thus saved to the women and children of men who had been accustomed to drink a considerable portion or sometimes practically all of their wages and leave their families to get on as best they might is almost incalculable.

A still more important result of Father Matthew's work was the demonstration that men who are the victims of even such a habit and craving as that which is produced by indulgence in liquor may break it completely by a single powerful act of the will, when to that is added the strong suggestion that they will surely be helped by divine favor to accomplish what they have purposed. Literally hundreds of thousands of men under Father Matthew's inspiration, and touched by the example of others around them, broke off once and for all from liquor habits to which they had been enslaved sometimes for years.

Professor William James in his essay on the "Energies of Men" first published in the *American Magazine* under the title of "Powers of Men" (October, 1907) — it was originally the presidential address delivered before the American Philosophical Association and therefore written not for popular reading, but as a serious contribution to science — has on this, as on many other subjects, a paragraph that is valuable in this regard. It is not only interesting but is eminently suggestive with regard to the effect that can be produced on a man by deep emotion, and when that emotion is based on profound religious feeling it can be not only immediate but extremely enduring in its effect. This is what proved to be the case for the vast majority of those who took the pledge from Father Matthew.

Professor James said: "The normal opener of deeper and deeper levels of energy is the will. The difficulty is to use it, to make the effort which the word volition implies. But if we do make it (or if a god, though he were only the god Chance, makes it through us), it will act dynamogenically on us for a month. It is notorious that a single successful effort of moral volition, such as saying 'no' to some habitual temptation, or performing some courageous act will launch a man on a higher level of energy for days and weeks, will give him a new range of power. 'In the act of uncorking the whiskey bottle which I had brought home to get drunk upon,' said a man to me, 'I suddenly found myself running out into the garden, where I smashed it on the ground. I felt so happy and uplifted after this act, that for two months I wasn't tempted to touch a drop.'"

Nothing is so capable of giving a fillip to a sluggish will, arousing it to efforts that even its possessor never dreamt it capable of, as religion. The change of life known as conversion has not infrequently revolutionized an existence that seemed hopelessly and helplessly committed to the baser aims of living. Instances are in every one's experience, and the veriest self-missioned exhorter has many of them to his credit.

Religion has listed temperance among the four cardinal virtues, and though it is usually named the last — prudence, justice, fortitude and temperance — it is considered by no means the least in importance, and the cardinal virtues, as the etymology of their descriptive epithet signifies, are literally the "hinge virtues" on which the religious life depends. Religion has not, however, ever favored that complete prohibition of the use of the milder alcoholic beverages which have such a definite place in life. Life is, as a rule, too hard a thing for most people without the opportunity for escape from the tension of existence represented by mild alcoholic stimulation. At the very beginning of Christianity Paul advised his disciple Timothy to take a little wine for the stomach's sake, and in this religion is only helping nature, provided there is no abuse, for natural digestion is accompanied by the production of a certain amount of dilute alcohol. Absolute prohibition of very natural indulgences that are not in themselves wrong is so likely to be followed by a reaction in the opposite direction that abuses are almost sure to occur. Temperance and not prohibition represents the true religious aspect of this question.

Unfortunately very serious abuses had followed the interesting developments of modern human ingenuity in the making of strong liquors. Natural processes only make liquors of various kinds that do no harm unless taken in great excess and that have a very special place in the human economy. From the abuses no argument holds against the use, but it was the very reaction produced in religious minds against the serious associations of the drink traffic that led to the enactment of laws against it. In themselves they represent a great benefit for humanity, for it is perfectly sure that we shall never want the saloon back again, nor the free consumption of strong alcoholic liquors which are not stimulants but narcotics and have done not so much physical harm as moral harm. They have caused the workman to neglect his family and bring them very often to the point of starvation; they have filled our jails, have made the need for charity greater than it would otherwise be; have fomented passion and only too often encouraged vice, and we must never have them back. Even the exaggerated religious reaction has done great positive good, and when it settles down to moderation in prohibitive laws we will set a magnificent example for the rest of the world, the first hints of which are already manifest.

What is true for the alcoholic craving can be just as true for addictions of all kinds and particularly for drug addictions. In our day a great crusade is needed for the relief of this evil, for in spite of efforts at repression, drug addictions are growing in frequency rather than decreasing. We have tried to use material repressive measures and have failed. It is time for us to realize that there remain moral and religious motives, appeal to which can produce almost incredibly strong effects. These can prove effective against many of the most unfortunate habits of mankind which are likely to turn out extremely deleterious to health if persisted in. Religion can thus be a source of power — virtue is the word the Romans used for this and its full form is not translated by our English word virtue any more — to help in the neutralization of human tendencies more prone than any others to shorten life or be the origin of serious disease.

It would be too bad to reduce religion to the rôle of merely a scavenger of bad habits, a sweeper up of the unconsidered trifles which if allowed to act tend to the deterioration of physical existence, but what happens when religion does bring about improvement in the victims of these unfortunate habits is that a great new incentive is given to life, and men, realizing what they have been rescued from, may now turn the new energies they have found to great purposes. Some of these at least have learned to devote themselves unstintedly to work for others which proves a source of the greatest possible good. How many a rescued drunkard has, after reform, given himself whole-heartedly to helping others out of various unfortunate conditions in which both body and soul were being pulled down to the very lowest that was in them. Some of these "rescued" ones for twenty or more years devoted themselves, in the midst of what might have seemed almost inevitably compelling temptations to their former habits, to the care for others until their names became household words in the great cities of their time because of the good they were accomplishing. Jerry Macaulay was an example of this that New York will not soon forget, but we have had many humbler fellow workers of his.

The human will, stimulated by religious motives, can change the whole course of man's life when his character would seem to have made it inevitable that this could not be changed for the better. How true the maxim of conduct in life is: "plant an act and reap a habit; plant a habit and reap a character; plant a character and reap a destiny." What seemed the almost unescapable destiny of many men has been changed by the influence of religion over habits, so that a natural disposition which by habit had become a personality fraught with evil for self and others has been changed into an individual that proves an asset instead of a liability to the community.

Not only in the matter of substances harmful in themselves, but in those which though good and even necessary when taken in moderation, yet are greatly harmful when consumed in excess, the regulations of religion have been particularly helpful to mankind. Fasting has been encouraged and indeed set down as an absolute obligation for all those who are in health. Mortification, that is, self-denial with regard to things that people like very much, was counseled and the counsels so often repeated that people were almost sure to practice some of them and many were taken quite seriously to heart. Moderation in eating was advised at all times, and any serious excess set down as gluttony, one of the seven deadly sins. How much the religious counsels against excess may be needed nowadays even with regard to things quite harmless or even valuable for mankind will perhaps be best appreciated from the present status of sugar consumption in the world. One hundred and twenty-five years ago a few thousand tons of sugar supplied all the needs of mankind. Now nearly twenty-five million of tons are scarcely sufficient to maintain prices for the commodity at a level low enough so that people may continue to buy it in the quantities they desire.

Sugar is an artificial product made from starchy substances, not unlike alcohol in certain ways and capable of doing at least as much physical harm as alcohol. There are at the present time half a million people in this country who either have now or will have before they die, diabetes. This is a serious disease; when it occurs under thirty it is practically always fatal. Under forty it may shorten life seriously. It always greatly weakens the individual and makes him subject to certain other serious diseases. We need self-control in the use of sugar; the habit of taking it grows on one.

The use of sugar and milk in tea and coffee is an occidental abuse that the orientals who originally began the drinking of these substances find it extremely difficult to understand. Tea with milk and sugar in it a Chinaman would be likely to think of as sweetened milk soup. The reason for adding milk and sugar was to cover up the defective qualities in poor tea or coffee, or mistakes in their making by which certain bitter astringent principles not meant to be in solution had their taste covered up by the sweet milkiness. The habit of using tea without sugar often formed by the practice of a little mortification would probably result in more good than merely the absence of the sugar.

Every one of the seven deadly sins represents excesses in bodily or mental propensities against which religion set up the attitude of utter disapproval and pointed out their inevitable tendency to part a man from what was best in him. Teaching children from their early years that pride, covetousness, lust, anger, gluttony, envy and sloth were serious offenses made for an early realization of the necessity for guarding against them. All of them represent extremely unfavorable factors for health. Pride goes before a fall, and the disappointments which it almost inevitably brings with it represent more occasions for depression and melancholic tendencies than almost anything else. The inordinate desire for money has brought down on many a man serious nervous prostration. With regard to lust and its awful consequences to health nothing need be said here, and not much needs to be said even in the chapter on Purity. We have had its baneful effects dinned into our ears particularly in recent years. Anger is not so serious, and yet many an older man especially has shortened his life quite materially by giving away to ungovernable bursts of temper. Nervous people who do not control their tempers often suffer from serious lack of nerve control as a consequence of their lapses of temper. Gluttony has already been touched on and needs no illustration as to its extremely bad effect on health. Envy often makes most of the functions of the body perform their work incompletely because nothing so disturbs even such apparently purely physical functions as digestion and nutritional metabolism generally as the wearing of a grouch. The grouchy man almost never digests well and quite inevitably his state of mind interferes with other functions. Little need be said about sloth and its effect upon health but the fact that from the very earliest times religion has pointed out that the mere doing of nothing could of itself become a serious, even capital offense, for a healthy person represented an excellent stimulus to that activity of mind and body which is so important for health. It is only lately that we have come to realize how dangerous a remedy rest may be, to be prescribed with great care, for it is a habit-producing remedy nearly as risky as opium and never to be prescribed on any general principles. There has been ten times as much harm done to health by rest as by vigorous exercise or even hard work. The hard workers are nearly all long lived, but the sons and daughters of rest pass away from the scene, not of their labors, but of their languors, rather early, as a rule.

Religion then has been an extremely valuable factor for the control of excesses, or at least for their limitation, and thus has been of great significance for health. Religious counsels and prohibitions have not entirely prevented excesses even in those who were adherents of religion, for man is so constituted that it is not quite possible to have all men follow the wiser course. Even the best of men have to confess, like St. Paul, that sometimes, though they know the better path, they follow the worse. If to do good were as easy as it is to know what it is good to do, life would be a much simpler matter. Not knowledge, but will power is needed, and religious practice builds this up and strengthens the will so that it is able to resist many temptations that would otherwise prove difficult to surmount. The contest between good and evil has gone on in spite of religion, and will go on, but there is no doubt at all that evil would have accomplished much more of harm only for the help that religion has been to mankind, and this has been particularly manifest in the limitation of the excesses which so often prove detrimental to health.

The old saw of English tradition which in some form or other is many centuries old is well worth recalling in this regard.

> "Virtue, temperance and repose
> Slam the door on the doctor's nose."

We hear much of the vicious circles that are formed by which things go from worse to worse, one unfavorable factor helping on another, but we forget apparently that there are virtuous circles according to which "all things work together for good." This means good not only for the soul and the mind, but also for the body and for health. Religion makes for health and health promotes religion, and the virtuous circle is completed.

CHAPTER X

PURITY

NOTHING has worked so much detriment to the health of mankind for many centuries as the habits that may be generalized under the term impurity. Until recent years it has been the custom to suppress the knowledge of the immense physical evil that was being worked to humanity by the venereal diseases. A generation ago it was only imperfectly known, but now we recognize that no set of diseases are more important for the race and its health than those which usually occur as the direct result of violations of the moral code. Their ravages have increased just in proportion to the gradual diminution of the influence of religion during the past few generations. They have probably worked greater havoc on the better classes than on the poorer classes. There are nations like the Irish, over whom religion has a strong hold, in which the injury worked by these diseases has been almost negligible. There have been classes of men like the clergymen, deeply under the influence of religion, who have escaped almost entirely the awful, destructive effects of these affections. We have only just waked up to the realization of how much this element of conduct, so profoundly influenced by religion, has meant for suffering and death among men.

In spite of the fact that there was a conspiracy of silence with regard to the venereal diseases, something of their fearful effectiveness in adding to mortality lists came to be known, at least by those who were interested in the subject, a generation ago. Though every possible excuse was taken not to list death as due to these diseases during the twenty-five years before nineteen hundred, when, just after the smug mid-Victorian period, the conspiracy of silence was at its highest and was particularly hide-bound in England, no less than sixty thousand deaths from venereal disease were registered by the English registrar general. Nearly twenty-five thousand of these were females. Over two thousand deaths a year is a pretty heavy toll, but such statistics give only the very faintest hint of the awful ravages of these diseases. It is not alone death that occurs as a consequence of them but long years of suffering and crippling of various kinds, the blinding of children and the birth of dead or idiotic children, or of other poor little ones who grow up to be epileptic or to become insane in early adult life, or to exhibit other sad marks of the diseases of their parents.

Civil statistics of these diseases mean very little, especially in English-speaking countries, because of our prudery with regard to them. Army medical statistics, however, have had to be rigorously kept because of the amount of military inefficiency due to these affections. The statistics of the last generation in England show that it was not an unusual thing for nearly one in four of the soldiers in a regiment to be admitted to the hospital each year because of venereal disease. Actually nearly one in five of the effective strength of regiments was constantly in a hospital because of these diseases. It is improbable that soldiers are notably more immoral than civilians of the same class, except that perhaps there has been in the army a tradition of greater contempt for these affections. So far as large cities are concerned, many good medical authorities are convinced that the average young men of the population suffer to about the same extent as soldiers. Actually something more than three out of five in the English army suffered at some time from these diseases, and as they are extremely difficult to cure and often continue to have serious effects for years, as well as being contagious for others, we get some idea of what an immense amount of harm has been worked by them.

It might possibly be thought that conditions in America were better than in Europe in this regard, but our experience during the war did not justify any such optimism. Nearly six per cent of the men mobilized for the army in the United States actually showed signs of these diseases when they were admitted for examination on arrival in camp. This percentage does not include those who had been cured prior to their examination. From some of the cities of this country the proportion of young men actually suffering at the time of their enlistment from these diseases was more than one in ten, and from certain of the southern cities it actually approached very close to one in five. According to the statement of the Surgeon General of the War Department, diseases due to impurity constituted the greatest cause of disability in the army. When the physicians were given the opportunity to make a more careful examination of the second million of the draft than had been possible for the first, the percentage of diseased men ran up notably, in spite of the fact that warnings in the matter led a great many of those who were drafted to seek proper treatment before presenting themselves at the camps.

We have waked up at last to something like the full significance of these diseases in the destruction of the race.

The American Social Hygiene Association in its Publication No. 250, " Conquering an Old Enemy ", dared to tell the story of these affections very straightforwardly. There are many physicians connected with this association and its opinions are thoroughly conservative and not at all hysterical. We get a striking idea of the destructiveness of these diseases from an early paragraph of the publication:

" In these United States and in this year of peace 1920, more lives than the whole empire of Great Britain lost during any year of the Great War will be flicked out by two diseases which are curable and preventable diseases. Nor will the year 1920 stand alone. In the four and a half years of intensive warfare between 1914 and 1918, the fifteen civilized nations which fought at Armageddon gave to these twin scourges a heavier toll than they did to bullets, shells, gas, air-bombs, all the ghastly, wholesale killers of modern battle."

The more important of these diseases is estimated by authorities to kill annually in the United States more than 300,000 people. It is far more deadly than tuberculosis and carries off every year nearly, if not quite, as many lives as influenza at the height of its epidemicity. France lost during the four years and four months of Armageddon 1,350,000 lives in battle. We lost almost as many during the same time from this affection which a few years ago we were ostrich-like hiding from ourselves by refusing to look at it. The other of these affections is probably responsible for more serious suffering in women and female complaints that require operation as well as blindness in children than any other single factor that we have in modern life. There is no element that has so seriously interfered with the simple joys of existence, the raising of children and family life in peace and happiness, as this affection.

When it is realized how many complications and sequelae may develop from these diseases, but above all how much harm may be done to innocent wives and children, some notion of the suffering that has thus been inflicted on mankind will be obtained. The one significant factor in the control of this source of ill health has been religion. Just in proportion as religion has lost its hold over the rising generation, there has been a marked increase in this particular mode of ill health. The only effective brake on human passion has been religious feeling, but above all religious training. If religion had done nothing else than limit to a noteworthy extent the irregular living consequent upon yielding to passion, that would be sufficient of itself to make not only personal but community health greatly indebted to religion. Other motives have at times been appealed to and sometimes with apparently good results for the time being, but never with any enduring effectiveness against the flood tide of feeling which comes over those who have had no practice in self-repression and who have not learned to appeal to the higher motives to help them in this matter.

For a great many young men, "sowing their wild oats" has been sowing a crop of seeds whose products have meant the ruination of their own lives, but unfortunately also only too often of the lives of their future wives and their unborn children. We know now that the great majority of all the blind children in our blind asylums owe their blindness to one of these venereal affections. Three out of five at least of the imbeciles and epileptics in our institutions derive their mental trouble from the other of these diseases. We hear a good deal about young folks "seeing life", but for many the process which has been thus lightly glossed over should be described literally as "seeing death."

Since the unfortunate breakdown of religion to a considerable extent in the last few generations and its tendency to change into a mere social influence at most, there has been a great increase in the prevalence of these diseases. Some of this is undoubtedly due to our modern city life and its temptations, but the individual attitude toward life means more. St. Theresa said, "When the individual is well grounded in faith, the temptation means little." An attempt has been made to control the power of temptations and repress the passions of men by other means. Above all, knowledge of the awful sex disease dangers which they were running has been turned to as a hopeful remedy in this matter. It was thought that young folks could be terrified by the knowledge of the hideous possible consequences of their acts into avoiding the lapses which occasion them.

In spite of the fact that practically all of our prominent psychologists have opposed any such method as this, a great many people who have very little right to an opinion have insisted that this policy must be followed in our schools. There is probably nothing that could do more harm than this. The diffusion of the knowledge of the immense amount of serious, even fatal, disease consequent upon sex irregularities suddenly thrust upon the world has made a great many people a little hysterical and has tempted them to turn to remedies which are not only not likely to be helpful but are almost sure to be vicious in their consequences. It is like finding that a child has swallowed some poison and in the excitement administering another with the vague hope that one may neutralize the other.

Professor Foerster of the department of psychology and ethics at the University of Munich does not hesitate to say that such teaching is sure to do harm and not good. He has suggested that "in making use of the intellect to restrain sex instincts there is every danger of the intellect itself, through excessive familiarization with details of such knowledge, being captured and employed in the service of the enemy." He praises the older teachers, "The great educators of the past who have all been instinctively aware of this truth and have hence strongly insisted on the importance of cultivating a sense of shame; for they have realized that the chief task of sexual education is not to attract the attention of the young to sex matters, but as far as possible to distract them from it."

Professor Münsterberg of Harvard University took very strong ground against the teaching of sex hygiene in public schools and stated his opinion quite as emphatically as Professor Foerster that such teaching, even though it be given with the best of intentions, is sure to do much more harm than good. He said: "The cleanest boy and girl cannot give theoretical attention to the thoughts concerning sexuality without the whole mechanism for reinforcement automatically entering into action. We may instruct with the best intention to suppress, and yet our instruction itself must become a source of stimulation which unnecessarily creates a desire for improper conduct. The policy of silence showed an instinctive understanding of this fundamental situation. Even if that traditional policy had had no positive purpose, its negative function, its leaving at rest the explosive sexual system of the youth, must be acknowledged as one of those wonderful instinctive procedures by which society protects itself. . . .

"A nation which tries to lift its sexual morality by dragging the sexual problems to the street for the inspection of the crowd without shyness and without shame, and which wilfully makes them objects of gossip and stage entertainment is doing worse than Munchausen when he tried to lift himself by his scalp."

It would be perfectly easy to give many other quotations from prominent psychologists who agree with Foerster and Münsterberg in this matter. What is forgotten is how large a rôle suggestion plays in all matters relating to conduct, but particularly sex conduct. The exhibition of such ordinary crimes as "second-story work", climbing porches in order to steal while the family are at meals, the picking of pockets and the like, on the reels of moving pictures has been found to be followed over and over again by the occurrence of such crimes among the boys and even the girls in the neighborhood where the exhibition was given. Girls see a woman's reticule cleverly rifled in a street car or on a crowded corner and, tempted by the cleverness of it, they are led to imitate the action. In many cities the police refuse to allow such reels to be exhibited unless the punishment for the crime completes the picture. Even with this, however, it has been found that such exhibitions prove criminally suggestive, for the young folks remember the cleverness and think of the fun that one can have with the money, while the punishment is, if not forgotten, at least so pushed into the background of memory as to have comparatively little deterrent effect.

If this is true with regard to indifferent actions of this kind, the temptations to which are more or less artificial or but of comparatively slight allurement, it is easy to understand how serious and profound can be the suggestive power of sex knowledge for which there is likely to be so prurient a curiosity and with regard to which there are in the best-regulated healthy individuals, bodily stirrings almost as soon as the mind begins to be occupied with them. For that is the danger, — that even in the best of men the physical sex impulse may be awakened. In those who for professional reasons are quite familiar with sex matters, as for instance the physician, the dwelling on sex subjects even in matters of disease may arouse physical elements in the system, and these may react to deepen the attention until other considerations may be quite pushed into the background of consciousness. If this is true for older people, how much more so for the young, who have not yet been disillusioned on sex subjects and whose inhibitions are likely to be so much weaker. A great many of the people who are so intent on sex education apparently do not realize that their very tendency to occupy themselves with this subject so much is due to unconscious physical stirrings within themselves, consequent upon the preoccupation of mind with these subjects to the exclusion of healthier considerations.

The imparting of knowledge often serves only to awaken sleeping passions unsuspected before in the organism. Everyday experience shows how little knowledge helps. The people whose sex divagations get most frequently into our courts are those between thirty-five and fifty years of age. There is no question at all that they know enough to keep them right if knowledge made for righteousness. I have said elsewhere, and I know it to be true, that medical students, in spite of their knowledge of the consequences of venery, are not better, but on the average a little worse in these matters than other students in the universities. Their knowledge, like all knowledge, acts as a suggestion to evil much more than as a protection against vice. When temptation comes they are likely to think of the possibility of avoiding the worst evils and of the powers of medicine, and anyhow youth always feels in the expressive French phrase, *On meurt! les autres!* People die! Oh, yes, other people.

The one factor in life that will give the most precious aid in the protection of humanity against sexual temptations is religion. All the higher religions have emphasized the virtue of purity, that is, of freedom from sex vice, as of the greatest importance. For Christianity this has been a corner stone of the spiritual life without which righteousness, to use the good old-fashioned word which indicated that a man went "right" in life, was impossible. We are a little afraid of these old-fashioned religious words in our time, and we use such expressions as "go straight", somewhat as during the war the soldiers used the expression "go west" in order not to have to mention the solemn word death, but the old-fashioned words express exactly the meaning that we want, and they often carry valuable suggestion with them. In the Sermon on the Mount, Christ held out His highest rewards in heaven for those who practiced purity. He insisted, however, not on purity of body alone, but on purity of mind and heart when He said, "Blessed are the clean of heart, for they shall see God."

The head master of Harrow, the great public school

in England, proclaimed a very great truth that we all know, but need to be reminded of, when he said to his young men at Harrow that "The Bible does not so much speak as thunder against impurity, and it is no injustice to a secularistic morality to say that purity received from the lips of Jesus Christ a dignity, nay, a paramount authority which it cannot receive from human lips. Nor is personal chastity the same thing if it be taken to be a sanitary, or conventional, or moral practice, as if it be a duty resulting from the sanctity of the body as the temple of the indwelling Spirit of God."

Doctor Norman Porritt, in his book on "Religion and Health", does not hesitate to say that religion is the only factor that can be helpful in this extremely important matter of the prophylaxis of sex disease. He goes so far as to say that "Give to the tempted the reinforcement of religion, and you place him in a position well-nigh impregnable." It has been well said that if the man who first wrote "honesty is the best policy" meant that people should be honest because that was sure to rebound to their own benefit in the end, he was a rascal at heart. In something the same way Doctor Porritt suggests that to teach that purity is the best policy is to take an extremely low motive for the purpose of combating one of the most alluring temptations that man has. He says very emphatically and yet surely with a great deal of common sense: "And what is to be the remedy for the scourge which is incapacitating and crippling a fifth part of the nation's manhood, checking the natural expansion of population and sweeping unknown thousands to untimely graves? There are many remedies. We may look to the creation of a public sentiment which shall regard immorality as a disgraceful thing, to be ashamed of rather than proud of; we may learn to point the finger of scorn at the tempter as readily as we spurn his victim; we may prove, both by precept and our own example, that chastity is compatible with health, and that impurity — even when no gross disease follows — tends to deterioration and disorder; that the reasoning which gives a sanatory sanction to immorality and vice is a subtle sophistry. We may cultivate the manly exercises and stamp out impurity by wholesome books, elevating amusements, and noble ambitions; we may endeavour to check the spread of these diseases by legislative restrictions; we may inculcate teetotalism and banish enervating habits and too stimulating foods. Each of these measures may do something. Some of them may do much. But all of them have one fatal defect. They are all tarred with the brush of expediency. Expediency, and not wrong-doing, is the danger signal they show. And when the hot blood surges through young veins in the struggle with an imminent temptation, what becomes of expediency?"

Many people are ready to declare that the conspiracy of silence which has characterized the old-fashioned attitude of mind with regard to sex matters generally is due to the Church more than to any other agency. I think that from what we have said the Church's insistence on reticence with regard to sex subjects as the policy most likely to do good in the long run is now recognized by psychologists as being founded on motives that are the basis of natural defense by human nature in an extremely thorny matter. Ignorance is not innocence, but a saving lack of knowledge may spare a great many evil suggestions that would otherwise work harm. You cannot neutralize sex temptations by the provision of knowledge, you cannot even minimize them, and you may tactlessly add not a little to their danger.

There is a prudery which is not proper reticence that is cultivated by some people who happen incidentally to be religiously inclined. They would not call a spade a spade for the world. They would not hint at the fact that conjugation is always the origin of life for worlds. They would not use certain plain words that must be used in order to express very definite ideas without the feeling that they had smirched themselves by saying such things. If they had gone through Europe in the old days and seen the public comfort arrangements, they would have collapsed then and there. All this is sheer prudery and when applied to sex matters represents really a neurosis of excessive precaution and inhibition with regard to some of the most natural things in the world.

Any one who understands even a little of the religious attitude toward marriage will appreciate readily that such a state of mind is as far as possible from being that of the Church. Marriage is termed holy and blessed, and the ministers of the sacrament are the married persons themselves. Only those who fail to comprehend religious teaching in these matters have suggested that religious reticence with its conservation of that supreme reverence which even the great pagan teacher Quintilian recognized as due to youth represented an unfortunate cultivation of harmful ignorance. On the contrary, it is a part of that great tradition of age-long reticence which represents the highest wisdom of humanity. Hence the reversion to that mode of dealing with the question which has characterized the teaching of conservative psychologists in the last few years.

The greatest safeguard of purity with all that it means for the preservation of health and strength is the practice of self-denial with regard to the luxuries of life. No element in life has emphasized that and encouraged its practice so much or so constantly, and so persistently tried to train her children in it from youth as religion. It is almost impossible, for young people particularly, to keep right in this matter if they constantly indulge in luxuries. The very word luxury has come to be defined as "lust and lasciviousness and indulgence in lust", because there is such an almost inevitable connection between the exuberance of animal spirits which develops in connection with indulgence in luxuries of various kinds that the two words have almost necessarily come to have an intimate association. The word is applied to the friskiness or wantonness of animals, and it is very easy to understand its application. Men as well as animals who take more food than their occupations in life enable them to dispose of properly become similarly wanton or out of control. In Scriptural words they "wax fat and kick."

Religion has encouraged innocent enjoyment of every worthy sort as a distraction of mind and an outlet for youthful energy, but has discouraged in every way possible that complete gratification of the senses or of bodily desires which is so likely to be fatal to such strength of will as will enable people to control themselves. Clarke says, "Luxury does not consist in the innocent enjoyment of any of the good things which God has created to be received with thankfulness, but in the wasteful abuse of them to vicious purposes in ways inconsistent with sobriety, justice or charity."

Professor Foerster, whose books on the subject of the

training of youth and especially on sex matters in youth attracted so much attention shortly before the war, faced frankly this problem of the necessity for the practice of mortification, or as he did not hesitate to call it, genuine asceticism, the exercise of the virtues of self-control and self-denial as the most important factor for the protection of youth. He said: "All solutions of the sex problem which tend to emancipate sex feeling from the control of moral and spiritual law (instead of making it the chief aim to place the spirit in a position of mastery over the sex nature) are essentially hostile, not only to our whole social evolution and to the development of individual character, but to actual physical health in the sphere of sex. To secure the mastery of man's higher self over the whole world of animal desire is a task, however, which demands a more systematic development of will-power and the cultivation of a deeper faith in the spiritual destiny of humanity than are to be found in the superficial intellectualistic civilization of to-day. To achieve such a result it will be necessary not only to have recourse to new methods and new ideals, but to make sure that we do not allow what is valuable and in any way worthy of imitation, in the old, to be forgotten. The ascetic principle in particular is to-day in danger of being undervalued."

The cult of the body which has become so much the occupation of the present generation, which refuses to make the necessary effort of mind to secure intellectual pleasures, has always been the special deprecation of the Church. A great many of the words in the language show the effect of that religious attitude very clearly. Sensuousness, while its original meaning is only anything connected with the senses, has come to mean the quality of being particularly alive to the pleasure that is received through the senses and therefore by implication, at least, not particularly intellectual. The *Edinburgh Quarterly* reviewer long ago, in the famous article which Byron suggested as having snuffed out the "fiery particle" of Keats' soul, hurt him most by suggesting his lack of intellectuality and declaring that he was "too soft and sensuous by nature to be exhilarated by the conflict of modern opinions", hence "he found an opiate for his despondency in the old tales of Greek mythology." Sensuality even more than sensuousness has come to mean under the sway of the senses and the bodily desires rather than of the mind. Pope spoke of men "sensualized by pleasure" like those who were "changed into brutes by Circe."

There is probably no epithet that a man of intelligence resents more than to be called a sensualist. Goldsmith summed it up when he spoke of "the vulgar satisfaction of soliciting happiness from sensual enjoyment alone." Religion has particularly emphasized the danger and the actual degradation of human nature which this brought about. Bishop Atterbury declared that "No small part of virtue consists in abstaining from that in which sensual men place their felicity." Longer ago Shakespeare summed up the degeneration of the sensualist when he said

> "Those pampered animals
> That rage in savage sensuality."

This is quite literal degeneracy, for as man is both animal and rational, overindulgence in the pleasures of the senses drags him down toward his animal nature, that is, toward the *genus* below the *genus homo* to which man belongs. No wonder men resent the epithet "degenerate."

As the result of the influence of religion other words such as carnal, worldly, have come to be stamped with a meaning which makes people understand much better than would otherwise be the case the real significance of indulgence in bodily or mere earthly pleasure. The words are no longer fashionable, but that is because the deeds which they represent have become quite fashionable, and those who affect them do not want to have the innuendo of decadence and wrongful indulgence which necessarily goes with them applied to their acts. Religion has thus created a state of the public mind that has been extremely helpful against sensual pleasures and their power to ruin health, so long of course as religion held its place of influence over men.

Above all religion has insisted, and it is almost the only agency which continues to do so, that there can be no purity with its power for good for the health of both mind and body if the excitants of sensuality are indulged in. There must not only be no doing of evil, but there must be, as far as possible, no thinking about it, and especially there must be no dwelling on sensual pleasure, for bodily cravings will almost surely be aroused that make temptation almost insuperable. To think of delicate viands when one is hungry causes a flow of saliva, making the mouth water, but we know now that it causes a flow of what are called the appetite juices in the stomach which adds materially to the feeling of hunger and would make it very hard to resist taking food if it were placed before one, even though there might be some rather serious dangers connected with its taking. The thirsty soldier finds it extremely difficult to obey military laws with regard to not drinking any water that has not been examined and declared wholesome by the medical régime of the army, and if he should dwell much on his thirst it would make it ever so much harder to restrain if water from outside military sources should be offered to him.

Other pleasures of sense are even more likely to become the subject of almost insuperable temptations if the objects of them are dwelt on. Religion therefore has insisted, and is still insisting, on the necessity of avoiding attendance at such theaters as quite inevitably set up sensual excitation.

Fashion, which is another word for the world — and religion has always pointed out that the three great enemies of the development of the spirit of man are the world, the flesh, and the devil — has always set itself in opposition to religion in the approval of sensual gratification. That conflict is unending. A great many people declare that they would rather be out of the world than out of fashion, and it is surprising what insensate things fashion leads people to. The present fashion for the slow dance with the partners closely wrapped in one another's arms, for that is of course the essence of all the modern dances, no matter what their varying names may be, is only another development of the unending opposition between fashion and religion. Here once more, as with regard to the theater, religion presents the only serious protest. Dame Fashion insists that she sees no harm in it, but that is of course only a fashion of speech. It is quite impossible for a physician to watch the dancing without becoming convinced that human passions must be aroused by such close contact of human bodies of opposite sexes.

In this, however, as in so many other phases of life, only religion can interfere or protest with any hope of success. Her protest remains often unheard; fashion may be almost all powerful even against the higher calls of duty as well as against common sense. Certainly religious influence has had more to do with keeping a great many women from following the dictates of fashion in emphasizing their sex and therefore exciting the men with whom they come in contact than any other single factor. It has not been entirely successful, it never will be; the conflict will go on and worldliness will constantly come to the surface in some form or other, often to the detriment of health; and religion when properly vital will continue to be the most important factor in keeping evil from gaining such ascendancy as would be seriously detrimental to the healthy mind in a healthy body.

Religion is the only agency in the modern time that tries to regulate the reading of young folks and indeed of others in this dangerous matter of sex excitation. A great many books seem to be written at the present time for no other purpose than to excite sex feeling, — and thereby to make money. They depend for their sale entirely on the fact that for a great many people there is a distinct physical pleasure in reading about sex subjects. This is particularly true of women. A great many of them, and especially those who have not very much else to do and who therefore have no proper outlet for animal spirits and for the energies that tend to accumulate in them because they feed well and sleep long, are prone to indulge in this sort of luxury. Most of them would resent the suggestion that it was wrong for them to indulge their feelings in this way, but religion has always taken a decided stand and insisted that the fomenting of desire and the toying with alluring thoughts and the inviting of temptation are of themselves actually sinful. As John Boyle O'Reilly said,

"Temptation waits for all, and ills will come;
But some go out and ask the devil home."

Physicians have always insisted that the sexual erethism which is excited by the reading of books on sex subjects, the attending of sex problem plays and of shows of various kinds is the worst possible background for healthy living. Such frequent titillation of delicate nervous mechanisms plays sad havoc with general nervous control. Unfortunately just those who are indoors a great deal, who take very little exercise, and who live on dainties are most likely to indulge in these habits of life with regard to reading and the theater and dancing and the like which are most harmful for them. They are irritable in the nervous sense and excitable, and this erethism increases their nervous instability which responds by craving further excitement. A vicious circle is formed which very often leads to nervous breakdown. Just now we are hearing much about sexual repression as the cause of nervous disorders, but sexual repression is as almost nothing in its tendency to produce neurotic or psychoneurotic affections compared to the partial tantalizing, sexual indulgence which comes from sensual reading or lascivious shows. The plays that are seen, the jokes that are heard, the sex problems that are dwelt on, the stories that are read must get more and more spicy and contain more and more sex "pep" to afford any satisfaction, and the consequence is a disturbance of delicate parts of the nervous system which react more or less seriously to lessen the control over the whole nervous mechanism of the body.

When Doctor S. Weir Mitchell pointed out two generations ago that not only headache, but rather serious nervous disturbance involving often the gastro-intestinal tract and sometimes other large organs like the brain itself, as well as even mental operations, might come from so small a cause as disturbance of accommodation in the eye, most physicians refused to believe that such far-reaching symptoms could come from what was apparently so trivial a factor. The accommodation mechanism of the eye is extremely delicate, however, and requires such nice adjustment that any interference with it causes a waste of nervous energy that is likely to make itself felt at almost any part of the nervous system. In our day disturbances of the eye are confessed by all to be extremely important. In something of the same way disturbances of the sexual system of the body are reflected throughout the whole nervous system.

Religion has counseled, commanded and thundered against any practices, however simple they might seem in themselves, that would serve as excitants for the sex feelings. Without her influence even more harm would have been done than has been. It is the waning of religious power over public morality and public opinion that has led to the orgy of indulgence in sexual excitation, which has had such bad effects and which unfortunately so often leads to sexual acts which are fraught with the hideous dangers of venereal disease, because passion excited will find its satisfaction. Society heedlessly arouses passion but apparently cares not what happens afterwards.

CHAPTER XI

INSANITY

THERE is a very prevalent impression that religion is a common, even rather frequent cause of insanity. This is founded on popular experience. It has often been noted that not a few of the people who go insane have delusions on religious subjects. It is also a very common observation that those who are on the road to insanity and have finally to be placed in an asylum have for some time been making themselves conspicuous by their excessive practice of religious observances of one kind or another. It is not surprising then that the familiar fallacy *post hoc ergo propter hoc*, "after this therefore the result of this", should have come to be applied in these cases, and that religion should be set down as a prominent factor of mental disease and perhaps one of the commonest causes of the condition.

Those who have given most study to the subject, however, know very well that this conclusion is quite as unjustified by the facts of the case as the corresponding one with regard to religion being a frequent source of nervous diseases. We will discuss that in the chapter on Nervous Diseases, and almost necessarily the closely related subject of mental disturbances is touched on somewhat there. Of course it is well understood that a great many of those who are on the road to such mental alienation as will eventually require their internment in an asylum will give many external manifestations of religious feelings, some of them exaggerated beyond reason, as perhaps the very earliest striking symptom of their mental alienation. Religion, as we said in the Introduction, is one of the most universal interests of men. When people go insane, some interest will receive exaggerated attention. The delusions of their insanity are dependent on what the deepest interest of the individual was. If he was interested in money, he will believe himself the richest or perhaps the poorest of men. If he is interested in science, his delusions will be associated with that subject. Delusions concerning some phase of science are probably even more common in our day than those based on religion. Electricity is the source of more delusions than anything else, though hypnotism and telepathy and other sensationally exploited modes of so-called psychology are a close second in this respect. If the patient has recently suffered a severe loss by the death of a friend, sorrow will be the central idea of his mental disturbance; if there has been a disappointment in love, that will be the focus of his mental troubles; if there has been a money loss, that disappointment will be the core of the depression. Almost any human interest may thus become the root of excitement or discouragement leading to mania or melancholia.

The Great War gave us some very interesting material as to mental as well as nervous disease. In nothing was that more interesting than as to the causes from which insanity develops. It might very well have been expected that a great many people would break down under the awful conditions in which they were placed during the war. For instance Poland was fought over some six times, and portions of Austria overrun three times, and Servia was, between war and the ravages of famine and disease, a veritable shambles of its people for three or four years. It is easy to understand the awful states of anxiety and solicitude and almost continuous terror to which the inhabitants of Belgium, occupied by the Germans, were subjected, particularly in the smaller places where they were utterly at the mercy of the German officials whose one idea, fostered by their military teaching, was that the end of the war would be brought about or at least greatly hastened by a policy of frightfulness.

Literally many millions of people were subjected to conditions which would seem to be impossible for human nature to stand for any length of time, and yet they had to bear them continuously for four years or more.

The records of the development of insanity among these people have been rather carefully gathered, and they reveal the astounding fact that the insanity rate was very little higher among all these intense sufferers from the war than it would have been under the ordinary conditions of civil life. Manifestly a certain number of persons had the insanities which would have developed in them in later years anticipated by the trials and the hardships of wartime conditions, but only those suffered from insanity as a rule who might have been expected to do so because their family or personal history revealed tendencies in that direction which would almost surely have made themselves manifest sooner or later even under the inevitable vicissitudes of peace time.

What modern medicine has revealed to us is that apart from certain infectious diseases which produce degeneration of the physical basis of mind and the absorption of certain poisons — alcohol is a typical example — which cause a corresponding degeneration to the infections, the supreme factor in insanity is the inheritance of a predisposition to the affection. Two things have become perfectly clear in the course of modern medical investigation, that insanity and longevity run in families, and that there is almost no other basis on which the two conditions may develop. Infections or intoxications in the broad sense of the word may produce conditions to foster or impair respectively either of them, but even they are of minor significance compared to the original inheritance in either case.

Clouston, the well-known English authority on mental diseases, whose opinion is founded on many years of personal observation, in his book on "Unsoundness of Mind"[1] has put the relationship between religion and mental disease very clearly. He said: "It is true that religion, touching as it does, in the most intense way the emotional nature and the spiritual instincts of mankind, sometimes appears to cause and is often mixed up with insanity. But in nearly all such cases the brain of the individual was originally unstable, specially emotional, oversensitive, hyperconscientious and often somewhat weak in the intellectual and inhibitory faculties and, if looked for, other causes will usually be found." He had said just before, "To talk of 'religious insanity' as if it were a definite and definable form is in my judgment a mistake."

So far from prayer — the principal exercise of religion, that is the raising up of the mind to God, either in petition or in resignation — unsettling people's minds, it has exactly the opposite effect. Professor William James, whom most people are not inclined to think of as likely to be an overstrenuous advocate of religion, in his well-

[1] Methuen, London, 1911.

known essay on "The Energies of Men" has a paragraph in which he quotes from a physician who had had long experience in the care of a great many insane and who did not hesitate to say that prayer was a benefit and not in any sense of the word a detriment to his patients.

"Doctor Thomas Hyslop, of the great West Riding Asylum in England, said last year to the British Medical Association that the best sleep-producing agent which his practice had revealed to him was prayer. I say this, he added (I am sorry here that I must quote from memory) purely as a medical man. The exercise of prayer, in those who habitually exert it, must be regarded by us doctors as the most adequate and normal of all the pacifiers of the mind and calmers of the nerves."

It is recognized as a general rule in asylum practice that when patients begin really to pray, a turn for the better has come in their condition, and they are on the high road to recovery. This does not mean, of course, noisy, wordy praying, but quiet raising of the mind to God and acts of resignation to their condition so long as they may be affected.

There is a very general impression among those who have had most to do with the insane as well as among psychologists in general that religion, instead of favoring the development of insanity, rather inhibits it. Professor Münsterberg, in his "Psychotherapy" dwells particularly on this. Almost needless to say Professor Münsterberg did not wear the special favor of religion in the lists and was in no sense her champion. He is proclaiming simply what he knows and feels to be true.

A very curious reflection on the relations of religion and insanity is to be found in the fact that the marked increase in the insane among the population of all the great modern civilized countries and most striking among our own has come since the decay of religion and the decrease of religious belief. The statistics of that increase in the number of the insane are very startling to those who are not familiar with the subject. During a single generation the number of the insane in our institutions has increased to five times what it was before in proportion to the population. There is no doubt that this is due to some extent to the fact that people are much less ready to care for their insane relatives outside of institutions than they were a generation and especially two or three generations ago. We are much less ready to make the personal sacrifices needed to keep our friends at home, which is probably also due to the lowering of our religious sense of obligation in the matter. Fortunately our insane asylums are much better conducted than they were, and this has made people more willing to confide their relatives to them. Giving all due allowance for this, however, there has been an enormous increase in the number of the insane. Such commonwealths as California and Massachusetts, in which there are very large proportions of educated people, present the highest increase in the number of the insane. There are certain critical spirits who would say that it is our education without God and without religion that has fostered this state of affairs, and that it is particularly people of a certain limited intelligence who, when overeducated, lose their faith, who are most prone to lose their minds.

The most important single factor in insanity, not dependent on constitution or heredity but on conduct, is that degeneration of the brain which brings on paresis or general paralysis of the insane. Taken by and large throughout the world generally, nearly one in five of all those who die in insane asylums die from this affection. It is the result of an infection usually consequent upon sexual immorality. The disease is inevitably fatal and once it begins it is steadily progressive from the delusions of grandeur so common at the beginning through various delusional states up to absolute dementia and death, which usually takes place in a little more than three years from the beginning of the disease; five years is a long time for a patient to survive. Nothing has done so much to limit the occurrence of this disease as religious influences, and it has increased to become the modern scourge that it is just in proportion as religion has lost its hold upon the mind of the rising generation. The disease is particularly infrequent among clergymen, and while *lues* from which the disease develops may be contracted innocently, it is very evident that a regular moral life such as is led under the sway of religious principles is the best possible safeguard against the spread of the disease.

After paresis the most serious form of acquired insanity in modern life is that known as alcoholic insanity, due to excess in the taking of spirituous liquors. It is not necessarily inevitable that a man who frequently indulges to excess in alcoholic liquors will become insane any more than that he will suffer from alcoholic neuritis, but a large number of individuals prove susceptible to the toxic effects of alcohol in these ways. There is an inherent liability in their brain and nervous system to degenerate under the influence of alcohol acting as a poison. This is an extremely common form of insanity, but almost needless to say it occurs much less frequently in those who have any religious principles than in those who are without them, because religion protects from the excesses that predispose to these conditions. Clergymen very rarely suffer from them and though occasionally clerical patients have developed alcoholic insanity or alcoholic neuritis, these cases on careful investigation oftener proved to be due to certain patent medicines which contained alcohol in large percentage than to any direct consumption of spirituous liquor.

Religion by its calming influence keeps a good many people who have hereditary tendencies to insanity from developing outspoken symptoms of the disease. Religious conviction has a definite efficacy in making people humble instead of conceited, and this is an excellent factor for preventing the tendency to insanity. Nearly always the preliminary sign of insanity is an exaggeration of the *ego* and a hint at least of delusions of grandeur. People who overrate their importance are often on the road to the asylum. Religion, by inculcating humility, at least lessens this tendency and puts off developments that are inevitable so that many more years of reasonable sanity are enjoyed than would otherwise be the case.

Probably the worst thing in the world for those who have any inherited tendency to disequilibration of mind is to have an occupation in life which involves strains and stresses of emotion. The gambler, the speculator, the man who risks his all on some attempt to make a great deal of money, are much more prone to develop insanity than those who have occupations in life at which they work from day to day for a moderate wage, and who get their joy in life out of the fulfillment of domestic duties. Almost needless to say religion has always discouraged gambling and such speculation as resembles it very closely, and the whole tendency of religious influence is to make people so satisfied with their lot in life that they will not take the risks which involve the vehement mental emotions so likely to disturb those with inherited predispositions toward irrationality. Undoubtedly religion has in this way saved a great many men from serious developments in mental alienation which might have come had they felt themselves free to take up the riskier avocations in life from which they were deterred by the feeling of religious disapproval.

After the tendency to exaggeration of the ego and delusions of grandeur, the most common symptom of incipient insanity is delusion of persecution. As regards this, once more, the religious feeling of trust in Providence and the conviction that God will somehow take care of them keeps many people from allowing their delusions of persecution to manifest themselves so soon or so violently as would otherwise be the case. Only comparatively rarely do religious minded people in the midst of their delusions of persecution commit crimes, being deterred therefrom by the underlying consciousness of the wrongness of their acts in taking judgment on their persecutors into their own hands, even though they may have yielded to a belief in their delusions. It is true that a certain number of religious-minded people do commit crime under the influence of delusions, but these are rarer than the cases which occur in people who have never had any sense of religious morality.

In a word religion has meant a very great deal for the limitation of insanity and the tendency to it, for putting off its development and giving patients years of sanity they might not otherwise have enjoyed, and it has had a very definite effect in limiting the crimes consequent upon insanity. It has a very marked tendency to create the atmosphere of placid trust and confidence which means so much for the preservation of sanity. Far from being a provocative of irrational tendencies it soothes patients' minds, prevents them from running into such excesses of emotion as are dangerous for mental balance, and it predisposes those who allow themselves to be deeply influenced by it to live such quiet satisfied lives without inordinate ambition and disordered desires as make for health of mind and body during prolonged life.

It has often been said that religion unfortunately proved harmful to insanity and the insane in the old medieval days, because ecclesiastics, sometimes for the sake of the fees that they might secure for exorcisms, taught very generally the doctrine that the insane were possessed of the devil, and that the one thing to do for them, besides exorcising the evil spirit, was to chain them up and keep them in manacles in dungeons until there was assurance that they had been released from the devil that had gained possession of them.

In spite of the fact that this is a rather common teaching in medical books and is frequently asserted even by physicians and sometimes indeed by specialists in nervous and mental diseases who are supposed to know the subject on which they discourse, there is very little foundation for this prevalent impression. Undoubtedly there was the belief in the possibility of possession by the devil and some such modern scientific minds as Alfred Russel Wallace and Professor Barrett of Trinity College, Dublin, have reverted to that belief because of their studies in spiritism and some of the curious results that follow from overdevotion to the cult of spirits. There was, however, a very definite recognition of the fact during the later Middle Ages that the insane were just ailing persons who had to be taken care of, properly treated, kept from hurting themselves or others, just as delirious individuals would have to be guarded, but who must be looked upon as sick in mind, just as a number of people were sick in body and with more than a hint that the bodily condition had more to do with the insanity than anything else. I have discussed the subject at some length in my volume on "Medieval Medicine" recently published in London.[1] Paul of Aegina wrote in the seventh century of melancholy as a primary affection of the brain to be treated with frequent baths and a wholesome and humid diet, together with suitable exhilaration of mind and without any other remedy unless when from its long continuance the offending humor is difficult to evacuate, in which case we must have recourse to more complicated and powerful plans of treatment. Paul was a very popular author much read in the Middle Ages.

The Church's view of the subject of insanity is very well expressed in Bartholomew's Encyclopedia. This was a work written particularly for the information of the clergymen of the time, in order to explain to them all references in Scripture and to give them such details of knowledge as were necessary for preaching and for the teaching of their flocks. Bartholomew was very widely read and went through many editions before printing, was put into print very early, and some of the editions are among the greatest of bibliophilic treasures. Bartholomew, usually called the Englishman — his Latin name of *Bartholomæus Anglicus* is well known — boiled down all the knowledge of insanity into a single paragraph. He has nothing at all to say of possession by the devil, and his discussion of the whole subject of madness is as modern as can be.

The causes of insanity which this clergyman writer

[1] Black, 1920.

of the middle of the thirteenth century enumerates are those which psychiatrists of the present day are insisting on. The symptoms of infection, considering the brevity of the passage, are very well and clearly described, and the treatment suggested is the very latest in modern practice and consists of improvement of nutrition and the diversion of the insane. With all our supposed advance in knowledge no physician, even of the twentieth century, could have expressed the whole subject of insanity any better than Bartholomew did. This paragraph is a complete refutation of the objections that the Church by its insistence on diabolical possession as the principal cause of insanity did a great deal of harm. Bartholomew said:

"Madness cometh sometime of passions of the soul, as of business and of great thoughts, of sorrow and of too great study, and of dread: sometimes of the biting of a wood (mad) hound, or some other venomous beast; sometimes of melancholy meats, and sometimes of drink of strong wine. And as the causes be diverse, the tokens and signs be diverse. For some cry and leap and hurt and wound themselves and other men, and darken and hide themselves in privy and secret places. The medicine of them is, that they be bound, that they hurt not themselves and other men. And namely, such shall be refreshed, and comforted, and withdrawn from cause and matter of dread and busy thoughts. And they must be gladded with instruments of music, and some deal be occupied."

CHAPTER XII

NERVOUS DISEASE

JUST as with regard to insanity, there is a very common impression that religion increases the amount of nervous disease in the world and is responsible for a great deal of what has been called hysteria. Not a few who think they have a right to an opinion in this matter, and some of them are physicians — though usually they are rather young — are quite ready to assert that religion is a fruitful source of nervous symptoms and very often of rather serious nervous conditions. We saw in the chapter on Insanity how false is the prevalent impression as to religion producing tendencies to insanity, though of course a great many insane people have religious delusions. It is very much the same with nervous diseases. Many nervous people pay a certain amount of attention to religion, and not a few of them cling to straws of hope that they may be able to overcome their neurotic tendencies by superficial attention to prayer or to some practices of religion which they seem to look upon about in the same light as patent medicines recommended for the cure of nervous diseases. People who are deeply religious, however, very seldom suffer from nervous affections, and they have in their religion the most beneficent of helpful resources, if by nature, that is, by heredity or unfortunate development, they have neurotic tendencies.

So far from religion increasing nervous disease, then, it has exactly the opposite effect. We have a number of testimonies to this purport from prominent neurologists, many of whom were themselves not believers in religion but who recognized its influence for good over others. Such expressions are to be found in the writings of men of every nationality. Not infrequently, in spite of their own religious affiliations, they acknowledge what a profound influence certain forms of religion have over certain people. These testimonies have been multiplying in our medical literature in recent years, because apparently physicians have come to appreciate by contrast the influence for good of religion over some of their patients, since they see so many sufferers from nervous diseases who have not this source of consolation to which to recur.

In America we have a number of such testimonies. In his "Self Help for Nervous Women", Doctor John K. Mitchell of Philadelphia, who may be taken to represent in this matter the Philadelphia School of Neurologists, to which his father lent such distinction, said:

"It is certainly true that considering as examples two such separated forms of religious belief as the Orthodox Jews and the strict Roman Catholics, one does not see as many patients from them as might be expected from their numbers, especially when it is remembered that Jews as a whole are very nervous people and that the Roman Catholic includes in this country among its members numbers of the most emotional race in the world.

"Of only one sect can I recall no example. It is not in my memory that a professing Quaker ever came into my hands to be treated for nervousness. If the opinion I have already stated so often is correct, namely that want of control of the emotions and the overexpression of the feelings are prime causes of nervousness, then the fact that discipline of the emotions is a lesson early and constantly taught by the Friends would help to account for the infrequency of this disorder among them and adds emphasis to the belief in such a causation."

In writing a "Textbook of Psychotherapy"[1] eight years ago one of the appendices was devoted to the relations between religion and psychotherapy. One of the paragraphs, written for physicians, and I may say that it has been read by many thousands of them, puts my own opinion on the dual subject of the nexus between religion, insanity and nervous disease, as succinctly as I can hope to put it. There is no doubt that an abiding sense of religion does much for people in the midst of their ailments and, above all, keeps them from developing those symptoms due to nervous worry and solicitude which so often are more annoying to the patient than the actual sufferings he or she may have to bear. While religion is often said to predispose to certain mental troubles, it is now well appreciated by psychiatrists that it is not religion that has the tendency to disturb the mind, but a disequilibrated mind has the tendency to exaggerate out of all reason its interest in anything that it takes up seriously. Whether the object of the attention be business, or pleasure, or sexuality, or religion, the unbalanced mind pays too much attention to it, becomes too exclusively occupied with it, and this overindulgence helps to form a vicious circle of unfavorable influence.

While many people in their insanity, then, show exaggerated interest in religion, this is only like other

[1] Appleton.

exaggerated interests of the disequilibrated, and religion itself is not the cause but only a coincidence in the matter.

Some who are interested particularly in this subject, on reading this will at once revert to the fact that scruples are extremely common among the religiously inclined and that these are, after all, as a rule, only nervous symptoms which are surely fostered by religion. To say this, however, is to misapprehend the real meaning of scruples. The word is a very old one and means a little sharp stone, as if in trying to make progress the scrupulous found themselves hindered by having to walk over little sharp stones which so disturbed them that they were hampered in getting on. Above all, scruples put them into a state of mind where they hesitate as to whether they can go on at all or not.

The subject of scruples was very thoroughly worked out and carefully described by the older spiritual writers centuries ago. They wrote elaborate treatises on it, while it was not until our own time that physicians by their careful study of corresponding conditions entirely apart from religion came to appreciate that these conditions of the spiritual life were only expressions of a rather common set of tendencies altogether independent of religion. They are prone to develop in people with certain physical and mental characteristics who are possessed of dispositions and nervous systems particularly likely to be the subject of these hesitancies and doubts and difficulties for which there is very little basis in actuality.

The whole chapter of phobias and the other chapter on obsessions and the third on what the French call *la folie du doute*, the doubting mania in our modern textbooks of neurology, are really so many chapters in the literature of scruples of the old time, now transferred to the textbooks on functional nervous diseases. Some nervous people who are religiously inclined get into a very disturbed state of mind from the fear that they may commit sin almost unknown to themselves or that they may be in sin unawaredly and cut off from their Creator, and they become extremely miserable as a consequence. This is, after all, a very familiar picture to the neurologist accustomed to see patients suffering from functional nervous diseases. I have patients who suffer quite as much from the dread of dirt as these scrupulous people do from the dread of sin. Women often suffer from this dread of dirt — misophobia is the scientific name derived from the Greek — to an exaggerated degree. A woman patient of mine makes it extremely uncomfortable for the conductors on the street cars because, for fear of contaminating her hands, she dreads to touch the handle bars by which she could mount or descend easily. This adds greatly to the risks she takes every time she boards a car. She is constantly washing her hands to get the dirt off, so that in cold weather she sets up severe skin irritations and makes herself very uncomfortable. I have a male patient who would not touch the handle of my door for the world, and whom successive maids have come to know very well because he stands outside the outer door and has to have that as well as the inner door opened for him. He has said to me over and over again, "Doctor, don't ask me to shake hands with you, because you shake hands with so many people." I have seen him standing outside of a large department store with the temperature around zero, waiting for some one to open the door so that he might slip in without touching it. Nor are such states of mind confined to the uneducated; on the contrary, they are commonest among those who have a good education and are quite sensible in other things.

Obsessions were originally described as super-religious states of mind in which some idea assumed a terrorizing character. The victims of them dread that they might commit some awful crime and as a consequence were profoundly miserable. Instead of being confined to religion, such mental states are quite common in conditions altogether apart from religious feelings. Women read of a mother killing her child in some awful way or perhaps accidently poisoning it or burning it badly with some escharotic external application. They become obsessed with the idea that they may do something of this kind and fear that they may not be able to resist the suggestion. Medical literature is full of such cases. A typical case is described by Tangi in his textbook on insanity:

"A young married woman suffered from nervous exhaustion after her first childbirth. She watched day by day her husband cutting up meat for his parrots with a pair of scissors, and the action filled her with disgust which later increased to positive horror. Thus a repulsive obsession was produced and this in turn engendered the morbid suggestion to cut the tongue of her dearly loved child in the same way. The fear that she would not be able to resist this suggestion made the suggestion more vivid and the idea more imperative, causing an agonizing struggle each time."

Then there are accounts, some of them most poignant, from Catholic patients of my own, who were sure that sometime while in the midst of their devotions or even at the very reception of the sacraments they would blaspheme. They are people who fear that every pious act of theirs may just expose them to the risk of committing some awful sacrilege.

Almost needless to say such states have nothing at all to do with religion, and when similar conditions occur among the religious minded, they must be attributed to the general neurotic condition and not to the incidental religious tendencies. The doubting mania occurs among the religious minded when they keep on fearing that they have not done something that they should do. Some of these individuals get into a profoundly miserable and disturbed state of mind, but that must not be blamed on religion.

This sad state of mind in people who have no religion at all is extremely familiar to the neurologist, and it has no necessary connection with religious practice or religious belief. I have a patient who has been coming to me for many years now from a city in the Middle West; he is a broker, and every time there is a panic in the money market I am almost sure to see him. Whenever he gets very much disturbed over business matters, as is likely to happen in panic times, he develops a very striking *folie du doute*, or doubting mania. He will take a letter to a post box and go back three or four times, first to see if by chance he did not drop it on the way, secondly to be sure that it did not get caught in the slot; then, if the letter is important, he will go back to see if perchance there may not be some bolts or other obstructions at the top of the box that may catch it and delay its collection. I have even known him to wait for some time at the post box to see if the postman might not possibly drop it when he came to collect the mail. But then he does other things just as foolish. Occasionally he will get home from his office and suddenly have the feeling that he forgot to lock his safe. He will go back and then get part way up town when he is overcome by the fear that he may not have locked the door after him as he came out. At times when his *folie du doute* is at its worst, he has been known to go back three or four times to close windows or for some other trivial reason. When he is in reasonably good condition there is very little of this state of mind manifest, but he can make himself supremely miserable when the obsession is on him.

It is often said that the declaration by the Church of the idea of possession by the devil rather encouraged the development of certain mental and nervous states and thus fostered neurotic manifestations of many kinds. This whole question of the possibility of direct diabolic influence over mankind, that is, of some evil spirit deeply influencing certain human beings, is yet a matter that is not nearly so settled as a great many physicians who have not been following scientific work in allied lines seem to think. So distinguished a scientist as Alfred Russel Wallace, the co-discoverer with Darwin of the theory of natural selection, had the feeling that spirits interfered much more in human affairs than a great many people were willing to admit, and that the evil spirits probably could, under certain circumstances, deeply affect individuals. Professor Barrett of Trinity College, Dublin, is even more outspoken in what he has to say in this regard, and now there is a very general feeling among those who have investigated spiritistic phenomena most carefully that if spirits do actually communicate directly with men, it is commonly not the spirits who claim to do the communicating who are actually present. Almost needless to say any such conclusion as this would, if maintained, throw even scientists back to the old idea of diabolism, which the Church, on the strength of many centuries of experience, still teaches.

One thing is perfectly sure: that if overzeal on the part of certain ecclesiastics rather encouraged neurotic manifestations because of the alluringly suggestive quality of the thought of diabolic possession, they did no more than physicians did in more modern times by their suggestive methods in the study of hysteria. A great French neurologist of to-day has pointed out that major hysteria as studied by French neurologists of a generation ago has practically disappeared, or occurs very rarely in our day because it is no longer unconsciously suggested to patients by physicians that these major symptoms are being looked for. Overzeal in medicine raised up a whole series of symptoms that had no existence except in the heated imagination of their patients under the influence of strong suggestion.

Another extremely interesting phase of this subject is that in the old days many of the sensible ecclesiastics and some of the civil authorities came to recognize that people supposed to be possessed of evil spirits could be cured of their condition not infrequently by roundly whipping them. Sir Thomas More particularly called attention to how much good could be effected in this way. In writing an article on "Psychoneurosis and the War" (International Clinics, Volume II, Series 29) I called attention to this in a paragraph that may be helpful in the understanding of the discussion of diabolic influence.

It has been the custom for many years now, indeed for more than a generation, to think that the old-fashioned methods of treating many of the psychoneuroses by punishment and the infliction of pain were founded on an entirely wrong principle. Sir Thomas More, for instance, tells the story of a number of folk in his time who suffered from rather serious complaints; some of them were dumb and some deaf, and some thought they could not see, and others could not walk. He says that some people considered them possessed of the devil, and that it was the presence of this very undesirable spirit that hampered their activities in various ways and made it impossible for them to use their powers properly. The description of the cases makes it very clear that he is referring to hysterical conditions of various kinds and the sequel as to the successful treatment which he says was frequently employed on them more than confirms the inference of hysteria and demonstrates the very definite hysterical character of the affection. Many a physician down through the ages has been inclined to think that these people were possessed of a bad spirit of some kind, even though he might not be quite ready to think that a personal devil had taken hold of them and was seriously hampering their functions. We recognize that the real trouble is with their own spirit, to which may be applied whatever epithets come to mind, and no one will think them exaggerations; this spirit has lost its control of their activities, rendering them incapable of exercising their functions properly.

There is a very widespread tradition, which has found its way into medical literature especially, that the fervent practice of religion in women has a very definite tendency to make them neurotic. Particularly when religious devotion is associated with mortification and fasting, it is supposed to be serious in its effects. It is the custom to make references to such pious women as St. Catherine of Siena and St. Theresa of Spain as typically exemplifying this neuroticizing tendency.

Any one who really knows the lives of either of these women will not be likely to think that they were neurotic in any proper sense of that word at all. Both of them were not weak but had immensely strong characters, veritable towers of strength in supremely difficult times, supporting not only their own heavy burdens but helping others around them to bear theirs. Of Catherine of Siena, Swinburne, the English poet, surely not a sanctimonious person, whose sentimentality might lead to admiration for the hysterical bizarre, but who had studied her career because so many incidents in her life have been the subject of great paintings by a number of the greatest painters of Italy, said:

> "Then in her sacred saving hands
> She took the sorrows of the lands,
> With maiden palms she lifted up
> The sick time's blood-embittered cup,
> And in her virgin garment furled
> The faint limbs of a wounded world.
> Clothed with calm love and clear desire,
> She went forth in her soul's attire,
> A missive fire."

The great hospital at Siena was rebuilt in honor of Catherine shortly after her death because of the fact that she had spent many years of her comparatively brief life there; she died at thirty-two in personal service of all kinds to the patients suffering from every manner of disease, even leprosy, who were in the institution. (The lepers were housed apart from the others.) She placated so many feuds among the noble families of Siena, feuds that were the cause of as many murders as the worst of our own in Kentucky, that she was asked to be the envoy of peace when cities were at war, and it was she who eventually by her influence brought the Popes back from Avignon to Rome and thus put an end to the great disorders in the Italian peninsula.

St. Theresa, the great Spanish mystic of the sixteenth century, the other "horrible example," held up even by some neurologists, of hysterical tendencies due to religion and mortification, proves, when studied in real life, to have been at least as great and strong a character as Catherine of Siena. She well deserves the name of saint as a leader in unselfishness, but besides she had a fine sense of humor. That is what neurotic people lack above all — a sense of humor. All sorts of distinguished men in the Spain of her time — and in the sixteenth century Spain was by far the greatest country in Europe, her sovereigns ruling most of Europe and the greater part of America, and the nation gave birth to great art, literature, architecture and philosophy — turned to consult St. Theresa in their difficulties. She wrote a series of books that have been republished in every cultured language in Europe at least once a century ever since, and our own generation has been sedulous in the study of Theresa's writings. No less than a dozen lives of her have been written in English in the twentieth century. This Spanish lady who died three hundred and fifty years ago is still a very living force in the world.

Owing to the special conditions under which much of my work is accomplished, I am brought in contact with a great many religious women every year. For some twenty years I have spent some days each summer with groups of religious communities where large numbers were assembled for special intellectual and spiritual work. The mother superior has often consulted me with regard to some of her daughters who had special nervous manifestations, but it is a never-ending source of surprise to find how few of them suffer from the nervous symptoms so common in our time. Considering the fact that they spend their lives very largely indoors, that they live on very simple food — and sometimes I have been inclined to think with scarcely enough nor sufficient variety to make them capable of the amount and demanding nature of work they have to do — fewer of them suffer from nervous symptoms or affections than women of the same class who are living at home and on whom the demands are not nearly so strenuous. Their religious duties, instead of being in any way a drain on their nerve force, though I have often heard it said that teachers ought not to be required to give quite so much time to their religious duties, represent a reservoir of energy from which they draw strength and above all placidity of mind and consequent power to accomplish more than would otherwise be the case.

My duties often bring me into contact with numbers of sisters during their hours of recreation, so-called, and I do not think that I have ever seen a happier, heartier group of people than they make during these periods of relaxation. I have always considered it a privilege to share recreation after dinner or supper with a dozen sisters when I am lecturing in one of the smaller towns, and we have often laughed so heartily together that I have sometimes wondered what the neighbors would think of us. People with a sense of humor like this are not likely to have hysterical tendencies. Nervousness is at bottom selfishness, and there is always a great deal of conceit in it. Religious women are likely to be humble, and that means much in keeping them from various magnifications of their ego which so often result in nervous and mental symptoms.

I have often ventured to say that I was quite sure that a religious house, especially where there were many young people, in which laughter came easily and was heard frequently during the times appropriate for it, was sure to be a place of real spirituality and happiness. I have often dared to remind them that the one place where one hears no real laughter, though sometimes sounds are made resembling it, is an insane asylum. People who are ready to laugh are usually eminently sane. Above all, they do not take themselves too seriously. It is taking one's self and one's feelings too seriously that is the root of a great deal of nervous and mental disturbance in this little world of ours. Certainly the discipline of heart and mind and body and the feeling of satisfaction from duty well done that comes in connection with that complete sacrifice of themselves in a great religious cause which members of religious orders make, so far from predisposing them to nervous disease has just exactly the opposite effect.

Nervous diseases, instead of being fostered or fomented by religion, are on the contrary repressed rather effectually and equilibrium given even to those in whom some hereditary elements might have proved disturbing. This does not mean that all the religious minded are free from nervous symptoms, and it must not be forgotten that not every one who says "Lord, Lord," gets into the kingdom of heaven, either on earth or hereafter, but religion must be counted as an asset and not a liability in this matter. It will not overcome strong hereditary tendencies, and it will not help efficaciously those who do not submit to the discipline that true religious feeling entails, and of course religion is not a panacea for the ills of mankind, though it must be counted a therapeutic adjuvant and not a nervous irritant.

Professor Foerster, whom one is tempted to quote because of the thoroughgoing thoughtfulness of his treatment of many of these subjects and his wise conservatism founded on that deep consideration, has discussed the question of repression of self in matters of purity as a possible source of nervous troubles of various kinds. Freudianism, as it is called, which has attracted so much attention in recent years, would seem to suggest the conclusion that a great many of the nervous symptoms of humanity are due to the repression of sex impulses. Foerster has pointed out that just the opposite is true, and that there never was a time when there was so little real self-repression and also never a time when there was so much functional nervous disease. He said:

"From this point of view there can be no doubt that the modern theory of 'living one's nature out' is largely responsible for the nervous degeneration of to-day, and that the widespread hysteria in modern life does not spring from those remnants of discipline and idealism which are still operative amongst us. One is compelled to ask indeed with astonishment, with what right Freud finds the dangers of repression so alarming in an age which is conspicuous for self-indulgence. In reality there has never been an age which was less influenced by the spirit of abnegation and repression than is our own. The present age is one of disintegration, in which natural instincts have largely broken away from their controlling higher ideals; if, therefore, it suffers to a peculiar degree from nervousness, one can hardly look for the cause in the fact that it constitutes a high-water mark of control and discipline. The precisely opposite conclusion would be nearer the mark."

Professor Foerster admits, however, that it is perfectly possible that people who have no good motive for self-repression and who suppress instincts only out of the merest human respect and cowardice as to results, may very well suffer some of the consequences that Freud has pointed out. He says:

"There is one point, however, in which one can entirely agree with Freud, or at any rate allow oneself, through him, to be led to the recognition of an important psychological and pedagogical truth. There are to-day certain circles who cling to the old ethical tradition only through considerations of an outward description, as the result of a species of timidity which keeps them from breaking with respectable customs; and yet these people are, at the bottom of their hearts, believers in a view of life of a totally different description — one which attaches no value or meaning to self-mastery and self-denial."

Almost needless to say this obscuration of religious motives with the result of leaving the individual too much at the mercy of the merely physical without adequate principles for self-control is not the fault of religion but of its very opposite — irreligion. Foerster's words are all-important for the understanding of an important phase of the discussion of the cause and cure of nervous and psychic symptoms of various kinds which has attracted much more attention outside of medical circles than it deserves.

The danger of the absence of religious motives in the world, because of the persuasion that new discoveries are doing away with the necessity for faith, has also been emphasized by Professor Foerster, who said:

"Along with the disappearance of belief in a spiritual world arises the danger that even earnest and noble men and women will be influenced in their consideration of the deeper things of life by the newest and most tangible facts alone, and will be inaccessible to all arguments going beyond the scope of mere practical sense and expediency. It would appear as if the preponderance of an intellect directed towards external things destroyed not only belief in the invisible world in a religious sense, but also undermined the power of grasping the full value and reality of certain *imponderabilia* in earthly life, and of understanding the deep-growing spiritual injuries which may proceed from apparently harmless and even outwardly beneficial things."

CHAPTER XIII

DREADS

THE most fruitful source of neurotic affections and especially of what have come to be termed in recent years the psychoneuroses, those disturbances of nerve function due to an unfortunate state of mind, are the dreads or, as they have been called, the fear thoughts of mankind. Men as well as women develop, in the sense of fostering, often almost unconsciously to themselves, a dread of the ulterior significance of some symptom, or feeling, or disturbance of function, which serves to make them extremely uncomfortable. The physical sensation which they experience and which is the basis and the source of the dread may be only a quite normal physiological feeling common to all humanity, heightened by overattention to it, but the fearsome state of mind will cause it to assume the significance of a definite symptom of some serious disease or, what may be worse, an indefinite symptom of some impending affection which, in the opinion of the sufferer, may be as yet too inchoate for the physician to recognize its real significance.

It is not a question of an imaginary ill, as a rule, and there is but seldom a real hallucination or creation by the fantasy out of nothing, of the ailment from which these people suffer, but there is an exaggeration of some slight or at least comparatively insignificant feeling to an extent that makes it assume a serious aspect. This inhibits normal function, lessens appetite and exercise, at times even disturbs sleep, and so brings about some at least of the ailments that are dreaded.

Not infrequently these dreads are very vague. People wake in the morning with a sense of depression and the feeling that something is hanging over them. As a result they feel out of sorts, their appetite for breakfast is blunted and they begin the day very badly just because of this incubus of vague disturbance of mind. Almost anything that happens during the day will emphasize their depression; as a consequence lunch may be skimped, they do not get out as they should, and a vicious circle of influences is begun. Perhaps they eat rather heartily for dinner and then fall asleep in their chair afterwards over the evening paper, and then find that when they go to bed they do not sleep promptly as they expected to. They worry over it, feeling there must be something the matter with them, since they cannot sleep lying down though they could sleep so well in the chair, and if there should be a repetition of these feelings the next day, it is easy to understand how a psychoneurosis would be started which might easily, if eating and outing and exercise were to continue to be neglected, develop into a serious condition. Many a case of nervous breakdown has a beginning as simple as this, and people of nervous temperament must be constantly on guard against it.

Such patients — and they are much more common than might be thought and they have been with us for thousands of years, for Plato describes some of them and the oldest prescription in the world is a fumigation that was directed to curing just such a neurotic condition — need to have faith in themselves and faith in their Maker and to stop hesitating and doubting and thinking and dreading. I have known men, but particularly women, who had been suffering in this way, become converted so that they took up the practice of religion which they had neglected before and proceeded to get immensely better. Of course, there are any number of hypochondriacs among people who profess religion, but they are the exceptions which prove the rule that fewer people who have a real sense of religion and who take it seriously as a guide of life suffer from dreads and the symptoms which result from them than are to be found among the people who have given up the belief and practice of their religion. This is particularly true of those who belong to the old orthodox forms of religion which require self-denial and self-control as part of the practice of religious duties. As we have shown in the chapter on Nervous Diseases the Quakers, the strict Methodists, the Roman Catholics, the Orthodox Jews, get their reward for their submission to their religion even in this world by lessened solicitude about themselves.

Indeed there is nothing that is more likely to dispel dreads than an abiding sense of religion. If a man or a woman is convinced that there is a Providence that oversees human life as well as the universe, in Whom "we live and move and have our being" and of Whose infinite knowledge and power we can have no doubt, the unreasonableness of dreads comes home to him. The man who prays every morning, "Thy will be done on earth as it is in heaven", must have the feeling that His will *will* be accomplished, and that is all that any of us can ask for. Somehow that is for the best, though we may not be able to see just how. "If not a sparrow falls to the ground but your Heavenly Father knoweth", and if, as the Master said, "Are not five sparrows sold for two farthings and not one of them is forgotten before God? But even the very hairs of your head are all numbered. Fear not therefore: you are of more value than many sparrows", surely the believer will keep himself at least from being overworried by dreads. His disposition may be such that he cannot dispose of them entirely, but at least the best source of consolation and strength is to be found in that strong faith for which there are so many strengthening expressions against the fears and dreads of life to be found in the sacred writings.

How many striking sentences there are in the Scriptures to help against these solicitudes: "And which of you with taking thought can add to his stature one cubit? If ye then be not able to do that thing which is least, why take ye thought for the rest?" How one is tempted to quote others of the expressions in that same wonderful chapter of Luke (XII). "The life is more than the meat and the body is more than raiment. Consider the ravens; for they neither sow nor reap; which neither have storehouse nor barn; and God feedeth them; how much more are ye better than the fowls. But rather seek ye the kingdom of God; and all these things shall be added unto you. Fear not, little flock; for it is your Father's good pleasure to give you a kingdom." All over the Scriptures are passages that are meant to be fear-dispelling and that have been for many men and women in many generations. For fear is often the state of man unless he has something to cling to. "Fear not, I am with thee." . . . "Fear ye not, nor be afraid, have I not told thee." . . . "Fear not, I am the first and the last, for I the Lord thy God will hold thy right hand, saying to thee fear not, I will help thee."

Scientists have recognized that religion and science

were coördinate factors for the neutralization of the dreads that disturb humanity. Professor H. D. Seeley, who was for many years professor of geography, geology and mineralogy at Kings College, London, and who was a distinguished Fellow of most of the important English scientific societies, the Royal, Linnean, Geological, Zoölogical and Geographical, stated in his little work, "Factors in Life", his views as regards the place of religion in dissipating the fear thoughts of life, and places it side by side with science itself in this respect. He said:

"To the religious neither life nor death has terrors, and in freeing existence from its greater anxieties the influence of Religion works on the same foundation of moral efforts as Science. The sciences are the sisters of Religion in that they unfold something of the laws by which the universe is governed, and by which man's life is directed. They are thus far the stepping-stones of faith. And those who have learned that health is the reward which man may gain by moral discipline, that mental vigour may be augmented by the wise (or moral) use of food, and that education is the systematic exercise of moral responsibility in any or all the affairs of life, may find that in the practice and pursuit of the truths of Science they are conscious of a religious education which is a light to the feet. Such matters are factors in life, which may educate us in a reverent appreciation of religious truth and divine government of the world."

Many physicians of large experience have recognized the value of an abiding religious faith as a remedy for many of these dreads and doubts which so pester mankind and make so many people suffer even from physical symptoms that seem surely to have only material causes as their basis because they so hamper the will to live. Sir Dyce

Duckworth, the distinguished English physician, once wrote to a friend: "What is always needed is a reverent study and a full acknowledgment of God as a Father and as the great 'All in All.' In my experience the only solution of all our difficulties is to maintain a humble, child-like faith and a confident trust in the perfect love of God, who 'knows whereof we are made, and remembers that we are but dust.'

"With that and perfect love, there need be no fear, and all will come right in His own time. That is the faith to live by and to die with, and the happiest people (and the happiest of the dying) are those who hold firm by that faith.

"This is my experience after much thought, much knowledge of human nature, and not a little study of all the difficulties you relate to me."

But it must not be thought that these dreads cause only the trivial instances of nervous breakdown in which people never very capable give way before the strenuous call of commercial life in the large cities of our time. Nor must it be thought that education is dispelling them. Some idea of the important rôle that dreads may play in the production of human ills that seem to be very serious and that often prove quite incapacitating for mental and physical work, even in men of fine abilities and proven powers, may be gathered from what happened during the recent Great War. The Allied nations had to maintain some fifty thousand beds behind the lines for the accommodation of patients suffering from functional nervous affections really founded on dreads. At the beginning these cases were misunderstood, and they were unfortunately called "shell shock" because they seemed so serious that it was thought that they were due to some concussion of the nervous system, that is, some shaking up of its elements that made it impossible for it to function normally, even though there were no external signs of injury. After a time, however, it came to be appreciated that the great majority of these patients were suffering from major hysteria due to loss of control over the nervous system as a consequence of the almost inevitable dreads which developed in the awful conditions of warfare in the trenches, with its terrifying sights and sounds, and with the intense strain put upon the nervous system because of the demands made upon physical energy almost to the point of exhaustion.

After loss of sleep and irregular eating, wet feet for days at a time, exposure to the inclemencies of the weather and then having to withstand an enemy attack, often at dawn after a fearsome barrage had been laid down on them for hours, it is no wonder that in many cases men's nervous control did give way. They were not cowards, they were not malingerers; on the contrary they were often brave men who had volunteered for the service, giving up important positions at home to take up the defense of their country; and yet after a time their dreads dominated them and they suffered from all sorts of symptoms. Some of them could not see, a number could not hear; some could not use their legs, and some could not employ their arms properly; some walked with a limp, some had tremor that made their usefulness as soldiers absolutely at an end. Nearly all of them had a series of complaints which they wanted to detail in all their minuteness to every physician who came near. Their stories of what had happened were mainly untrue or utter exaggerations of the actual events, and yet these men were not liars and they were not the doddering idiots that they sometimes seemed to be; they were just fellow mortals who meant to do their best, and who had been affected in this way because they were asked to stand what was beyond their strength of soul to withstand.

The educated suffered more than the uneducated. There were four times as many "shell shock" cases among the officers of the British army in proportion to their number as there were among the privates. Neither ambition nor nobility nor any artificial distinction of any kind seemed to make any difference, for all classes and conditions of men came down with it. Its frequence can be very well judged from the fact that one third of all the dismissions from the British army, not counting the wounded, was for "shell shock", which of course should be called by its proper name of major hysteria. One seventh of all the dismissions, if the wounded were included, was for this reason. It had been the custom to think before the war that only a comparatively few men, mostly those of a certain feministic appearance and delicacy of constitution, were likely to suffer from hysteria. It was found, however, that college graduates who stood at the head of their classes, athletes who held records, broad-shouldered, healthy men who had been considered to be the very acme of common sense, men who were supposed to be without a nerve in their make-up, all these proved to have "nerves"; and when the war "got on their nerves", they suffered from the complaints which we have mentioned and many others, including pains and discomforts of all kinds, and inabilities and incapacities; motor and sensory as well as of the memory, of the mind or the will.

This recent significant experience will give some idea of how potent dreads may be in the production of symptoms which seem surely to be due to physical rather than merely mental conditions. Most people would probably be inclined to think that in so far as dreads produced diseases by the exaggeration of minor symptoms, at most scarcely more than mental conditions of discomfort would result from them. What are called the psychoneuroses, that is, the neurotic affections dependent on the state of mind, may simulate almost any of the organic conditions and may seem to be serious diseases. Through the creation of unfortunate habits, they may give rise to a great many rather severe physical symptoms. The war neuroses emphasized this for us. Inability to use limbs, either legs or arms, is quite common in connection with them; disturbances of sensation, such as defective hearing and eyesight, or even what seems to be complete blindness and deafness, may develop. Tremors are quite common, and pains and aches in connection with the disabilities of the limbs are extremely frequent.

A very usual experience is to find that a patient has as a preliminary suffered some injury. This may not be very severe, but it is enough to cause the sufferer to spare the limb that is affected; and unfortunately physicians sometimes put a limb with a minor affection in plaster of Paris or in a splint for a time. The patient's own solicitude with regard to the hurt may cause almost as effective splinting of it as a plaster cast or wooden slat and a bandage. Whenever this happens, the unused muscles lose some of their nutrition. This is due partly to the fact that the circulation is interfered with because the active contraction of muscles, especially of the legs, is depended on by nature to help the venous or return circulation by bringing about compression of the veins. The valves in the veins are so arranged that when the veins are compressed and the blood thus pressed out of them, it cannot move away from the heart but is impelled onward toward the heart. Besides, the sending down of nervous impulses for the active use of muscles increases the size of the arteries to the part by direct action on their walls, and whenever there is failure to send impulses down, the arteries do not carry as much blood as usual, and the nutrition of the part suffers as a result.

If this inactive state of the muscles continues for a few days, they will become somewhat flaccid, and after a week or more will actually begin to decrease in size. As a consequence of this, they cannot be used to as good advantage as before, and use of them sets up an achy condition as soon as the limb is set free for use, whether it has been splinted by the physician or by the patient's mind. If the patient is still solicitous, he notices this condition of pain and concludes that it means that the muscles are not yet in the condition of health where they should be used, and he puts on the splints, metaphorical or literal, once more. The muscles grow more flaccid and eventually atrophic as a consequence, until sometimes there will be a difference of more than an inch in the girth of two limbs at the same point, and this atrophy may proceed much farther. It seems almost impossible to believe that men and women could thus make a limb useless, but this is actually what happens rather frequently. The effects of the original injury will pass off in a few days, but the effects of the disuse of the limb may remain for months or even years because of the disturbance of circulation and of nerve impulse. It is probable that the nerves themselves have a trophic or nutritional — that is, vitalizing — influence upon muscles. Some physiologists actually talk of there being trophic fibers in the nerves, though it would seem more reasonable to think that the nerve trophic effect comes from the modification of the circulation to the part.

Whenever muscles have to be increased in size or won back from an atrophic condition, the individual to whom they belong must go through a period of soreness and tenderness in those muscles which often is very hard to bear. The young fellow who, after a rather relaxed summer, begins training for the football team in the fall, knows how sore and tender his muscles have become. After the first day or two of training, each time he wakes up at night he turns over in bed with the feeling that every bit of him is full of tenderness. Any number of people under similar circumstances are inclined to think that they must have caught cold. They usually reason thus: "I got into a perspiration and sat down for a while and then took cold, and that is the reason for all this painful condition that has developed."

That word "cold" is as unfortunate as "shell shock." There is no such thing as taking cold. We catch infections, but much more frequently in fall and spring than in winter. The young man who is in training usually pays no attention to such unfavorable suggestions or dreads, since he knows that he must take his medicine of further hard exercise until he has *hardened* and developed his muscles and then, instead of their causing discomfort, nothing in the world gives him so much satisfaction as their active exercise.

Older people, however, and especially those who have what may be called a "dready" disposition, do not call their muscle discomfort soreness and tenderness; they speak of pains and aches. The very words carry a suggestion of evil with them, and above all they carry with them an inhibitory suggestion which keeps muscles from being used normally. If, then, certain older people get an injury, even though it may not be very serious, so long as it causes them to give up the use of a limb for a while, or sets them to using the muscles of it a little differently from before, a psychoneurosis on the basis of a dread, but with the physical basis of somewhat atrophied muscles to keep it up, may develop and persist for weeks and months and even years. As a consequence of this state — much more of the mind than the body — men may walk lame or be very awkward in the use of one arm, or they may have a little stoop, or they may dread very much the using of some group of muscles. Such conditions occasionally occur in the neck or in various parts of the back, and especially in the lumbar region, with strikingly visible effects.

It might seem impossible that such conditions should develop and persist for any length of time in sensible and above all intelligent people, and yet I suppose that every physician's case book contains a number of examples. After he has been in practice for ten years or more this will surely be true, if he has had much to do with nervous patients. One of the most distinguished scientists that we had in this country, possessed of one of the finest intellects of our generation, thoroughly sensible and noted for his executive ability, suffered from a slight attack of sciatica, to which he had been predisposed by some unusual work in connection with a heavy fall of snow when he had to go out and do the shoveling himself, since labor was not available. He never quite got over it. For some time he carried two crutches because he had so little confidence in putting down the foot on that side, after having spared it for a while. Then for several years he carried a single crutch. In the meantime he was examined by half a dozen of the best physicians in the country, who could find nothing the matter with him except that disuse had rendered the muscles of that leg slightly atrophic, and he would have to push through a period of soreness and tenderness while exercising them. He carried a cane ever afterwards, walked a little lame and favored that leg.

Persistent sciaticas of this kind and lumbagoes are much more common than they are thought. It was a case of this kind, undoubtedly, that brought about Bernheim's interest in hypnotism at Nancy and initiated that wave of attention to hypnotism at the end of the nineteenth century which did so much harm. A patient who had suffered from sciatica for some years and walked a little lame as a consequence came under Bernheim's care, and he tried without success every therapeutic resource at his command to make him better. Finally his patient gave up calling on him, completely discouraged. He had gone to a great many physicians before Bernheim, and all of them had failed to do him any effectual good. They could relieve his discomfort for a while, but when he stopped taking drugs, that returned and his limb could be used no better than before.

Some months after Bernheim missed the patient from his clinic he met him on the street one day, walking perfectly straight without his cane and evidently entirely well. He was so much interested that he stopped to ask what had cured him. The patient told him he had gone around to Liebault, who, almost alone in Europe, was still practicing hypnotism, for the practice had been greatly discredited by certain exposures in England shortly after the middle of the century. Bernheim, who had ignored

Liebault's work before, now took an interest in it and found of course that hypnotism — or indeed, though Bernheim did not know that, anything else that would give these patients the confidence to push through a period of tenderness and soreness in regaining the use of their muscles — would cure them. The incident began that period of reawakened interest in hypnotism which now constitutes such a ludicrous series of events in the medicine of the end of the nineteenth century.

Such cases are by no means so uncommon as they might be thought. I have known the teacher of a high school to slip while coming out of school, fall on his knee, bruise it rather badly, and then have this bruised condition heal very well, only to develop in the course of a few weeks a distinct inability to use the muscles of that leg properly, until he had to walk with a marked limp. The circumference of the limb above the knee reduced distinctly in size, it suffered more from cold than did the other one; it perspired more freely; it was distinctly more sensitive to the touch, and it would seem as though there must be some serious underlying nervous condition. He passed through the hands of several specialists, including one who wanted to remove a cartilage in the knee joint which he said had been dislocated, and another who insisted that he was suffering from a neuritis of a branch of the sciatic nerve, and who wanted to inject water within the sheath of it or at least lay it bare and stretch it. Fortunately we persuaded him to join an athletic club and take more exercise than usual and above all exercise that limb. He had had massage and passive movements for it, but these are of very little service in these cases, because the nervous impulses must come down from above. It would almost seem as though the will sent down some of its own creative energy through the nerves which lead to the part. He is now entirely well, though he suffered for several years, and absolutely nothing was done for him except to make him eat better and make him push through a period of soreness and tenderness — he used to call them pains and aches before we explained the condition to him — until he had properly recovered the use of his limb.

On the other hand, I have known a good clergyman with a rather similar condition to this, who had bumped his shin bone not far below the knee and after recovery from that had developed a marked psychoneurosis in the muscles above the knee, refuse to be cured by any such simple procedure as merely exercising himself back to health. He could not bring himself to think that it was only his own lack of will power that had caused the condition to develop. Above all he needed something external to cure him. He finally went to a bone-setter, one of these old fellows who claim to be the seventh son of a seventh son, or something of that kind, possessed of marvelous hereditary power and instinctive intuition in the matter of setting bones right, and who cure nearly everything under the sun and a few other things besides by their supposed bone-setting processes. My clerical friend was sure that he had been cured by the bone-setter, but any physician would have told him that what had happened was that his faith in his healer had released his inhibition of his muscles and given him the confidence to go on and use them as they should be used, — that is, of course, as far as he possibly could at first. Then they were gradually restored to their former condition of health and strength. That is what happened, and he has had no recurrence. He is quite sure, however, that the trouble was a subluxation of his hip joint, which the bone-setter set right, thus allowing nervous impulses and the blood to flow properly through the part once more. His own will was the only obstacle and it was that alone that had to be overcome and used as a therapeutic agent.

These patients are the stock in trade of all sorts of irregular practitioners. Whenever they think anything is the matter with them they must be "cured"; they never get better of themselves. They need something or somebody to which to pin their faith. It is the hardest thing in the world to find out what is the matter with a man who has nothing the matter with him except a state of mind and its consequences in his physical condition. He must have his state of mind changed first of all, and usually he requires some rather strong suggestion for that purpose. What is likely to affect him most favorably is some novel or unusual method of treatment, or some new discovery in science recently applied to medicine, or some new method of healing, or some supposedly new invention or discovery in therapeutics. These patients are a veritable nuisance in medicine. It is the cures of them, made by all sorts of new-fangled remedies, which make it so difficult for physicians to judge whether a new remedy has a positive favorable physical effect or only a mental influence.

Very probably the best appreciation of the place of dreads in life and how much of good is accomplished by their neutralization can be obtained from the number of sufferers of all kinds who are cured by all sorts of new remedies which prove after a time to have no physical effect at all. We have discussed this subject of the remedies that have come and gone in medicine in the volume "Psychotherapy." It has been very well said that the most important chapter in the history of medicine is that of the cures that have failed. It illustrates very thoroughly how much influence the mind has over the body, and particularly how much dreads have meant for the production of symptoms which have been relieved whenever the patient had his dreads lifted, no matter what might be the agent to accomplish this purpose. Instead of decreasing, dreads have increased just in proportion as popular education has spread and more people have been able to read and receive unfavorable suggestions of all kinds. This has been particularly true with the diminution of the influence of religion over people's minds.

All sorts of religious substitutes which would give people enough confidence in themselves to enable them to throw off their dreads have gained vogue and have come to be very popular institutions in recent years. Dowie, who claimed he was Elijah returned to earth, and Schlatter, who said that he was divinely inspired to cure people, were as successful in the twentieth century as Greatrakes "the stroker," who said that the Holy Ghost appeared to him in a dream and told him to heal people, in the seventeenth. Metaphysical healing of all kinds has been successful, and spiritualistic healing and new thought and magnetic healing, with as little magnetism about it as Mesmer's famous battery which had no electricity, — all these have cured people. All sorts of healers are successful just because they lift the dreads and make people forget the inhibitions that they have been exercising over their functions. Indeed this state of fear thought is one of the most prolific sources of symptoms, or rather let us say of complaints, that medicine has to do with at all times, hence the importance of the chapter of the cures that have failed. Almost any religious feeling will be helpful in the matter, but an abiding sense of rational religion will save many people from being imposed on by all sorts of upstart theories and religious systems which base their claim to recognition on these cures of human beings.

These patients furnish a great many of the cures made at shrines. That is why at every shrine there are so many crutches and canes and braces and belts and splints and supports of various kinds to be seen. They have been left there by grateful patients who were able to drop them as the result of the change of mind that came over them during their devotions. Many cures besides these occur at shrines, and I have taken a good deal of pains to assure myself that most of the affections that are healed at them are quite different from these psychoneuroses. Over sixty per cent of the cures made at Lourdes, for instance, are of tuberculosis processes. Many of these are of external visible lesions. Some of them, after years of progress in spite of all sorts of treatment, heal over in the course of twenty-four hours. I have seen this happen to a lupus, at Lourdes, during my stay there, and I do not know how to explain that incident by any natural process. To me it seemed surely supernatural. I know that there are some physicians who suggest that we do not know all the possibilities of the therapeutic effect of the mind on the body, and somehow there may be included in the psychotherapeutic armamentarium the power to heal tissues rapidly, even when they have been the subject of a chronic granulomatous process for years, but I cannot but think that is merely an effort to retain what seems to me plainly miraculous within the domain of the natural.

I know too that Doctor Boissarie's experience, so carefully noted and written out in his clinic at Lourdes, shows that there are cases of real joint trouble which have been cured with similar rapidity, but these are very rare. Most of the halt and crippled who are cured at shrines have simply been the victims of an attitude of mind which has affected their muscles and their use of certain joints unfavorably, so that they had to carry crutches or canes or wear braces. The deep influence of religion will cure them very often, but it is not a miracle in any supernatural sense of the word, though it is a wonderful event, and that is all that miracle means by etymology. Indeed, professors of neurology have occasionally foretold that certain of these patients would perhaps be cured at shrines, and their prophecies in specific instances have been fulfilled. The cures are examples of what faith can do in lifting a dread, but that faith may be exercised with regard to much less worthy objects than are presented at shrines and yet work successfully. When George Cohan, in the "Miracle Man", had the cure that attracted attention to the "new prophet" occur with regard to a lame boy, he was eminently wise in the selection of just the type of case that could very readily be cured that way, and yet the fact that the boy had been lame for years and now walked perfectly made the healer seem a veritable wonder worker.

Dreads have always been with mankind, and their effects upon human bodies have been the stock in trade of the medicine man in primitive tribes and among savages and of his successors in suggestive medicine among educated and even cultivated people down to our own time. They can be conjured away by almost any impression that is deep enough to produce a favorable suggestion. Religion of all kinds has been appealed to successfully to neutralize them. The one rational cure for them is a deep sense of confidence in the Almighty and in an overruling Providence which serves to dissipate the phobic state of mind with its inevitable inhibitions on bodily functions. It may be necessary for its successful working that the correction of many minor physical ills should be secured, but the all-important basis of successful treatment for the psychoneurosis and the many ailments of mankind which are complicated by psychic states is a thoroughgoing belief that God is in His heaven and all is well with the world, even though there may be difficulties to be overcome, hardships to be borne, and many things that are far from easy to understand.

CHAPTER XIV

SUFFERING

THE problem of the meaning of suffering and evil in the world is the greatest natural mystery that man has to face. It has raised the question as to whether life is worth living or not in some minds. It causes a great many people to be disturbed about the meaning of life and has led some sensitive people to conclude that there cannot be an overseeing, all-wise Providence since otherwise He would surely prevent all the needless suffering there is in the world. Biologists, owing to their occupation with the thought of the struggle for existence in current theories of evolution, have been particularly inclined to say that they could not think that there was a Providence because there was so much of carnage in nature, so much ruthless destruction of life amid suffering for which it would be hard to find any satisfactory reason. There has been no little exaggeration in this view, for a calm review of conditions as they obtain in nature shows not so much of active contest as a healthy competition for the means of existence, in the midst of which death comes to the weakling without anything like the suffering so much emphasized.

It must not be forgotten that the supersensitiveness of the sedentary student must be taken into account in the appreciation of the significance of such a declaration, for the recluse scientist often shrinks from trials that the active outdoors man finds only a stimulus to action, which serve to develop powers and give satisfaction rather than any real suffering. The incentive to have life and to have it more abundantly which this affords to heartier natures makes the poet's expression, *forsan et haec olim meminisse juvabit*, "perhaps we shall be glad to recall these hardships in the time to come", easy to appreciate. Life without suffering would lack that contrast which saves it from the dull monotony that might tempt to waste of energy in dissipation.

Perhaps the best illustration of the actual benefit to man which accrues from suffering is to be found in the fact that one of the surprising results of the presence of the mystery of suffering in the world is that meditation over it has given rise to the five greatest dramatic poems that were ever written. Men contemplating it have been led to the expression of the deepest thoughts that have ever stirred minds. These great poems have come at longer and shorter intervals during four thousand years, from Job, the essential ideas for which probably date from about 1800 B.C., though its literary form is much later, through Æschylus' "Prometheus", Shakespeare's "Hamlet", Calderon's "The Wonder-working Magician", down to Goethe's "Faust." Of these five dramatizations of the mystery of human suffering, recurring poetic impersonations of Hamlet's

> "The time is out of joint: O cursed spite,
> That ever I was born to set it right!"

the greatest, as conceded by all the critics, is not — as might be expected from the very prevalent impression that man makes wonderful progress down the ages — the last one, Goethe's "Faust", but is the first one, Job. No one has ever expressed so well the only reasonable attitude of mind that man must take in the presence of evil and suffering as this "man of the land of Hus whose name was Job and who was simple and upright and fearing God and avoiding evil", yet who had to bear some of the severest trials that man has ever been called upon to undergo.

Mr. H. G. Wells has recently, in one of his thought-stimulating novels, shown us that verisimilitude of the most modern type could be woven into a story which followed the outlines of the book of Job very closely, so that far from being dead, even the novelty-seeking fiction readers of our generation have brought home to them the fact that Job is still a very living piece of literature. Job's answer to the mystery of evil is that man must confess his inability to understand it, but he can trust the God who "thunders wonderfully with His voice" and "doth great and unsearchable things", "who commandeth the snow to go down on the earth and the winter rain", "who knoweth what ways the light spreads and heat divideth on the earth", "who joins together the shining stars, the pleiads, and can stop the turning about of Arcturus" and "who created behemoth and leviathan and can bind the rhinoceros and has fashioned the ostrich." All that Job can say is, "I know that Thou canst do everything and that no thought can be withholden from Thee", therefore for any impatience that he may have displayed over his suffering he reprehends himself and promises to do penance in dust and ashes, — "and after this Job lived one hundred and forty years and saw his sons and his sons' sons, even four generations. So Job died, being old and full of days."

In any consideration of suffering, above all in connection with the related subjects of health and religion, we must not forget that suffering has always been a badge of the race, the common lot of men, so that this very community of it greatly reduces human reaction toward it, since the sufferer cannot help but note that every one else must submit to it as well as himself. At times among those who fail to think deeply enough this may be doubted. The poor may even envy the rich because they suppose that they must by their riches escape suffering, but most physicians soon learn to appreciate very well that the mental discomforts of the wealthy, their disappointed social ambitions, their thwarted aspirations after greater wealth, their envy of their more successful neighbors, but above all their frequent disappointment in their children, though it is almost invariably their very wealth that has spoiled the children and brought their greatest griefs on them, are really the source of much more genuine suffering than the poor have to bear. The worries of life increase with possessions, not decrease, as is fondly hoped, and as the author of the "Romance of the Rose" said some seven centuries ago:

> "And he who what he holds esteems
> Enough, is rich beyond the dreams
> Of many a dreary usurer,
> And lives his life-days happier far;
> For nought it signifies what gains
> The wretched usurer makes, the pains
> Of poverty afflict him yet
> Who having, struggleth still to get."

Suffering must ever remain a mystery, especially when we take into account the fact that all of us are profoundly possessed by the desire for happiness. We can never probe to the bottom of the mystery and know all its meaning, but at least we can readily understand that in the vast majority of cases, instead of being an evil, it is a good. Nothing so deepens and develops character as suffering. Take the case of our young men who went to the war — so many of them scarcely more than boys, feeling but little of the responsibilities of life — and see how they have come back to us matured by the hardships and sufferings through which they had to go. Thucydides said nearly twenty-five hundred years ago, "There is very little difference among men, only a few of them rise above the great mass because they have gone through hard things when they were young."

It would seem as though we had changed all that, for we are deeply intent on making things just as easy as possible for the young, but a generation ago Gladstone repeated Thucydides' expression with heartiest approval, and twenty years ago John Morley, writing the life of Gladstone, agreed with both of them. I wonder if there are two men in our time who have known men better than Gladstone and Morley.

In that sense suffering is no mystery, and it is easy to see how it is quite literally true that "Whom the Lord loves He chastises." It is the chastisement of suffering that brings out the powers of men. Any one who has not had to suffer in life is nearly always a self-centered egoist without sympathy, but above all without that fellow feeling that comes only from having gone through similar experience. He who has not suffered has not really lived below the surface of his being at all, and he does not know himself. To "know thyself" is the most important thing in the world and the only way to know others. The men who have done great thinking for us have nearly always been men who had to suffer much. It was a blind Milton who wrote "Paradise Lost." When Camoëns wrote what German and French critics think — and when Germans and French agree about anything there is probably a deep underlying truth in it — the greatest epic in modern time, he was starving in a garret, and his old Indian servant was begging for him on the streets to secure enough to keep body and soul together until the great work was finished. Cervantes wrote what Lord Macaulay called "incomparably the greatest novel ever written" in a debtor's prison, out of which it seemed he might never be able to secure his release. Dante wrote what many think the greatest poem ever written during a long exile in which he learned "how bitter it is to eat the bread of other's tables." *Poeta laudatur et alget*, "the poet is praised and starves", is as true in our time as when Horace said it three thousand years ago.

Goldwin Smith has brought out very clearly the fact that suffering and evil are really a necessity in the world if this is to be a place of trial, as every one believes, for of course such a belief represents the only satisfactory explanation of life as we have it. Man must have something to strive for and against if there are to be stepping stones of our dead selves to higher things, and so it is not surprising that Doctor Goldwin Smith should have said:

"At the same time, so far as we can discern, character can be formed only by an effort which implies something against which to strive; so that without evil or what appears to us evil, character could not be formed. The existence of evil in fact, so far as we can see, is the necessary condition of active life."

Suffering has been with us from the beginning and it will always be with us; instead of an evil it is one of God's great gifts to man, and yet it sometimes makes little souls bitter and swamps the efforts of those who cannot rise above its trials. Religion is the one element that is supremely helpful in this. Above all in the terminal sufferings of mankind, when there is no longer any question of pain that has to be borne in developing character for this life, the only consolation is that to be derived from religion and a firm belief in a hereafter and an acknowledgment of the fact that somehow God knows best and all is for the best. Without this the awful suffering from cancer which is increasing rather than diminishing, and which seems to be so rooted in human nature that we shall probably never solve its mystery or at least be able to secure human nature against it, as well as ever so many other chronic sources of pain that will never cease entirely until the end of life comes, become hideous specters for humanity, and suffering has very little meaning.

No matter what our attitude of mind may be with regard to suffering, there is no question but that we have to stand it under present conditions in this little world of ours. During the next twelve months scarcely less than one hundred thousand persons will die of cancer in this country and a million and a half victims of the disease will breathe their last throughout the world. When we add up all the accidents in industry and transportation, all the wounds in war and civil life, and then add the affections which in one way or another cause mechanical stoppages of processes in the body, for these are the exquisitely painful conditions, it is easy to understand that we need consolation for suffering. An old medical axiom is that "the doctor can seldom cure but he can often relieve and can always console." There are a good many physicians, however, who feel their ability to console sadly hampered by the fact that so many men and women in our time do not believe in a hereafter for which their sufferings in this world can be a preparation, and that therefore the terminal suffering of existence, of which there is and manifestly always will be such an amount, can mean nothing for them except just so much pain that has to be borne without any good reason that they can see, except that somehow or other things were so arranged in this world that there is ever so much more of pain and suffering than of joy in it.

Two thousand years ago Cicero said in his own oratorical way that it was better for all of us to believe in immortality, for if there was no immortality we should never live after death to know it — which comes very near being an Irish bull by anticipation — while if there was, and we had not believed in it, there would come a very rude awakening to the truth of things. Something of the same problem has been put in much more flippant and yet very expressive way in modern slang. "If there is no other world than this, then some one handed us an awful lemon when we were sent into existence." That is, I suppose, one answer to the mystery of suffering so sure to come to all men in some way or other, and it is one that counsels us to seek the only real consolation for suffering, — that which is to be found in the religious feeling that somehow or other, somewhere, there is some one who knows and understands, and suffering has its meaning. "God's in His heaven and all's well with the world" in spite of the fact that "nature red in tooth and claw" works such sad havoc with her creatures.

What the belief in immortality and the feeling that this life is merely its portico can accomplish in giving a man equanimity in the face of disappointments and patient fortitude under even atrocious pain is very well illustrated by what Professor William James has to say of Thomas Davidson in his essay on him.[1] Davidson died of cancer at a comparatively early age, considering the length of life that many scholars enjoy, and for many years "he had prepared a large amount of material for that history of the interaction of Greek, Christian Hebrew and Arabic thought on one another before the revival of learning which was to be his Magnum Opus. Davidson was destined never to finish the work. Professor James, who had been an intimate friend and was so close to him in the organization of the Glenmore School of the Culture Sciences on Hurricane Mountain at the head of Keene Valley in the Adirondacks, had felt the possibility of this accident of destiny and had inquired of Davidson with regard to his great prospective work.

"Knowing how short his life might be, I once asked him whether he felt no concern lest the work already done by him should be frustrate, from the lack of its necessary complement, in case he were suddenly cut off. His answer surprised me by its indifference. He would work as long as he lived, he said, but not allow himself to worry, and would look serenely at whatever might be the outcome. This seemed to me uncommonly high-minded. I think that Davidson's conviction of immortality had much to do with such a superiority to accidents. On the surface and toward small things, he was irritable enough, but the undertone of his character was remarkable for equanimity. He showed it in his final illness, of which the misery was really atrocious. There were no general complaints or lamentations about the personal situation or the arrest to his career. It was the human lot, and

[1] "Memories and Studies", New York, 1911.

he must even bear it; so he kept his mind upon objective matter."

Only a profound conviction of personal immortality will enable a man who feels that he is cut off in the midst of his work to bear with patience the final ailment which by its very progress is precluding the possibility of accomplishing the task that he had set himself. Yet this interruption of their chosen labor inevitably comes to a great many men; for death, no matter how late it may seem to onlookers to occur, happens untimely to most of humanity, even though they may count up years far beyond the threescore and ten of the Psalmist.

The greatest resource in the midst of the suffering caused by the war for soldiers and civilians has been religion. It was sadly needed, but it was magnificently employed. Any one who saw how much their religion meant to the soldiers who really had faith will appreciate very well how valuable it was for them. Many a man who had given up his faith, and this was particularly true of the French, found a new power to dare and to do, and also to bear and to "carry on" in the religion that it had seemed they could so readily dispense with before.

Colton, writing a series of aphorisms in "Lacon", a century ago, declared that there are three arguments for atheism more effective than any others, — health and wealth and friends. When we have our health and an abundance of money at command, besides many and powerful friends who seem willing to do everything that they can for us, we feel but little need of God and then many men refuse to believe in him. Necessity is a very precious thing, the mother not only of invention, but of reverence and many other good qualities. But when suffering comes, especially if wealth, and in that case of course, friends, have disappeared, God is a very firm support to lean on. Many a man has found his faith again under such circumstances and has realized how flimsy were the veils which he had allowed to come between him and his recognition of his obligations to his Creator.

The presence of suffering and evil in the world has provided us with one of the most striking arguments for the existence of God and of a hereafter that we have. As Goldwin Smith said:

"This at all events is certain: if death is to end all alike for the righteous and for the unrighteous, for those who have been blessings and for those who have been curses to their kind, the Power which rules the universe cannot be just in any sense of the word which we can understand."

Doctor Carroll, in "The Mastery of Nervousness"[1] has summed up the value of suffering as a revealer of power and a bracer of strength in words that are worth remembering. "None knows his real strength till he has faced failure and tasted the bitterness of defeat. Physical and mental suffering and soul pain come to all that endurance may be developed, for without this the strength which conquers can never be. The master man laughs in the face of personal hurts; offenses fail to offend, insults fail to embitter; he turns with shame from the so-called depths of suffering; for him honor and majesty of soul are found upon the heights of suffering." In a word the really brave man does not let himself sink under the burden of suffering but maintains his place and stands up firmly under it. Under these circumstances suffering, instead of being an evil, is a good. After the showing of mercy, man is likest to God when he stands suffering bravely and brings good out of evil even as Providence does.

[1] Macmillan, New York, 1918.

CHAPTER XV

PAIN

PAIN is one of the very hard things of life which most people find it extremely difficult to bear with equanimity. I suppose that the majority of human beings, especially when they are young, do not feel nearly so much dread of death as they do of the possibility of years of discomfort preceding it or even a short period of very acute pain when nature is preparing for dissolution. Older folks learn to bear physical pain better and come to appreciate how much harder to stand is mental anguish. Modern life, with its cultivation of comforts and conveniences and the elimination of discomforts of all kinds, has greatly fostered the dread of pain. We hear much of the progress of humanity founded on the increase of comfort, but that way lies degeneracy and failure to take life seriously. Human character develops under the stress of pain and even the body acquires self-control through it and is trained under the discipline of pain not to react so disturbingly as is the case when there has been no experience with it or but very little.

We find it almost impossible to understand, now that we have cultivated the comforts of life so sedulously, how men and women stood the discomforts to which they were subjected in the ordinary run of life practically every day two generations ago. A great many of them slept in little stuffy attics with scarcely any chance for the free movement of air on the hot days of summer, often immediately underneath a roof which had been exposed to the direct rays of the sun all day long. In the winter not infrequently they broke the ice in their pitchers to secure water for washing. Their heating arrangements were so imperfect that in the colder months at least there was very little possibility of comfort. A grate fire makes a very charming ornamental addition to a room which is heated by steam or some other modern heating arrangement, but when it is the only means of heating it is not very efficacious except in milder weather. On very cold days an open fire will heat one side of the individual, but not the whole person, and at best the feet are likely to be cold because the open fire must be fed with an abundance of air and the draft runs along the floor in order to get to it. The story is told of an English public school in the old days where the head master met one of the smaller boys crying because of the cold; on being told what was the matter, the head master simply remarked that "this was no young ladies' seminary, and young gentlemen are expected to stand things without tears." Twenty years later in India, during the Mutiny, just before that boy who had cried from the cold led a forlorn hope of a charge with the idea of saving the lives of women and children, he remarked to his commanding officer who was himself also from that same public school, "This is what old . . . " — naming the head master — "would have said is no young ladies' seminary." And then he went out without more ado to accept death in a great cause.

It is extremely difficult for us to understand how the people of the older time, young and old, endured all these trials and hardships, though it is not difficult to comprehend that if one were exercised daily in standing things of this kind it would be much easier to bear pain and even serious discomfort than it is at the present time, when many people can bear only the touch of silk on the skin and the sybarite's complaint of his utter inability to sleep because there was a crushed rose leaf underneath him has become almost a literal reality. More and more we are eliminating discomforts from life and making things as comfortable and easy as possible. From the carefully tempered water of the morning bath to the warm foot bath just before sleep, in a bedroom where the temperature makes it possible to undress for bed without a shiver, all is arranged for the avoidance of the slightest discomfort.

Pain has become a veritable nightmare to most people as a consequence of the lack of the necessity to stand things in life, and it is therefore all the more interesting to see what an effect religion can have in enabling people to stand pain. In my volume "Health through Will Power" I have told the story of the second last General of the Jesuits and the very serious and intensely painful operation which he insisted on standing without an anæsthetic. The story is worth repeating here as showing what a habit of prayer and practice of self-control can do for a man in the face of some of the severest pain a human being is asked to stand. Generals of the Jesuits have usually found their way into literature for very different reasons from this.

He had developed a sarcoma of his upper arm and was advised to submit to an amputation at the shoulder joint. As he was well on in the sixties the operation presented an extremely serious problem. The surgeons suggested that he should be ready for the anæsthetic at a given hour the next morning and then they would proceed to operate. He replied that he would be ready for the operation at the time appointed, but that he would not take an anæsthetic. They argued with him that it would be quite impossible for him to stand unanæsthetized the elaborate cutting and dissection necessary to complete an operation of this kind in a most important part of the body, where large nerves and arteries would have to be cut through and where the slightest disturbance on the part of the patient might easily lead to serious or even fatal results. Above all, he could not hope to stand the exaggerated pain that would surely be produced in the tissues rendered more sensitive than normal by the increased circulation to the part, due to the growth of the tumor.

He insisted, however, that he would not take an anæsthetic, for surely here seemed a chance to welcome suffering voluntarily as his Lord and Master had done. I believe that the head surgeon said at first that he would not operate. He felt sure that the operation would have to be interrupted after it had been begun, because the patient would not be able to stand the pain, and there would then be the danger from bleeding as well as from infection which might occur as the result of the delay. The General of the Jesuits, however, was so calm and firm that at last it was determined to permit him at least to try to stand it.

The event was most interesting. The patient not only underwent the operation without a murmur, but absolutely without wincing. The surgeon who performed the operation said afterwards, "It was like cutting wax and not human flesh, so far as any reaction was concerned, though of course it bled very freely."

Professor William James has noted this same power with regard to that most painful of all diseases in which pain seems so much harder to stand because it is hopeless, and there is no possibility that the endurance of it can lead eventually to any improvement. The patient must just stand being racked to pieces until the end comes. No wonder then that the professor of psychology should note with commendation the effect of religion in bringing about a sense of well-being in spite of the constantly progressive physical condition which was so painfully eating life away. He said:

"The most genuinely saintly person I have ever known is a friend of mine now suffering from cancer of the breast — I hope that she may pardon my citing her here as an example of what ideas can do. Her ideas have kept her a practically well woman for months after she should have given up and gone to bed. They have annulled all pain and weakness and given her a cheerful active life, unusually beneficent to others to whom she has afforded help. Her doctors, acquiescing in results they could not understand, have had the good sense to let her go her own way."

Many physicians, I am sure, have had the opportunity to witness instances very like that which is thus recorded with whole-hearted sympathy by Professor James. I count it as one of the precious privileges of life to have known rather well a distinguished professor of anatomy at Professor James' own university. He suffered from incurable cancer and two years before the end knew that nothing could be done for him and that it was just a question of time and pain and the most poignant discomfort until the end would come. He continued his lessons at the university; he finished up a book that he had long wished to write and had begun several times; he maintained his simple, social relations with friends in such a gracious spirit that none of them suspected his condition and continued until the very end bravely to go on with his work quite as if there were nothing the matter.

I shall never forget how shocked I was when I once presumed to invite an addition to his labors by asking him to make a public address, and he told me, as a brother physician, just how much he had to be in the trained nurse's hands every day so as to keep himself from being offensive to others. I had met him at lunch in the bosom of his family and spent several pleasant hours with him afterward without ever a thought of the possibility of the hideous malignant neoplasm which was constantly at work making a wreck of his tissues and which no one knew better than he would never be appeased with less than his death.

He himself would have said that whatever there was of courage in his conduct was due to the strength that came to him from prayer. It was his consolation and the sources of the energy which enabled him to stand not only the pain he had to suffer but to suppress any manifestations with regard to it and keep on with his work.

There is an impression in many minds that as time goes on and medicine and surgery advance and science scores further triumphs, pain and ill health generally will decrease, and there will not be nearly so much necessity for standing pain as there is even at the present time. Besides, it is thought that the discovery of new modes of stilling pain will still further eliminate the necessity for patience. As a matter of fact, all our advance in hygiene and sanitation and scientific medicine has served rather to increase than lessen the amount of pain. People now live longer than they used to. They live on to die of the degenerative diseases which are slow running and often involve a great deal of pain over a prolonged period. One reason, probably the most important one, for the great increase of the number of deaths from cancer in recent years is the fact that ever so many more people now live on to the cancer age than before. Every year beyond forty which a human being lives increases the liability of death from cancer in that individual. There are some enthusiasts in the field of medicine who are inclined to think that we may discover the cause of cancer and eliminate the disease, but after a generation of special effort in that direction with absolutely no hopeful outlook, this is at least a dubious prospect. Indeed, there are many good authorities on the subject, who are inclined to feel that cancer more often represents an embryologic or developmental defect than almost anything else and that in so far as it does we can scarcely hope ever to eliminate it.

While the death rate from other acute diseases has been decreasing in recent years and especially from the infectious diseases, the mortality from affections of the kidneys, heart and brain has been increasing. Almost needless to say, these affections are practically always chronic, involve definite discomfort when not positively acute suffering, and not infrequently produce bodily states in which people must bear patiently a great deal of discomfort, sometimes for years. When people live beyond middle life they become more and more liable to be affected by these diseases, so that instead of needing less consolation for pain, our generation and the immediately succeeding generations at least are going to need more. It is particularly the people who are stricken with chronic disease who need the consolation afforded by religion, above all when they know that their affection is essentially incurable and that the only absolute relief they can have will come from death.

It is with this as with regard to hospitals and charity. The greater the advance in medicine and the longer people are kept in life, the more need there will be for hospital care and consequently for the exercise of charity in the best sense of that word and also for patience in pain and suffering. In these matters, as with regard to knowledge, science, instead of lessening the need of religion and its influence, is multiplying it. There is not the slightest reason for thinking that a man will ever make here on earth a heaven in which he may be perfectly happy, and even those enthusiastic advocates of modern progress who are inclined to think of the possibility of this set the date of it so far forward in the future, especially since the disillusionizing process of the Great War, that even the fulfillment of their prophecy is not likely to do very much good for our generation or for many subsequent generations. We are going to need the consolations afforded by religion even more than our forefathers did in the past, now that physicians are able to prolong life and yet cannot entirely do away with suffering.

Above all it must not be forgotten that the cult of comfort and convenience and what may well be called the habit of luxury in the modern time has greatly increased sensitiveness to pain. There are two elements that enter into suffering, as we have said in the chapter on that subject. The one is the irritation of a sensitive nerve and the other is the reaction to it in the mind of the sufferer. If, for any reason, the nerve has been rendered insensitive, or the mind put in a condition where it cannot receive the irritation, the subject will not feel the pain. If anything has happened to increase the irritability of a nerve, as happens, for instance, when continued irritation has brought more blood to the part than usual and the affected area is hyperemic and swollen, the pain will be greater because the nerve is more sensitive. If anything happens to make the mind more receptive of pain, and especially if the pain message that comes up along a nerve is diffused over a large part of the brain because there is a concentration of attention on it, then too the pain will be ever so much worse. We are, in various ways, adding to this subjective element of pain and therefore increasing it. We are going to need then all the possible consolation that can be afforded by religious motives.

In an article written for the *International Clinics*,[1] on "Neurotic Discomfort and the Law of Avalanche", I called attention to how much even comparatively mild pains can be increased by concentration of attention.

The law of avalanche is a term employed by Ramón y Cajal to indicate the mode by which very simple sensations at the periphery of the body may be multiplied into an avalanche of sensations within the brain. In a lecture of his for *International Clinics*[2] Professor Ramón y Cajal said: "Impressions are made upon single cells at the periphery. As the result of the disturbance of the single cell, an ever-increasing number of cells are affected as the nervous impulse travels toward the nerve-center. Finally the nervous impulses reach the brain and are spread over a considerable group of pyramidal cells in the cortex."

In his paragraphs on attention he says that if conscious

[1] Series 23, Vol. IV. [2] Series 11, Vol. II.

attention is paid to the sensation a great many other cells throughout the brain become affected by it. It may be that every cell which subtends consciousness will at a given moment of intense attention be tingling from a single sensation. If it is unpleasant, the unpleasantness is multiplied to a very serious degree. The "law of avalanche" has a very large place in disturbing the lives of those people who have much time on their hands to think about themselves and who are always solicitous lest some serious condition should be developing.

Our self-conscious generation, as religious impressions have been diminished in recent years, is making its pains ever so much more difficult to bear than they were before. Paying attention to slight discomfort will quite literally turn it into a veritable torment. Prayer of itself, by distracting the attention, will act in an actual physical manner to reduce the pain, and the habit of prayer could accomplish very much in that direction. The feeling that somehow the pain that is being borne is not merely a useless torment but has a dual beneficial effect in strengthening character and storing up merit for the hereafter, as the religious minded believe, will do a very great deal to make the pain more bearable. As we are not going to have less pain for humanity, and suffering and death are to be always with us, not even the most roseate dreams of medical scientists contemplating their elimination, it is easy to understand how valuable religious motives will continue to be. Meantime physicians have abundance of experience of how much religion can do to make life, even under the most trying circumstances, not only useful for self and others, but even satisfying for those who would otherwise find it an almost intolerable burden.

Probably the most fruitful source of consolation to be found in life is contained in the profound conviction that the Lord and Master said to those who would come after Him that if they would be His disciples they must take up their cross and follow Him. One of the very great books of world literature is "The Imitation of Christ", the keynote of which is contained in its title.

This little book, which has chapters bearing such titles as "That a Man Must not be over Eager about his Affairs" and "That a Man has Nothing Good of Himself" and which suggests "That True Comfort must be Sought in God Alone" and "That All care Should be Cast upon God" and "That Worldly Honor must be Held in Contempt" and "That All Things, however Grievous, are to be Borne for the Sake of Eternal Life" and "That a Man ought to Consider Himself more Worthy of Chastisement than of Consolation", has been the favorite reading of more of the men and women whose opinions are worth while in the world's history than probably any other, with the exception of the Bible itself. It has been placed next to Homer and Dante and Shakespeare among the books which scholars would preserve if, by a cataclysm, all the other books in the world were to be destroyed. When, some years ago, there was a spirited discussion in the English newspapers and magazines as to the ten books which should be selected if one were to be on a desert island for the rest of life with only these ten books for company, the "Imitation of Christ" almost invariably found its way into the list and usually among the first five.

If the little book which emphasizes the pain and suffering of life has come to be looked upon as one of the greatest books of the world, by the very fact of its profound treatment of this subject in lofty poetry, then it is easy to understand the place that pain bears in life. It is at the very heart of it. Nothing so reveals its meaning and makes it so bearable as religion. Just as it is true with regard to suffering, as stated in the chapter on that subject, that the five poets who at long-separated intervals in the world's history dared to take the mystery of suffering in the world for the subject of their poems, made by that very fact the greatest dramatic poetry that has ever been made, so this humble member of the Brethren of the Common Life, Thomas à Kempis, working just as the Renaissance was beginning, and writing the spiritual conferences for "those humble-minded patient teachers and thinkers" as Hamilton Mabie said, "whose devotion and fire of soul for a century and a half made the choice treasures of Italian palaces and convents and universities a common possession along the low-lying shores of the Netherlands", composed what his contemporaries called "ecclesiastical music", and what all subsequent generations have agreed in thinking the most wonderful expression of the significance of life in terms of Christianity that has ever been written.

CHAPTER XVI

SUICIDE AND HOMICIDE

No book on religion and health would be complete without a discussion of the effect of religious influence on these two very important factors in modern mortality statistics, especially in our own country, — suicide and homicide. One of the most disturbing features of public health work is the occurrence of such a large number of deaths every year in our great city life from murder and self-murder. It is discouraging to have the death rate from nearly every form of disease coming down while these are going up. Any factor which promises, however modestly, to remove even to a slight degree this stigma from our modern civilization is worthy of consideration. The moral factors in life are most important in this regard and over these religion has the most direct and potent influence.

One of the most disturbing features of our modern life is the fact that in spite of the notable progressive increase of comfort in life far beyond what people enjoyed in the past, there has been a steadily mounting growth in the number of suicides every year in civilized countries. Comforts and conveniences have become widely diffused, so that the luxuries of the rich in the older time have become the everyday commonplaces of the poor or the simple necessities of the middle class, and life would seem to be ever so much more easy than it used to be. Yet more and more people find it so hard that they are willing to go out of life by their own hands to meet untimely the dark mystery of the future. It has become quite manifest that comfort of body and peace of mind are by no means in such direct ratio to one another as is usually thought, but rather the contrary. Our suicides take place more frequently among the better-to-do classes than among the poor who might possibly be expected to find life so hard that they could not stand it any longer. Even chronic suffering does not cause so many suicides as the various disappointments of life, most of which are only transitory in their effect.

Perhaps the most disturbing feature of the suicide situation lies in the fact that the average age of those who commit suicide every year is constantly becoming younger. Suicide used to be the resort particularly of the discouraged beyond middle life, but now it is becoming ever more and more the mode of escape from an immediate future of unhappiness which ever younger and younger folk foresee for themselves. Disappointments in love have always been occasions for suicide, but other causes have multiplied in recent years to an alarming degree, and now high-school children with the suggestion of sensational newspaper accounts of suicide in their minds turn to self-murder over failures in examination or setbacks in school work or over a scolding at home. Even below the age of fifteen suicides are reported rather frequently, because children have been punished or have been refused something that they had set their hearts on. The generation is engaged in producing many oversensitive young folk who cannot stand being disturbed in their hopes and aspirations.

Suicides have increased just in proportion to the decrease of attention to religion and the absence of religious teaching and above all of religious training, that is, of such practice of self-denial and of mortification for religious motives as leads to formation of character. When children and young folks are always given their own way and are not taught that denying themselves is of itself a virtue because it leads to strength of will power and enables one to stand the inevitable hardships of later life, no wonder that their first serious disappointments come to them as such disturbing misfortunes that they can scarcely picture to themselves a time when they shall be happy again. Above all a great many of them have no real belief in immortality and therefore face the future life with no feeling as to its mystery and no proper sense of their obligation toward a Creator who gave them life to use to the best advantage possible and who wants them to play the game of life fair, taking the ill with the good and "carrying on." The lack of religious feeling has left them with nothing to cling to in the midst of their trials, and though they may have friends, all human beings are eminently alone, and we must go through what is hard in life by ourselves. We never feel our loneliness more than when some severe trial comes. We almost resent the pity of others, and Emerson's phrase that we are "infinitely repellent particles" becomes a very grave reality.

It is the easy custom of our time to blame nearly all the social ills on what is called our present-day strenuous existence. There are a great many people who seem to think that men never worked so hard as they do now, though as a matter of fact in what concerns the accomplishment of things worth while our generation is sadly backward. He unfortunately grows preoccupied with trivial narrow concerns and keeps on working at them so continuously that we have become very fussy folk because we have no variety of occupation to relieve the strain of daily life. It must not be forgotten in this regard that some of the men who have lived the longest have been extremely hard workers, accomplishing so much in a number of lines of thought and endeavor that it has seemed almost impossible to understand how they did it, yet they have been healthy and hearty in mind and body until fourscore years, and sometimes, like Ranke, the great German historian, and Pope Leo XIII and Chevreul, the distinguished French chemist, even beyond ninety years of age and more. The strenuous existence is a good excuse, however, and a great many people are sure that it is the overtiredness and the disturbance of health and the depression which comes in connection with this that causes suicide or at least contributes greatly to the increase of it in our time.

Only a little analysis of suicide statistics, however, is necessary to make it very clear that it is not physical factors which contribute most to the increase of suicide, but that it is the state of mind of the individual. If the physical counted for much then it would be confidently expected that suicides would be commonest in the winter and least frequent in the summer, particularly in the pleasanter months of the summer time. The statistics show, however, that the month which has the most suicides is June. June is probably the pleasantest month of the year in most ways in our climate. July is likely to be very hot, May often has cold and rainy days at the beginning, but June has often a succession of almost perfect days. James Russell

Lowell sang, and it has been reëchoed many times, "What is so rare as a day in June", yet this is the month which more people take to put themselves out of existence than any other. Brides have chosen it as the favorite month for marriage because all nature looks so lovely and in sympathy with their own joy and because there are fewer rainy days in it than any other. Happy hearts are beginning a new existence with the brightest possible prospects just when so many others are voluntarily getting out of what seems a hopeless life.

December, which has so many gloomy days and which naturally is likely to be so much more depressing than the succeeding months of the winter, for the clear, cold days of January and February are bracing, might on physical grounds be expected to be the month with most suicides in it. Christmas with its celebrations and the announcement of peace and joy to men of good will might be expected to lower the number of suicides for the latter third of the month, but even the joy of that occasion could scarcely be hoped to neutralize completely the depressing effect of the weather. Just exactly the contradiction of these anticipations is what happens. Suicides are least frequent in December of any month in the year, and the last ten days of the month have the most of them because it is not so much the individual's own sense of hopelessness in life, complicated by physical suffering and material trials of various kinds, that tempts to suicide, as the contrast of the joy of those around him with his own feelings which emphasize his depressed state of mind until he feels that he can stand it no longer. June's gayety with its happy brides adds to the number of suicides and the Christmas festivities have a like unfortunate tendency. Gloomy weather has exactly the opposite effect from what would surely have been expected on the general principle that the physical plays the most important rôle in the production of suicides.

This is brought out still more clearly by the careful review of the effect of the weather on suicide which was made some years ago by Professor Edmund T. Dexter[1] of the University of Illinois.

He followed out the records of nearly two thousand cases of suicides reported to the police in the City of New York and placed beside them the records of the weather bureau of the same city for the days on which these suicides occurred. According to this, which represents not any preconceived notions but the realities of the relationship of the weather to self-murder, the tendency to suicide is highest in spring and summer, and the deed is accomplished in the great majority of cases on the sunniest days of these seasons. It is not at all a case of heat disturbance of mind or tendency to heat stroke, for as has been seen June is the month of most suicides and while it often has some hot days it does not compare in this regard with July and August or even September as a rule.

His conclusions are carefully drawn, and there is no doubt that they must be accepted as representing the actual facts. All the world feels depressed on rainy days and in dark, cloudy weather, but suicides react well, as a rule, against this physical depression, yet allow their mental depression to get the better of them on the finest days of the year. Professor Dexter said:

"The clear, dry days show the greatest number of suicides, and the wet, partly cloudy days the least; and

[1] *Popular Science Monthly*, April, 1901.

with differences too great to be attributed to accident or chance. In fact there are nearly one in three (31%) more suicides on dry than on wet days and more than one in five (21%) more on clear days than on days that are partly cloudy."

In reviewing the subject of suicide in my book on "Psychotherapy"[1] I suggested that this subject of depressed weather conditions as the contributing cause of suicide might be carried still further and the lack of the dispiriting influence of dark, damp weather, as a suicide factor, could be seen very strikingly from the suicide statistics of various climates.

The suicide rate is not highest in the torrid or in the frigid zones, but in the temperate zones. In the north temperate zone it is much more marked than in the south temperate zone. Civilization and culture, diffused to a much greater extent in the north temperate zone than in the south, seem to be the main reason for this difference. We make people capable of feeling pain more poignantly, but do not add to their power to stand trials or train character by self-control to make the best of life under reasonably severe conditions.

Severe physical suffering of any kind, provided it is shared by a whole people, reduces the suicide rate. Famine, for instance, though it might be expected that people facing starvation would surely take the easier way, rather reduces the tendency to suicide. Earthquakes followed by loss of life and intense suffering have the same effect. It might possibly be thought that this would be true only among less well educated people, the orientals or perhaps certain of the South Americans where lack of education made them less poignantly sensitive to physical suffer-

[1] D. Appleton & Co., New York, 1912.

ing than among the more refined people in our western civilization, but the earthquake at San Francisco demonstrated very clearly the effect upon average Californians who, I suppose, must be considered to have been rather a little above than below the general run of Americans in what we are accustomed to call civilization and education. Before the catastrophe, suicides were occurring in that city on an average of twelve a week. After the earthquake, when, if physical sufferings had anything to do with suicide, it might be expected that the self-murder rate would go up, there was so great a reduction that only three suicides were reported in two months. Some of this reduction was due to inadequate records, but there can be no doubt that literally a hundred lives were saved from suicide by the awful catastrophe that leveled the city. Men and women were homeless, destitute and exposed to every kind of hardship, yet because all those around them were suffering in the same way, every one seemed to be reasonably satisfied. Evidently a comparison with the conditions in which others are has much to do with deciding the would-be suicide not to make away with himself, for by dwelling too much on his own state he is prone to think that he is ever so much worse off than others.

If life were always vividly interesting, as it was in San Francisco after the earthquake, and if all men worked and suffered as the San Franciscans did for a few weeks, suicide would not end more than ten thousand American lives every year, as it does now. The one hope for the man who is contemplating suicide is to get him interested in others, to arouse him to the realization of the fact that there are others suffering even more than himself, but above all to get him to feel that he can relieve the suffering of others. Selfishness is the root of suicide, usually pathological in its utter preoccupation with self as the most important thing in the universe, but often only the result of a fostering of self-interest and a failure to train the mind to think of other people, which is of the very essence of religion.

It is not when things are made easy for mankind, but on the contrary when they are passing through times of difficulty and severe stress that the suicide rate goes down. War always brings a striking reduction in the number of suicides. Our Spanish-American War reduced the death rate from suicide in this country over forty per cent throughout the country and over fifty per cent in Washington itself, where there was most excitement with regard to the war. This was true also during the Civil War. Our minimum annual death rate from suicide from 1805 (when statistics on this subject began to be kept) to the present time was one suicide to about twenty-four thousand people, which occurred in 1864, when our Civil War was in its severest phase. There had been constant increase in our suicide rate every year until the Civil War began, then there was a drop at once and this continued until the end of the war. In New York City the average rate of suicide for the five years of the Civil War was nearly forty-five per cent lower than the average for the five following years. In Massachusetts, where the statistics were gathered very carefully, the number of suicides for the five-year period before 1860 was nearly twenty per cent greater than for the five-year period immediately following, which represents the preliminary excitement over the war and the actual year of the war. This experience in America is only in accordance with what happens everywhere. Mr. George Kennan in his article on

"The Problems of Suicide"[1] has a paragraph which brings this out very well. He says:

"In Europe the restraining influence of war upon the suicidal impulse is equally marked. The war between Austria and Italy in 1866 decreased the suicide rate for each country about fourteen per cent. The Franco-German War of 1870–1871 lowered the suicide rate of Saxony eight per cent, that of Prussia 11.4 per cent, and that of France 18.7 per cent. The reduction was greatest in France, because the German invasion of that country made the war excitement there much more general and intense than it was in Saxony or Prussia."

Above all the sense of patriotic duty, the recognition of the fact that there are things in life worth more than life itself, lifts men out of the depression into which they have permitted themselves to be plunged as a consequence of their utter absorption in themselves and their own narrow interests.

Old-fashioned religion has a distinct effect in the reduction of the suicide rate, and all over the world the orthodox Jews who cling to their old-time belief and above all to their orthodox practices and mode of life have undoubtedly the lowest suicide rate of any people in the world. This is true, though almost needless to say a great many Jews, not only in the foreign countries but here in our own great cities, have to live under circumstances that are the most trying that it is possible to imagine. A great many of them live in slums, doing intensely hard work in sweat shops — though, thank God, these are fewer now than they used to be — and yet the Jews cling to life in the midst of trials that would seem almost impossible for human nature to bear. The Jewish

[1] *McClure's Magazine*, June, 1908.

suicide rate is the lowest everywhere in spite of racial differences, for after all there are German Jews and Portuguese Jews and Russian Jews who have lived among the respective peoples after whom they are called for centuries and who might therefore be expected to take on the characteristics which their environments have brought. There is a very great difference in the suicide rate between the orthodox and unorthodox Jews, that is, those who have given up the beliefs and religious practices of their forefathers. It is in favor of the orthodox Jews, though of course the record is complicated by the prosperity of those who have given up their religion. Wealth and speculation greatly favor the occurrence of suicide.

It is well known that Roman Catholics the world over have much less tendency to suicide than their Protestant neighbors living in the same communities. It is true that where the national suicide rate is high, many Catholics also commit suicide, but there is a distinct disproportion between them and their neighbors. The suicide rate of Protestants in the northern part of Ireland, as pointed out by Mr. George Kennan, is twice that of Roman Catholics in the southern part. He discusses certain factors that would seem to modify the breadth of the conclusion that might be drawn from this, but in the end he confesses that their faith probably has most to do with it and that, above all, the practice of sacramental confession must be considered as tending to lessen the suicide rate materially. It is the readiness to give their confidence to some one on the part of these patients, for that is what they really are, that seems to the physician the best hope of helping them to combat their impulse, and Mr. Kennan's opinion is worth recalling for therapeutic purposes:

"In view of the fact that the suicide rate of the Protestant canton in Switzerland is nearly four times that of Catholic cantons, it seems probable that Catholicism, as a form of religious belief, does restrain the suicidal impulse. The efficient cause may be the Catholic practice of confessing to priests, which probably gives much encouragement and consolation to unhappy but devout believers and thus induces many of them to struggle on in spite of misfortune and depression."

It is not surprising that in countries where attendance at church and adhesion to religious organizations has dropped very seriously, the suicide rate should be higher than in countries where the great mass of the people are still faithful churchgoers, take their religious duties very seriously and therefore are subjected to the deepest influence of religion over the heart and mind at regularly recurring intervals. They find consolation in their suffering, advice in their trials, strength for their difficulties and a fount of hope almost for their despair. Above all they are deterred by the thought of another world than this and the possibility of punishment in it, if they have not had the courage and the manly strength of soul to face their difficulties in this.

It has come to be the custom rather to minimize the effect of deterrent motives on human beings and to say that men cannot be scared into doing good or avoiding evil, and it is quite true that a policy of frightfulness pursued out of mere malice to effect a human purpose will have exactly the opposite effect over the great majority of mankind, but when men realize that they are bringing punishment on themselves by their own acts, and that those acts are unjustifiable on any rational grounds, they have a very different feeling as a rule with regard to punishments that may be impending over them for their conduct. It is quite one thing to be unjustly punished and resent it and quite another to feel that the punishment we are incurring has justice in it, though we may not be quite able to understand all the significance of it or plumb its mystery entirely.

Shakespeare has Hamlet discuss that whole question in his soliloquy so well that it deserves to be quoted here:

> ". . . And by a sleep, to say we end
> The heart-ache, and the thousand natural shocks
> That flesh is heir to, — 't is a consummation
> Devoutly to be wished. To die, — to sleep: —
> To sleep, perchance to dream: — ay, there's the rub;
> For in that sleep of death what dreams may come,
> When we have shuffled off this mortal coil,
> Must give us pause. *There's* the respect,
> That makes calamity of so long life:
> For who would bear the whips and scorns of time,
> The oppressor's wrong, the proud man's contumely,
> The pangs of despised love, the law's delay,
> The insolence of office, and the spurns
> That patient merit of the unworthy takes,
> When he himself might his quietus make
> With a bare bodkin? Who would fardels bear,
> To grunt and sweat under a weary life,
> *But that the dread of something after death, —*
> *The undiscovered country, from whose bourn*
> *No traveller returns, — puzzles the will*
> *And makes us rather bear those ills we have*
> *Than fly to others that we know not of?*
> Thus conscience does make cowards of us all."

We have come to resent somewhat the suggestion of deterrent motives as helpful for the doing of good, and the dread of punishment as unworthy of men, but the religious beliefs of a hereafter of suffering for the coward who dares not face the trials of life are still and have always been valuable in keeping people up to their duty. The war restored some of the sadly needed old-fashioned attitude toward punishment as a help to discipline, and we are now more in sympathy with old-fashioned religious ideas in the matter.

There has been an even greater increase of homicide than of suicide and for very similar reasons. Our homicide rate here in America is a disgrace to a civilized country. Ambassador Andrew D. White, whose long experience in European countries made his opinion of great value, declared that for homicide we were the worst country in the world, with more killings of human beings to our credit than even vendetta-ridden Corsica. This is not due to any persistence of "wild west" conditions but obtains in the east as well as in the west. Indeed our large cities are by far the worst in this regard. New York and Chicago have many times as many murders annually as London has, though there is no very great difference in the composition of the population of these cities, for all of them house large numbers of foreigners of all kinds and they have about the same sort of slums and very nearly the same social conditions. Poverty is worse in London and if anything that ought to add to the homicide rate. Reverence for human life has very largely broken down, and the taking of it is not considered to be anything like the serious crime that it was even a few years ago.

This increase in homicide in civilized countries, like the increase in suicide, has come after the serious breakdown of religion. That the rise in the homicide rate is not a question of the familiar fallacy *post hoc ergo propter hoc*, "after this therefore because of this", is the opinion of a number of men who have a right to have opinions on this subject, and who insist that it is the obliteration of religious feeling with its emphatic insistence on the awfulness of the crime of murder that has largely served to make homicide the very common event that it is.

One powerful factor in this matter is undoubtedly the failure to punish murder properly, and as far as may be adequately, that has developed in recent years in this country. Very few murderers are executed. Less than five per cent altogether of those who have committed deliberate murder are ever executed, and in some States it is actually only two per cent. When but two out of every hundred men who take life deliberately lose theirs, it is easy to understand that men, in times of intense anger, will not have the restraint which would otherwise be exerted over them by the fear of prompt loss of life under disgraceful circumstances for themselves. Many a man will take his chances of having a long prison term for murder shortened by executive clemency or a pardon board who would hesitate very much over the thought of having to die himself by prompt legal measure. I have heard a distinguished jurist say that they execute nine out of ten of their murderers in England, while we execute a little more than two out of every hundred on the average of ours, so that there is little reason for wonder why we have ten times as many murders.

The real reason for this decrease in the number of executions and the growth of the opposition on principle to capital punishment in this country is the increasing obscuration of the belief in immortality. People have become afraid to do the irretrievable act of sending a man out of life because, thinking only in terms of this life, they feel he should have a chance for reform here and above all because they hesitate to think that men ever have the right to deprive another of existence, for if there is no other world than this, the end of physical life means annihilation. If life is but the portal to eternity, however, at longest a brief period of trial before entering upon another and much more important stage of existence, then the execution of a criminal done with all the dignity of the law, exacting a compensation as adequate as possible for a wrong that has been done, instead of being a dreadful thing has a very definite nobility about it. Of course, if there is no other world, the question of execution becomes a very different consideration, — the obliteration of a fellow human being. This feeling is often not consciously reflected upon, yet it is effective in suggesting conclusions and ruling the mental attitude.

The old religious orders had a tradition that certain men, because of the circumstances in which they died and above all the fact that they had sufficient warning as to the end of life and the chance to prepare themselves for eternity, were predestined to heaven, though they might have to go through a great deal of suffering, quite as Dante foresaw, before getting there. Among these the most prominent classes were men and women afflicted with an incurable disease which it was recognized would surely bring on a fatal conclusion with but a few months' or years' delay, and then those who were condemned to death had their weeks and months of preparation in prison for that event. This intense belief in a hereafter made the outlook on both murder and execution a very different thing from what it is without it.

Sentimentality reigns now where the sentiment of justice formerly ruled. A man who has committed an ugly sex crime capped with murder or who has often, after making her life miserable for months or years, murdered a poor wife in cold-blooded deliberateness, will be the subject of sentimental compassion during his trial from a crowd of silly women who will send flowers to his cell to lighten his solitude and who, if they can obtain permission, will visit him in the death house. They forget all that his victim suffered and the necessity for producing a definite effect upon the minds of others who might have the temptation to follow in his path, and whose minds are of a caliber that they can only be deterred by holding up adequate punishment before them.

The gradual diminution of the place of religion in life has given rise to an unfortunate phase of popular psychology with regard to the effect of punishment in general on human beings. The wisest writings that we have, the Holy Scriptures, which even those who might deny their direct divine inspiration would confess readily to contain the most marvelous knowledge of man and his ways to be found in literature, have insisted particularly on the deterrent effect of punishment held up before men and the reforming value of it when properly inflicted.

Probably nowhere in modern social life is a revival of religion more needed to save men from unfortunate tendencies in their natures than in what concerns the estimation of the value of human life and the prevention of a further increase in our awful statistics of suicide and homicide. Religion is almost more needed for this than for the so-called social diseases.

CHAPTER XVII

LONGEVITY

In spite of the Psalmist's warning that threescore years and ten are the years of man and that life beyond that is likely to be filled with all sorts of discomforts, practically all men are anxious to live long lives. They are satisfied to take the diseases of advanced years provided only there are surceases from pain at intervals and they are able to occupy themselves for some part of the time with their usual interests. It is true that a certain sadly increasing number in our time shorten existence by their own hand, and at an ever younger age on the average and that some at least of those who do so are not insane in any justifiable legal sense of the word, but they are felt by all to be unfortunate exceptions who prove that the rule of love of life and desire to cling to it through sad and evil case is practically universal among men. Life may be, in the words of the cynic, a chronic disease, whose termination is always death, but most men prefer that the disease should last as long as possible.

The most important factor for long life is of course heredity. The man who wants to live long should have been careful to be born of long-lived parents and grandparents. Doctor Oliver Wendell Holmes once said that the physician would often like to be in the position to treat in the persons of his patient's grandparents a number of the diseases that he sees in his consulting room. Whatever truth there may be in that, there is no doubt at all that there is very little hope of a man living long if his parents and grandparents have been short-lived, unless of course their taking off has been due to accident. After family heredity, however, undoubtedly the most important factor for longevity is an abiding sense of religion. A great many religious people live beyond the average age, and a great many clergymen live to be very old men and yet retain their faculties and physical powers very well. They are not longer lived than other professional men on the average, because many of those who become clergymen are delicate by nature and only rarely so robust as other college men.

In recent years the insurance companies have come to recognize very clearly what is called the moral hazard in life. A man who lives a quiet, simple life without excesses in eating or drinking, getting his full quota of sleep and his meals regularly without temptations to high living of various kinds is much more likely to outlive his mathematical average of expectancy in life than the man who does not follow that sort of existence.

Almost needless to say it is seriously religious men — all clergymen do not necessarily come under this head — who live these very regular lives and do not allow themselves the occasional divagations in life which may not in themselves prove serious but which often lead to conditions and developments that impair health and shorten existence. There are undoubtedly a good many men who have sowed their wild oats very freely when they were young and who have continued all their lives to be rather free livers, and who yet have lived on to good round old age. What we speak of here, however, is the average length of life which in men who live without excesses and without over-solicitude about the future or the present is sure to be longer than in others.

The old proverb says that "worry and not work kills men." Undoubtedly worry rather than work ages men before their time and breaks down their vital resistance and makes them much more susceptible to the many diseases that may shorten existence as the years go on than they would have been liable to had they lived regular lives. Religion is the great salve for worries. When genuine it lessens the irritations of life, makes them more bearable, renders the disposition more equable and more capable of standing the stresses and strains of sudden trials or serious misfortunes than it would otherwise be. Religion does not change nature essentially, but it lifts it up and modifies it to a noteworthy degree. Even Christ did not come to change human nature; He assumed it and showed men how to live. Religion does not make a passionate disposition mild, but it confers upon the passionate man the power to control his passions to no small extent and often so thoroughly that even those who know him best have no idea of the storms which start to brew within him but are suppressed.

Almost needless to say the moderation in all things which religion counsels and which its training fosters is extremely conducive to long life, if there is any underlying basis for that in the nature of the individual. Religion is like oil for machinery. It lessens the friction, prevents the development of heat which would only be destructive and serve no useful purpose, soothes the temper against reactions and smooths out life's ways. Some one once suggested that it represented the rubber tires of the modern automobile, but that is not a good figure, for the inflation on which a man is smoothly carried may blow out at any moment and leave him to run on the rim. That is much better represented by sentimentality and the motives drawn from it rather than from religion.

The direct influence of religion on health can very probably be estimated best by the comparative death rate of occupations. Clergymen, according to English statistics which are gathered rather carefully, have the lowest death rate, even below that of gardeners and nurserymen whose constant outdoors life gives them such an advantage and whose simple laborious occupation without excitement is so favorable for long life. After these come the farmers and then the agricultural laborers, and then a long distance afterwards the schoolmasters and grocers and mechanics generally. The highest death rates in occupations occur not among the laboring classes occupied at the particularly unhealthy trades — plumbers and painters who are subjected to lead; file makers and knife grinders whose lungs are seriously hurt by dust; and earthenware manufacturers who are subjected to the influence of both dust and lead — but among the innkeepers, spirit, wine and beer dealers and above all the inn and hotel servants among whom the moral hazards of life are greatly increased and over whom religion fails to have the influence that would be beneficial.

Perhaps the best way to demonstrate the effect of religion in lessening the wear and tear of life, thus proving conducive to its prolongation, is to take the statistics of the lives of those who devote themselves so thoroughly to their religious duties that they are called by the name *religious*. They give themselves not alone to the daily but almost to the hourly practice of religion, and its influence has a thoroughgoing opportunity to exert itself over their lives. Most of them live very simply and abstemiously, and indeed many people would be inclined to say that they did not take quite sufficient food to nourish them properly and that they allowed their sleep to be interrupted by religious duties in such ways as not to afford themselves quite rest enough. They are all very early risers, at five o'clock in the winter at the latest and in summer at four, while not a few of them get up at some hour during the night to sing some portion of the office, the full round of which has to be completed every day. Their beds are usually rather hard; there is no carpet on the floor in their cells, their lives to most people would seem rather narrow and without adequate diversion, and yet they are noted for living beyond the average age, except in cases where work in hospitals or the like subjects them to the danger of infection.

The tradition with regard to this prolongation of life among the religious has existed since a very early time in Christianity and indeed was noted before the Christian era among the men and women who, as among the Buddhists, lived in monastic seclusion lives of great abstinence and occupation with the contemplation of the hereafter. In the very early days of Christianity a number of the men who withdrew to live the lives of solitaries in the desert regions of Egypt and of Syria exceeded the Psalmist's limit of life, though the account of their neglect of food would seem to make that almost impossible. A number of them lived to be beyond seventy and not a few beyond eighty and some of them over ninety. St. Anthony, who is often spoken of as the first hermit, lived to be beyond one hundred.

It is a matter of never-ending surprise to find how many

people who dwell in monasteries, where their occupation is mainly some simple work of the hands varied by long hours of reading and prayer during every day in the year, live to be very old. It might be surmised that their opportunities for introspection and thought about themselves would be so frequent and extensive that they would get on their own minds and probably be the victims of various nervous symptoms that would shorten existence through worries over trifles. So far is this from being the case, however, that some of the most striking examples of group longevity among people who are unrelated are to be found in what are known as contemplative monasteries, that is, institutions where there is only enough active life every day necessary to maintain health and supplies for the simple physical needs of a monastery, and the rest of the time is spent in reading, prayer, meditation and the saying of the Divine Office.

The modern religious orders, which imitate some at least of the austerities of the old solitaries and those who in the early days of Christianity lived in communities, have a record of longevity quite equal to that of their forbears. What an absolutely regular life under deep religious influences, where practically every hour of the day has its allotted task, where no meat is eaten and two Lents a year are kept — that is one third less is eaten for about one fourth of the year — will do to prolong human life, can be seen very well from the vital statistics of the well-known Trappist Monastery at Gethsemane in Kentucky, which are before me as I write. The average age at death of the members of this community for the last twenty-five years is nearly seventy-three. A number of them lived to be beyond eighty, and as the Abbot has written to tell me, the most satisfactory thing for the community lies in the fact that the old members, even at fourscore years and more, can practically always join in the common life of the community and do not need to be specially waited on or taken care of. Their death is likely to be quiet and rather easy, the flickering out of the spark of life rather than its extinction.

One of the Benedictines has furnished me statistics for that order here in America, for there might be the feeling that in other countries life would be different and that longevity would occur for different reasons than those which occasion it in this country. A great many among the Benedictines live to celebrate their golden jubilee, and life among them has been calculated to be at least ten years more than that of their brothers and sisters who remained in the world.

Of course it might be said that only the people of very placid disposition who take things very quietly and are not inclined to worry would enter such institutions as these, and there is some truth in the statement. It is not nearly so true, however, as most people would imagine, for a great many of those who enter convents and monasteries were rather lively and gay when they were younger; indeed it has often been said that it was the liveliest, happiest and most charming girls at the convent schools who were destined to enter the convents afterwards.

As regards the monasteries for men, the same rule of longevity holds, and yet a great many of these men were not only lively and gay, but some of them had rather stormy careers before they settled down to the contemplative life after something of remorse over the foolishness which had led them astray in their younger years.

The men and women who enter religious orders are of course the more serious characters who take life rather placidly, and this adds to their expectancy of life, for it is worry rather than work or suffering that shortens existence, but it must not be forgotten that not a little of their placidity is not natural to their dispositions, but is rather acquired as the result of their deep religious feelings and their recognition of the fact that God's Will will be accomplished anyhow and there is no use worrying about things.

Undoubtedly one of the principal reasons why the death rate among women at all ages is so much more favorable than might be expected, in spite of their apparent tendency to worry more, their nervousness about many things, and the dangers of maternity as well as their weaker physical constitution, is to be found in the fact that religious influences are much more profound over them and have a more calming effect than over men. A very old expression calls women the devout female sex, and the influence of their devotion to religion is reflected in their mortality statistics. Doctor Woods Hutchinson, in his "Civilization and Health",[1] has a chapter on "The Hardy Nerves of Women" in which he brings out the fact that women resist the corroding effect of the strenuous life of modern civilization better than men and are not subject to the factors which have made modern health statistics so disturbing. For while we have been lengthening the average term of life and reducing the death rate in general, we have been shocked to find that the mortality above forty-five has been increasing rather than decreasing, so that men are being taken off just at the prime of life and at the height of their usefulness more than ever before, in spite of all our hygiene and the development of sanitary science.

[1] Boston, 1914.

The difference in mortality between men and women after the age of forty-five, that is, just at the time when religious feelings are likely to represent so much of a resource for the devout female sex, is so striking as to deserve to be noted particularly, and the contrast continues more and more to be emphasized as the years go on.

The average age at death has risen during the past generation from about thirty-three to slightly above fifty, but this improvement has been chiefly effected by saving the babies and children from death from unclean milk and the acute infectious diseases, and young adults from the great plagues of past generations, typhoid and tuberculosis. Doctor Hutchinson goes on to say:

"Naturally this preserves a much larger number of individuals to live to, say, the age of forty-five. And, as we must all die sometime, we begin to drop off somewhat more rapidly after this point has been reached — that is to say, the stupid and helpless creature, man, does. Woman, however, is far too shrewd for that. While man's mortality, after falling off markedly up to forty-five years, begins after that period to increase distinctly, woman's death rate, on the other hand, continues to decrease until fifty-five years of age, beating man ten years; then yields to the force of circumstances only to the extent of about one tenth of the increase man shows between fifty-five and sixty-five; and after seventy proceeds to decrease again."

Incidentally, it may be remarked that the total increase of mortality after forty-five in man is only about six per cent; besides which, the race need not worry much about what happens to the individual after fifty-five or sixty, provided he has done his share of the world's work. But women pass men three laps to the mile, for their increase of death rate after the age of fifty-five is barely one per cent, or one sixth of man's.

The lessened death rates among women at all ages are notable, particularly among those who have taken life seriously and religiously. Typical examples of similar longevity which they themselves would surely have declared to have been influenced more by their religious attitude of mind than by any other single factor are noteworthy in the lives of the two English cardinals of the nineteenth century, Newman and Manning. Both of them were men who accomplished a very great deal of work in their younger years and who then went through the serious mental strain of giving up friends and ways that had been very near and dear to them and making a great revolution in their lives. Both of them lived to be well past eighty, and indeed Newman lived to be past ninety in the full possession of vigorous power of mind until the very end of life. He himself had not looked for long life, but on the contrary had felt that he was one of those fated to die rather young; indeed, in the sixties, he had begun to think that he would give up work, and his friends had settled down to the idea that he would not be long with them, when an attack on his sincerity aroused him to a magnificent response that is one of the precious treasures of nineteenth-century literature and then for nearly thirty years longer he was a great intellectual force.

This same thing is very well illustrated in the lives of the Popes of the nineteenth century, that is, during the period when modern hygiene and sanitation have developed to such an extent as to make the conservative influence of religion on health felt to the best possible effect. The

Popes all down the centuries have lived far beyond the average of humanity, in spite of the burdens of responsibility placed on them, and even the shortening of life by martyrdom of so many of them at the beginning. Our nineteenth and twentieth-century Popes have proved wonderful examples of what placidity of mind can do under the most difficult circumstances in keeping worries from wearing out life energies, in spite of the fact that the life stream in some of the cases did not appear to be very strong at its source and long life seemed almost out of the question.

These long lives might very well be matched from the lists of old pastors from all the denominations and the sects who have outlived the years of the Psalmist without incurring the physical evils which he prophesied. Old clergymen are particularly likely to retain the full possession of their senses and to live on to a quiet, peaceful old age. I once heard one of them say — I believe that it was a quotation — that he used to think that all the pleasure of life was contained in the first eighty years, but now at the age of eighty-five he knew that there was a great deal of life's satisfaction to be found in the second eighty years.

There are exceptions to the rule, of course, and most of us would think that they are the sort of exceptions that prove the rule. There is an old saw in many languages which says that the good die young, but physicians are likely to think that this old-fashioned expression is founded on nothing more than the fact that a good many of the weaklings born without very much vitality develop into harmless nonentities who have no strong impulses to either good or ill, and who have but very little resistive vitality and die of the infectious diseases in early youth or are carried off by tuberculosis a little later. It must not be forgotten, however, that it is as much of an accident to run into a bacillus as into a trolley car, and indeed often more serious, and though all that too is in the hands of the Lord, in the order of Providence secondary causes work out their destined effects. Quite contrary to the tradition that the good die young is the world experience that a great many of the good, that is, men of sterling character and worth who have proved thoroughly capable of doing what is best in life for the benefit of others rather than for themselves, live on to be a source of inspiration to those around them for many, many years of a long and physically active life, even though sometimes they may run into the rule that whom the Lord loves he chastens, and they may have had many trials.

The Scriptural promises made over and over again were that the years of those who should keep His word should be long in the land. That promise has been fulfilled so often as to make it a commonplace. Three hundred years ago Shakespeare summed up at least the physical effects of keeping the law when he had old Adam say in "As You Like It":

> "Though I look old, yet I am strong and lusty;
> For in my youth I never did apply
> Hot and rebellious liquors in my blood;
> Nor did not with unbashful forehead woo
> The means of weakness and debility;
> Therefore my age is as a lusty winter,
> Frosty, but kindly. Let me go with you:
> I 'll do the service of a younger man
> In all your business and necessities."

CHAPTER XVIII

THE BIBLE AND HEALTH

FROM the very earliest times religious legislation has proved an extremely important factor for health. The book of Leviticus, one of the very oldest religious documents that we have, contains a sanitary code which is a marvel of completeness in its prescriptions for the maintenance of health and the prevention of disease. It anticipates most of the modern discoveries in this matter and the faithful keeping of its regulations has made the Jew the powerful personal factor that he has been so often in history, notwithstanding the fact that he belonged to a despised subject race. The orthodox Jew has kept his health in spite of the unfavorable conditions in which he was placed much better on the average than the Gentiles around him, and it is for that reason that his nation has been preserved. It would have seemed almost impossible for a people treated so badly as they were, crowded into unhealthy ghettos, often in the lowest and most insanitary parts of the towns, with no municipal care exercised for their health — except when it was feared that epidemics might spread from them to the Gentiles — to have maintained themselves for all these centuries; but they have not only survived but have been the most vigorous of people, at all times full of initiative and readiness to work far beyond the average of humanity.

The sanitary code of the Jewish people which is contained in the Old Testament is one of the greatest triumphs of sanitary legislation that the world has ever known. Doctor Alexander Rattray, in his volumes on "Divine Hygiene, Sanitary Science and Sanitarians of the Sacred Scriptures and Mosaic Code",[1] has brought this out very clearly. The Scriptural motto of his work, "That Thy way might be known upon earth; Thy saving health among all nations", is an excellent text for what he has to say. With regard to the sanitary code of the Hebrews, as compared with other ancient documents in sanitation, Doctor Rattray says:

"Indeed, contrasted with the teachings of modern times, the comprehensiveness and sufficiency of the rules and cardinal points comprised in the Hebrew Sanitary Code, primitive in time but not in practice; ancient, but not antiquated and obsolete; comprising a treasure of infallible truth, which is the admiration of all experts; and altogether so remarkable as to be comparable to, if indeed they do not surpass both in literary style and professional excellence, extracts from the best modern works on hygiene. So that savants, notwithstanding their increased anatomical and physiological knowledge, the accumulation of ages and the result of modern enlightenment and civilization, bringing with them vastly improved facilities for medical study, professional experience in hospitals and communities, may still quote his model work with approval; sit with advantage at the feet of the Jewish sage; and learn in language as concise and forcible as that of the best modern thinkers, not only the great base facts, but even many of the less important minutiæ of the art and science which they

[1] London, 1903.

study; if they would not continue to despise this authority because he is a Hebrew; ignore his work because it is Asiatic; slight the book in which it is found because it is not a rare, costly and abstruse volume; spurn instruction on a scientific subject because it comes from a Biblical source; and neglect the ready-made and divinely inspired code because it is ancient and a non-professional publication."

The question of the place that this health legislation of the Bible has in medical history is worth noting, for it makes very clear that it was no mere human development but something divine. Doctor Rattray said:

"Moses was no doubt learned in the medicine and surgery of that era, and could at least have taught his old Egyptian teachers, both theoretically and practically, especially in sanitary matters, a science of which they knew little, as the germ thought of preventive medicine had not then been begotten. But it was not to be his rôle to indoctrinate the Jews and Mankind in the least important sanatory or healing branch of medicine, but rather to initiate its higher and most philosophical department, the sanitary or disease preventing. And to shew both by precept and practice that this is the most philosophic and wisest policy to pursue regarding physical health, as it also is in moral, social and spiritual matters. Part of his beneficent and Divinely inspired mission was to inculcate in those early days the lesson popularly taught in modern times by the trite yet true proverb, 'prevention is better than cure': and to illustrate it on the Israelites; to shew that its scope is not only of private but of national, nay racial, import; and applicable not only to his day, but all-time: although grievously neglected in past ages even by medical men. From its

Biblical study does not medical science thereby appear in a new light, and come in the garb of one of the most incontrovertible aids to human faith in the veracity of Holy Writ; the truth of Scripture as the inspired word of the Almighty; God's medical message to Man, sent in His own method, at His own time, and by servants of His own choosing?

"The Sinaitic or so-called 'Mosaic' code and its hygienic sub-code, more ancient by five or six hundred years than Esculapius and the earliest human medical records, was not written and interpolated by any modern or medieval medical sage, but is as Moses says, an emanation of his era. And yet, as he himself affirms, it was not his conception, but strictly and entirely Divine in elaboration, codification, and delivery to humanity. Its true Author and Deviser was Jehovah, and Moses merely its earthly recipient, editor and human expounder and applier. For this most important educational information we are indebted to God's Holy Bible, and to that alone. What was the supernal object of the Code? It was humanitarian and tuitional."

The English physician discusses the origin of this code of laws and traces it to divine interposition:

"Viewed apart from its source, the Hebrew Health Code is an anachronism. And it must be evident that Moses was not a semi-barbarous Jew, but either a secularly scientific or an inspired man. And if we cannot accept the former hypothesis, and think it unlikely that imparted information and unaided intellect could have originated this consummate production; then we must avow the latter conviction, that he was truly 'a man of God.' But was the sanitary code that goes by his name, or styled the 'Sinaitic', his conception or not? This question Moses himself answers indirectly and often; and takes no credit for but disclaims it. Assuredly Moses was not only a man of science and the foremost sanitarian of his own or any other age; but also a man gifted by his Maker with the faculty to discover and appreciate not only the great fundamental facts and elements, but also many of the more important minutiæ of private, public, and national sanitation. Still he takes no credit for the sanitary utterances of the Pentateuch or even says or hints at their being partly, chiefly or wholly self-generated; and his own unaided creation; or that we are purely indebted for them to the genius of their practical expounder. Over and over again he insists and reiterates that they are solely heaven-sent and of Divine origin. Nay, more, what he says appears to suggest that his sanitary code was a premeditated and authoritative emanation, which in its elaboration probably occupied more years than any work that has since been handed down to posterity. In early times medical treatises were more slowly elaborated than now; and swayed only by the double patriotism of zeal for his Master and loyalty to his people, Moses had no need to give hasty and incomplete work to the world. In the desert he would have ample time to write his book of the law and the early story of Man and the Earth leisurely. From the Holy Bible alone we glean the great base facts about the Mosaic Law and its Hygienic portion. Here we learn, and by Moses' own handwriting, that he was not their author, but Jehovah Himself; that Moses only gave or wrote the law as averred by the Saviour (John, vii. 19); therefore, that it is Divine and inspired. Moses was merely its earthly recipient and transcriber and applicant. This great fact practically attested by over two millions of Hebrews, who heard the Voice of God delivering the Decalogue at Sinai, materially enhances the value of the bequest, as its supernal nature and origin attests its truth and infallibility. This great honour reserved for Moses, and the culminating fact in his earth history, stamps his character and place in history. Taught by the Divinity as no other man has yet been, Moses thus became Earth's greatest sanitarian and the Deity's ambassador and mouthpiece to Man in sanitary as in many other matters. What Moses wrote was revealed. He penned as he was inspired and wrote what Jehovah dictated in the Holy of Holies. Moses himself attests this, and thus wholly disclaims the authorship. Chapter after chapter begins thus, 'And the Lord said' (Leviticus, xvii). And thus the Hebrew leader and sage, as has been recorded by his successor Joshua, himself 'full of the spirit of wisdom' (Deuteronomy, xxxiv. 9), fully deserves this record, 'there arose not a prophet since in Israel like unto Moses whom the Lord knew face to face' (Deuteronomy, xxxiv. 10–11)."

The distinction between the meats allowed to the Hebrews and those not allowed remains down to the present day an extremely valuable canon of preventive medicine. The carnivorous animals were not to be eaten and were declared unclean. They are, as modern science has abundantly shown, much more likely to be the subject of parasites of various kinds than are the herbivorous animals. Any animal that died of itself or had been torn by beasts was not to be eaten, and this was an extremely wise provision, for those that had died were very likely to be the subject of serious disease, while those torn by wild animals, if they did not perish at once were likely to have pyemia or septicemia set in in their wounds, while if they had been killed at once and their bodies had been exposed for any length of time in the open air, they were likely to become the subject of serious putrefactive changes from the growth of bacteria in them. Any of these processes were likely to make the meat toxic, and the one safeguard was prohibition of their consumption. The Hebrews were not allowed to take the blood of animals, hence the necessity for having cattle butchered in their own way so that it might be *kosher*, and it is interesting to realize that this prohibition probably meant much for the prevention of disease. Meat that is well drained of blood keeps longer than that which contains the tissue fluids, and it has come to be felt that the protection of the Hebrews to a considerable extent against tuberculosis, so that their death rate from this disease is much lower than that of other races living under similar circumstances, is perhaps due to their abstinence from blood according to their law. They were forbidden to eat many of the fats, and this was hygienic in general, for the fat is a sluggish tissue and may contain parasites; but above all this was important for preventing the Hebrews from eating such an amount of fat as would make them obese and sluggish. The orthodox Jews of the present time who fail to keep this prohibition as to fat are weighted down with a load of surplus fatty tissue that takes away from their activity and shortens their lives. Obesity has certain relations directly with diabetes which also makes this fat prohibition of significance, and as the Jew is probably more subject to diabetes than most of those living in similar circumstances there is here another index of the value of this Mosaic law which prevented pathological tendencies of several kinds that now make themselves manifest.

The greatest weight was placed upon keeping food materials covered from the air, and the use of liquids kept in vessels that were uncovered is forbidden, as is likewise the eating of fruit with open moist cracks. It has often been said in modern times that the paring of fruits, when unbroken, constitutes the best possible safeguard against spoiling, and many have the feeling that this fact was discovered or its significance properly recognized only since we have been studying fermentation and putrefaction. It was known long ago, however. It was recognized also that food materials should not be handled except with the greatest precautions and that those who prepared them should practice careful cleansing. These regulations undoubtedly had much to do with the prevention of the spread of the infectious diseases. We have learned in recent years that cooks have had much to do with the spread of the intestinal infections, and we now recognize the need of the meticulous precautions on which Moses insisted. The place of the hands in conveying disease was emphasized very much, as for instance by Jewish writers who insisted on the rule that coins should never be placed in the mouth because they had been handled by so many people.

We have now come to appreciate this thoroughly, after having suspected for some time that the hands have more to do with the conveyance of contagion in many diseases than almost any other factor. A series of experiments made upon young sailors in the United States service after the Armistice was signed and when the "flu" was at its height demonstrated almost beyond doubt that influenza cannot be conveyed by breathing or coughing into the faces of others, nor in any way through the air. Most army surgeons came to the conclusion, therefore, that the mode of conveyance of the disease was by the hands, which in handling food and in touching the mouth and nose transmitted infectious material which had been gathered in various ways. It is interesting then to realize that the Jewish law insisted on careful cleansing of the hands before eating and on not touching the mouth or nose before the hands were washed in the morning, and that the Talmudic writings emphasized these regulations as regards the cleansing of the hands. They required that the finger nails, when pared, should be burnt. Some of the Talmudists suggested that if water could not be obtained gloves should be worn while eating, which would recall the use of surgical gloves in modern times, for the surgeons learned long since that the hands were by far the most dangerous media for the transmission of infection.

Some years ago Sir Benjamin Ward Richardson, one of the most distinguished of the English physicians of the latter half of the nineteenth century, pointed out that the records showed a very marked difference in the health and death rate of the Jews living in various cities of Great Britain as compared to their Gentile neighbors, and always in favor of the Jews. Other statistics gathered later in the nineteenth century and at the beginning of the twentieth emphasize the fact that there is manifestly something which enables the Jew to resist disease and maintain health under circumstances where the people around him suffer much more severely than he does. For instance, in Manchester the average annual death rate for three years in the two Jewish districts was over eight in one and over nine in the other below the death rate per thousand of the whole city. The two Jewish districts are among the worst slums of Manchester, yet not only do they exhibit a much lower death rate, but the morbidity statistics show that there is less sickness among the Jews from all the serious infectious diseases than among the Gentiles. They had a higher morbidity rate than all the other parts of the city for erysipelas, pyemia, and puerperal fever, showing that they were subjected to the influence of dirt and septic contagion, but in everything else they were much lower in the sickness rate than their neighbors. They had only about one half as many premature births, their children suffered from only half as many convulsions and scarcely more than half as much from diarrhea and dysentery.

The children in the Jewish districts proved to be particularly capable of resisting disease and their death rate is distinctly lower. The diarrheic diseases of childhood are practically all due to improper feeding, and the saving of children's lives in the unsanitary Jewish districts where poverty stalks abroad so openly is due to the more healthy feeding of the infants, but above all to the mother's very careful care of them. The Jewish mother is, by age-long tradition, an absolutely unselfish caretaker of her children. When they are ailing her devotion is constant, and nothing is too much for her to do. No wonder that she saves more of her children than the Gentile mothers around her. It is because of the presence of the Jewish mothers in New York and Boston that our Boards of Health have come upon the startling discovery that the foreign-born mother in this country raises one in seven more of her children than does the native-born mother. The reason, of course, for this is maternal devotion and readiness to sacrifice herself in any and every way for the sake of her children. At least twice as many of these foreign mothers — and among these of course every orthodox Jewish mother who can possibly do it — nurse their children, and that is by far the most important factor in securing the survival of children beyond the first year.

The Jews have been particularly careful for the lives of their infant children both before and after birth. It is considered a disgrace for a Jewish mother to have a premature birth, for it is felt that some blame attaches to the mother. As for the prevalent practice of abortion, there is almost none of it among the poor Jewish populations, and none at all until their orthodox Jewry begins to break down under the influence of contact with their Gentile neighbors. Human life is a very sacred thing to the orthodox Jew, and no matter how small or insignificant that life may be it has all the qualities of humanity for him and appeals to his protection. The solicitude of the Jewish mother for her children has been the subject of poet and painter all down the ages and is to be found as well developed and as strikingly manifest in the slums of the large cities of the west where it is so extremely difficult of exercise as it was in the Jewish towns of the olden time.

In Leeds, toward the end of the nineteenth century, there were some fifteen thousand Jews, the great majority of them belonging to the very poorest class. Most of them lived in the central ward of the city. As pointed out by Doctor Porritt in "Religion and Health", "that ward, one of the most squalid in Leeds, had a death rate lower than that of the whole city, the statistical records for which show all the advantages derived from the healthier or better class districts."

In London itself, in Whitechapel and Mile End, which were principally occupied by Jews, the death rates were only 18.5 and 19.3 per thousand of population, while in the neighboring districts of Limehouse and St. George, where there were many fewer Jews — Limehouse being practically without them — the death rates were respectively 23 and 24.6 per thousand. There was distinctly less morbidity from the infectious diseases in the Jewish districts, there being actually more than one fourth more in Limehouse than in Mile End on the average, and the infantile death rates were much lower among the Jews in spite of the fact that most of them were immigrants who had led very hard and anxious lives before settling in London and since coming had to work under unwonted, exceedingly unsanitary conditions, in a climate to which they were not as yet accustomed.

In other countries besides England the mortality and morbidity statistics favor the Jew even more strikingly than in England. In Frankfurt (on Main), as pointed out by Sir Benjamin Ward Richardson, where the influence of the Jewish ghetto still made itself felt about the middle of the nineteenth century and Jews were herded together under restricted regulations that would seem inevitably prone to hurt their health, they had as a matter of fact ever so much better health than the Gentiles around them. The average duration of life among the Jews was forty-eight years and nine months. Among all other classes it was thirty-six years and eleven months. More than half of the Jews reached fifty years of age, while scarcely more than one third of the other classes lived up to that. During the first five years of life Jewish children died at the rate of about thirteen per cent while Gentile children died at the rate of a little more than twenty-four per cent. One fourth of the Jewish population attained the age of seventy; one fourth of the rest of the inhabitants lived to be less than sixty.

In Furth the tenacity of life among the Jews could be noted at all ages. Of the Jewish children from one to five years ten per cent died, but among the rest of the population the infant mortality of the same age was fourteen per cent. At every stage of life Jewish mortality was lower until past the age of sixty, when, owing to the greater number of Jews who reached advanced age, the ratio was inverted. The number of Jews who lived to be above eighty and even ninety is strikingly larger than among the Gentiles. In Prussia, Legoit found that the average life of the Jew is greater than that of the Gentile by at least five years. The mortality among the population of the whole kingdom was a little over two and one half per hundred, while among the Jews it was only one and one half per hundred. The population in Prussia is increasing annually at the rate of one and one third per hundred among non-Jews, but at the rate of nearly one and three fourths among the Jews. The ordinary population requires fifty-one years to double itself, but the Jews require only forty-one and a half years for the same progression.

Sir Benjamin Ward Richardson, by a comparison of the ages of two thousand five hundred Jews buried in London in three years with the mortality of the whole population of London at different ages, found that under five years of age forty-four Jews died to forty-five non-Jews; from thirty-five to forty-five years of age, five Jews died to every eight non-Jews; and it was not until the age of eighty-five was reached that the ratio was reversed and two Jews were buried to every one non-Jew, there being considerably more than twice as many non-Jews alive at that age to supply the bodies for the burial.

CHAPTER XIX

HEALTH AND RELIGION [1]

RELIGION, as we have seen in the course of this book, does very much for health, but according to the great principle of nature, reaction is equal to action in compensation and health undoubtedly also accomplishes very much for religion. Indeed there are a great many troubles commonly presumed to be of the spirit and a great many supposed disturbances of the spiritual life that are really only manifestations of ill health of one kind or another, or at least of some hampering of bodily function reflected in the mind. This has always been recognized by all the great authorities in the spiritual life, and none have insisted more than the writers even of the highest mystical theology on the necessity for taking proper care of the body if the spirit is to be free for religious life.

Desolation, that is that feeling of utter dissatisfaction with religious exercises and difficulty in continuing them of which so much is said in spiritual literature, is very often nothing more than dyspepsia. What is familiarly called the "blues" or the "blue devils", that is the state of depression in which nothing seems hopeful and the future seems very blank indeed, is a common experience among mankind generally and is very often dependent on

[1] The suggestion for this chapter came from Reverend William J. Lockington's little book on "Bodily Health and Spiritual Vigour", Longmans, Green and Co., London, New York, Bombay and Calcutta, 1914.

some disturbance of the digestive tract. There is a well-known expression in English according to which the answer to the question "Is life worth living?" is "That depends on the liver", meaning not only the person that does the living, but also that large organ in the right upper abdominal quadrant, the largest, heaviest organ in the body, disturbances of which it is no wonder cause serious interference with a number of the functions of both mind and body. Many a long-faced person indeed who thinks himself pious is only bilious, and many a sad-eyed visionary who is quite ready to proclaim himself religious is only what the ancients called atrabilious and needs some liver regulator as badly as ever Horace thought he needed hellebore in the spring.

There are a good many traits of disposition or habits of life often supposed to be dependent on the state of the spirit that are really only symptoms of bodily indisposition. Many a fit of temper is consequent upon the condition of the digestive organs rather than the state of the soul. Suspicion and jealousy are not infrequently not so much vices as unfortunate feelings exaggerated out of all reason by some disturbance of health. There are certain times in women's lives particularly when almost any feeling that comes to them is magnified and takes on a significance quite beyond the reality. Physicians constantly have to remind their women patients to wait a few days and not let their inhibited feelings run away with them as they are so prone to do at certain periods.

Not a little of the irritability of life and especially the exaggerated response to minor irritations is due to insufficient oxygenation of tissues because the individual concerned is not getting out into the air sufficiently. At the end of a number of hours of mental work indoors, especially in a stuffy atmosphere, most people are inclined to be irritable. If instead of going out into the fresh air and staying out for some time when they get the chance, they think that they feel too tired for the effort which that involves, and prefer to rest in a comfortable chair or perhaps lying down, their irritability will often not be lessened but sometimes will even be heightened. On the other hand, if they get out into the brisk, bracing cold air of the winter time particularly, they come back with their irritability thoroughly dissipated as a rule and ready to go on with other work almost without a sense of weariness. Probably nothing makes a man say his night prayers more unsatisfactorily and with less devotion than to sit down in a nice comfortable chair after a rather heavy evening meal and smoke and read the paper or perhaps a magazine until he goes to sleep. He wakes up feeling all out of sorts, while if he played a game of cards with friends he would feel fine at the end of the evening and be ready to thank the Lord for another day and for the prospect of a good night's rest for the work ahead.

Above all, people who are living healthy, outdoor lives are much more prone to take a happy view of life, to see the bright side of things and to radiate good will and sunshine than those who are overmuch in the house. The cheerful givers whom the Lord loves come especially from among these. A great many of the people who want to pour out their ills perennially, because they like to indulge their self-pity by rolling the delectable morsels of their sufferings under their tongues, and who go around seeking consolation and sympathy whenever they are in even slight trouble are indoor people. They occur especially among those who spend a good deal of time sitting down and not exercising their bodies enough. The good old rule *ora et labora* is an extremely valuable precept, not only for the next world but also for this. Pray and labor, but be sure that labor gets a fair share of the time and be sure that the body has enough exercise to keep it going and to keep its functions in good condition, otherwise the prayer will be disturbed and life will be far from happy. Happiness comes to those who are healthily tired every day. Long ago Dooley said in one of those wise sayings of his which made even the *London Times* declare that the wisest man that was writing English in our day wrote under the name of Dooley in Chicago, that the one thing above all that made life worth living was to be tired enough at the end of every day so that one would sleep well every night. Without that life is indeed a burden.

The practice of hard work, some of it physical, is a very good rule for the physical as well as the spiritual life. A hard-working man has little time to be grouchy and to throw wet blankets over the good that others are trying to do. He is likely to be a lifter and not a leaner, a doer and not a talker. Nothing keeps people from finding fault so well as having so much to do that they can scarcely find the time in which to do it all. Especially is this important for those who have to spend a good deal of time in each other's company, and who must learn to bear with each other's faults and go on with their own work to the best of their ability. It must not be forgotten that a great many of the faults of others are to be attributed rather to the state of their health than to their disposition, and once this is rightly understood charity will readily help us to gloss them over or forgive them. Any one who makes his own faults the subject of excuse on the score of health, when his health is something that by a little care he could improve, is of course imposing on himself if he does it at all deliberately, and he is trying to impose on good nature if he thinks that other people do not appreciate that his ill health is really an excuse and not a reason for his faults.

In the chapter on Abstinence it is suggested that one of the best things that men and particularly women could practice to advantage from the standpoint of religious abstinence would be abstinence from excessive rest. Rest is one of the most dangerous remedies that we have, nearly as dangerous as opium and with a definite tendency for a habit to be acquired by the system for it whenever it is indulged in to excess, exactly as is true of the opiates. If mortification of the spirit were to be practiced by abstinence from overrest and by a definite amount of exercise every day it would be an excellent thing for the religious as well as the physical life. This is one of the most frequent advices of those interested in the spiritual life as well as the bodily health for many generations. What people need is to keep busy. This is good for both their minds and their bodies. It requires a great deal of mortification of the inclinations to keep at work and above all to take exercise voluntarily when one might sit around and enjoy the delightfully lazy feeling of doing nothing, but that way lies serious disturbance of health. The men who have been very hard workers, especially from a sense of duty and not for mere selfish reasons, taking a great deal of exercise and going to bed so thoroughly tired every night that they went to sleep as soon as their head touched the pillow, have been long-lived as a rule, unless they met with some accident or infection.

Above all, it is important for any one who wishes to retain his self-respect and keep from that sluggishness which is so fatal to the power to pray and to meditate not to permit his abdominal and flank muscles to become overstretched and to allow fat to accumulate within the abdomen until it is actually a burden. There is almost no excuse for any one permitting his waist line to become larger in girth than his chest, unless of course he happens to have some deformity that makes exercise very difficult or practically impossible. To keep these muscles in good condition prevents slouchiness and makes the individual ever so much more ready for activity of any kind. The only way that these muscles can be kept in tone to hold in the abdomen properly and keep the circulation within it in such vigor as will support the digestive tract so as to permit and encourage its proper activities is by exercising them. This requires the performance of certain exercises every day. Stooping, bending, stretching, all these must be practiced if the muscles are not to be allowed to degenerate. There is no harder task than to keep up the custom of performing these exercises regularly a couple of times a day, for though only from five to ten minutes is needed night and morning to maintain the muscles in condition or even to restore them when they have once begun to sag, all sorts of excuses come in to prevent the regular practice of the exercises, and it is the regularity above all that counts.

A man who keeps these muscles in good shape will be much readier for every sort of activity than if he allowed them to yield, and one of the secrets of the army officers' power as the years go on so that, quite contrary to the usual rule in life it is men well beyond sixty who make some of the greatest successes as leaders, is because their regular training and discipline keep them from letting their muscles lose tone and their powers deteriorate. The setting-up exercises of the army or navy indulged in for fifteen minutes a day — and this could be divided into two periods — would keep men in condition and prove at the same time a very salutary mortification and above all an exercise in self-control and persistent application to a good purpose that would constitute a magnificent factor for that training of the will that is so important for religion.

Nerve irritation is oftener a function of insufficient exercise and air with overfeeding than of any other factor. This same thing is true for suspicion and jealousy and envy and other of the supposed inner emotions of the soul. They will disappear very often before the fresh air, while they will be fostered by life indoors and by the coddling of ills by rest and high living generally. The passions, by which a great many people mean mainly the sexual feelings, though of course they also include the tendency to overeat and especially to stimulate one's self to eating in various ways, are all fostered by being much indoors and not getting enough fresh, outdoor air and particularly cold air.

There are a great many people who seem to forget that air is absolutely the most important requisite for life, and that when it is cold it takes heat away from the animal body and sets all the cell functions working at their best. Human beings are practically heat engines, and we keep on manufacturing heat all the time. As our temperature never rises except when we suffer from fever, some outlet must be found for this heat, and unless there is exposure to the air and especially air in motion that will carry heat away from us, the heat is consumed in various large organs and almost invariably succeeds in making us quite miserable. It is under these circumstances of sluggish indoor living particularly that irritability of all kinds is heightened and that the tendency to lack of self-control is most manifest. It is a form of intoxication actually that comes over people and would remind us not a little of the intoxication that follows from smaller amounts of alcohol with the resultant lack of inhibition.

When people are much out in the air it is surprising what they can stand in the shape of injury without great suffering. Our young soldiers learned during the war that their outdoor life in camps and at the front made the slighter wounds appear almost as nothing to them and even the severer wounds caused them nothing like the pain which they had anticipated or which they actually would have caused if the soldiers continued to be in the same state of mind and body as regards the reaction to pain which had been true during their civilian days. It requires much less courage to be heroic when one has been living the outdoor life and has been hardening muscles by exercise and plain food and not too much sleep than when one is living the indoor, relaxed overrested life. That does not lessen the merit of what they did, but helps to account for its development in just ordinary mortals and above all helps to explain why now they modestly prefer not to talk about it, for to them it seems to have been just all in the day's work.

Not infrequently oversensitiveness of disposition which resents even the slightest imputation and which is often prone to translate what was a mere conventional remark into a fancied insult is due to lack of sufficient outdoor air to keep the individual in good health. On the other hand men and women who spend a good deal of time outside are capable of standing even severe insults without wincing under them and sometimes this rebounds greatly to the benefit of the cause for which they are working. Father Lockington has dwelt on this in one of his chapters rather interestingly.

"Good health helps us to be patient and silent under insult and wrong, when this makes for duty better done. The souls for whom we labour are often unreasonable, often ungrateful, often crooked, but the trained worker never hesitates. Strong and self-contained he moves serenely on; no display of temper mars his work, no hasty word is uttered, however great the provocation. Like the missionary calmly wiping his face, when spat upon in the Japanese street, or that Little Sister of the Poor, who, struck across the face when begging food for her old people, calmly answered, 'That is for myself, and I deserve it; please now give me something for Christ's poor,' such a worker sees only souls here below, and Christ above, waiting for them. A healthy body will keep the mind broad and even; it has no place for brooding suspicion to lurk; it will help the soul to take a wide view of life and prevent that narrowness of thought, so fatal to work, to which our life of continual introspection tends."

A great many of the vicious impulses in connection with suspicion and jealousy and envy may be traced to a lack of diversion in life. There are some people who take no pains to organize existence in such a way that they have definite diversion at certain times. Every human being ought at some time on every Sunday to decide that on certain days of the following week, and above all on certain evenings, he will do things in which he is particularly interested and which he can look forward to with pleasant anticipation. Those who can should arrange either to go to the theater, or to a lecture in which they are interested, or to visit friends whom they care to see, or to go to a library and look up something that they have been wanting to find out about; or, if it is pleasant weather, to go for a short excursion or a boat ride or something of that kind and they should make two or three appointments with themselves for definite occasions of recreation for the ensuing week. As a rule all that is necessary for this is to make up one's mind to do it, though there is a tendency on the part of a great many people just to let each evening be like every other evening and because of lack of sufficient interest they lose that variety which is the spice of life. As a result existence becomes dreadfully monotonous, and those who live such narrow lives become the subjects of all sorts of unfortunate suggestions with regard to those around them.

Over and over again I have found that when women patients particularly were the subjects of various of these nervous irritabilities so that they were permitting themselves actually to be led into being deluded into various suspicions, there was a prompt disappearance or significant minimization of these thoughts when diversions were properly introduced into their lives. The founders of religious orders were very wise in this matter. In all the religious orders the members are required by rule to spend a certain time in recreation, that is in conversation and lighter occupation, usually several times every day. This must be spent in company with the others and the members of the house are not allowed to absent themselves without good reason. Young religious sometimes feel like resenting the rule requiring them to be present day after day at recreation as if it represented a waste of time, but they learn later on in life how wise it is. The various feast days of the Church are celebrated in such a way that there is a definite diversion from the usual routine of life and then there are special indulgences at table and in the matter of spending time in the open and receiving visitors and other things of that kind which mean a very great deal in breaking the monotony of the religious life.

Very often scruples are, as we have pointed out in the chapter on Nervous Diseases, only a manifestation of a nervous disposition sometimes on a hereditary, but sometimes on an acquired basis. The acquired basis is very often a lack of nutrition due to insufficient food, for people who are underweight are much more subject to dreads and obsessions of all kinds than are those who are up to weight. Living on the will, as it is called, when one is underweight and does not eat very much, certainly not sufficient to supply the energy for what has to be accomplished, is a fruitful source of irritability of any and every kind. It keeps people on edge, that is in a condition of unstable equilibrium, and almost anything that touches them has a tendency to put them into a state of disequilibrium. Bringing people up to normal health and especially up to normal weight is often the best possible means to lessen their tendencies to scruples and to various other manifestations supposed to be spiritual yet which represent only conditions and symptoms that are frequently seen in those who have no religion and no conscientious obligations with regard to anything.

It is surprising how often a sluggish state of the bowels proves to be seriously disturbing to the spiritual life.

People find it hard to pray without distraction or to meditate without getting sleepy, and they are liable to think of themselves as perhaps being the object of very special attention on the part of certain evil spirits who make it their business to distract and obtund those who are trying to put themselves in communication with the Most High, when all that is really the matter is that they are absorbing certain materials which ought to be excreted promptly but which are being delayed in their intestinal tract longer than is good for the individual.

I am not one of those who believe that intestinal auto-toxemia is a very serious condition which produces dire results, but I know very well that absorption in any quantity of residual materials from the intestinal tract that were meant to be excreted will produce langour and sluggishness. The present fad among certain physicians for attributing a great many serious symptoms to intestinal auto-intoxication has no basis in physiological chemistry and represents only one of those exaggerations of a minor truth for which medicine is so famous. The idea of self-poisoning, which is all that auto-intoxication means, is a very old one in medicine and the use of drastic purgatives such as calomel in large doses and the antimonial purges and then of blood letting represent the responses to this idea which doctors made in an older time. We know that they did harm and those who would exaggerate the meaning of auto-intoxication in our time are likely to do just as much harm, but there is no doubt at all that obstipation will make the majority of human beings uncomfortable and take away their initiative and keep them from being up to their best in mental and spiritual matters. To use some of the greatly advertised remedies or modes of treatment which are suggested for it, however, would probably do more harm than good. There are a number of simple sensible methods of treatment by which the affection may be overcome. Above all the formation of good habits, of taking an abundance of water, of eating coarse food, the peelings of baked potatoes and the parings of baked apples and an occasional orange with its peel, and using marmalade rather freely as well as eating whole wheat bread will gradually overcome the condition. The important thing is not to mistake the merely physical affection for a spiritual disturbance.

It requires persistence to form good habits and it is ever so much easier just to take something that will supposedly do the same good work "while you sleep" and are not bothered by the exertion of the will power necessary to form the habits that are required. Many a disturbance of health is due to sloth and laziness rather than to ignorance of what ought to be done or to any inherent tendency to ill in the body. Any number of people blame Providence for ills which they have brought on themselves by neglect of their own health and the habits necessary to maintain it.

Nothing so conduces to good health as the regularity of life without haste and without worry which the rational practice of religion brings in its train. The attitude of mind that a trusting faith in the Almighty fosters is particularly likely to prevent the neurotic symptoms and exaggerations of feelings which are responsible for so much of the modern suffering of mankind. It makes the real pains and aches ever so much more bearable and eliminates those which to a great extent are imaginary. The success of all sorts of curious therapeutic systems which prove after a time to be utterly without beneficial effect on the human body shows how much faith in anything may mean for health and restoration to health, even in the midst of what is supposed to be rather serious illness, and as men are bound to have faith in something and a living faith in a Providence that somehow, even though we may not be able to understand it, cares for men, drawing good even out of evil, can accomplish an immense amount in making men less amenable to suffering even in this world. It would be too bad to reduce religion merely to this status, but this should be one of its benefits. As the Scriptures said, "For it is not a vain thing for you because it is your life, and through this thing you shall prolong your days in the land."

INDEX

INDEX

N

O

P

Q

R